What people are saying about *When Gay Comes Home*

Never before have we faced such challenges in our culture with respect to issues of our sexuality and gender identity. Wilna van Beek is a voice of wisdom, strength, and courage in the desert. I have not seen this kind of profoundly important information presented so succinctly in any other format. Simplifying and bringing the confusion into an understandable place of dialogue and support, she has captured both the heart of the matter and the challenge of our culture.

Families facing the unexpected news of a child who "comes out," or someone dealing with their own internal battle, will find real answers as they wrestle through this emotionally charged topic. This is a must-read for every pastor, youth pastor, leader, and support worker who wants to have a relevant biblical perspective of the difficult societal challenge our world faces today. Wilna's bravery, character, and calling are for such a time as this. I thank God for her!

—Laura-Lynn Tyler-Thompson
Co-Host of *The 700 Club Canada*
and Host of *Laura-Lynn & Friends*
Author of *Relentless Redemption*

I recall a time when Wilna gave her testimony in a church while, outside, an angry mob was protesting. Why not treat them to a barbecue on the lawn? Of course! Before she spoke, they all were welcomed in, but few accepted the gracious offer. Starting her presentation with seeking forgiveness, she created an atmosphere of love and acceptance.

While some of us are fighting the culture war, firing defensive salvos on Facebook, Wilna has not lost sight of the fact that our warfare is not against flesh and blood, but against powers and principalities (Ephesians 6:2). She reserves her salvos for the likes of them, but as for her human detractors, she walks a path central to Scripture all but forgotten by the rest of us: *"If your enemy is hungry, feed him"* (Romans 12:20, NIV). It is that kind of authenticity that caused one protester to end up crying in her arms!

Many Christian authors have written about homosexuality, but Wilna has written from an angle that so badly needs to be shared—how to simply love those involved in it. Having been there herself, Wilna approaches this subject with winsome and disarming childlike innocence. If we would all approach the subject with the same compassion, how many more might end up crying in our arms and finding their way to the freedom so many secretly long for?

—Mark Sandford
Director, Elijah House USA
head of Elijah House Ministries International
Co-author of *Deliverance and Inner Healing*
Healing the Earth (with John Sandford)
and *Divine Eros* (with Joy Corey)

Wilna van Beek is one of my heroes. She courageously and vulnerably shares her own experience of growing up feeling *different* and the early wounds which led her to embrace a homosexual lifestyle. She explores the root causes of same-sex attractions and offers hope and healing for those who experience them, as well as the families who love them.

Her book is well researched and packed with relevant scripture, helpful diagrams, and other resources. Wilna graciously takes us beyond a discussion about homosexuality and heterosexuality to embrace *holy sexuality*. This is a must-read for people seeking to understand same-sex attractions in light of the Bible and anyone who longs to represent Jesus to the LGBTQ community in a loving, redemptive way.

—Donna Carter
International author, speaker, and broadcaster
www.donnacarter.org

The message of Wilna's book is critical for our time. She shares with openness and vulnerability her own journey of sexuality and then provides a framework of grace in helping others navigate their own journeys. This equipping is necessary for churches and believers as we seek to reach people with the gospel of our Lord Jesus. Great freedom will be found by those who read this powerful story.

—Lorie Hartshorn
Author, Speaker and Pastor
www.loriehartshorn.com

In *When Gay Comes Home*, Wilna van Beek beautifully weaves together two profound stories into a tapestry of faith, hope, and love.

The first story is her story. It is told with compelling courage and refreshing transparency and desperately needs to be heard today. Wilna's honest vulnerability projects us beyond the predictable and tired cultural norms of individualism, self-identification, and sensual pleasure and allows us to see that there is another, higher way to live: the way of humility and repentance, which leads to transformation and genuine life!

The second story is the well-worn but often misunderstood story of Jesus and how Jesus loves and cares for people… all people. It is Jesus who enables the transformation we all so desperately require.

In the book, Wilna capably serves as both a pastor and a prophetess. As pastor, she effectively explains Scripture to provide comfort, encouragement, and hope. As prophetess, she boldly proclaims truth. Be prepared to be uncomfortable as you read *When Gay Comes Home*. Truth has a way of making us feel that way.

The clear and timeless biblical foundations established in this book will enable the timely application of its truth in the lives of individuals, families facing real-life challenges, and Christian congregations seeking to reflect the fullness of both grace and truth.

—David E. Hazzard
General Secretary Treasurer, Pentecostal Assemblies of Canada

As I made my way through the pages of *When Gay Comes Home*, I sensed Wilna's feelings of brokenness and rejection, which started as a young girl and continued into adulthood. I could sense her feeling of separation from God. Then the door was opened and the love of Jesus was allowed to flow in and fill the emptiness. I could see the healing and redemption that took place in Wilna's life.

Often when we read a book related to the topic of homosexuality, we forget the people involved, what they think, how they live, and their fears and joys. *When Gay Comes Home* reveals Wilna's heart for the hurting, for those living the gay lifestyle, and for those walking this path with them.

When Gay Comes Home establishes very clearly what God's Word says on this subject and how Wilna has studied the Bible extensively to present the truth. This book will teach you the importance of maintaining your beliefs and not compromising your moral standards for the worldly view, but how to love and honor a gay son, daughter, or even a neighbor unconditionally.

When Gay Comes Home is a must-read for those dealing with a gay loved one, and for pastors and youth leaders. Very simply, it's for everyone. Very inspirational and educational.

—Jan, parent of a gay son

When Gay Comes Home is an inspirational and educational book which reveals the healing and restoration power of God from an unholy sexual lifestyle. Moreover, the book also gives crucial insights on how the body of Christ can reach out to persons within the LGBTQ community with compassion and love, without compromising the truth of the Word of God, which is currently the case in some Christian communities today.

This book is a masterpiece and a much-needed evangelistic tool in the body of Christ. Indeed, the author has been truly inspired by the Holy Spirit to write on such a sensitive topic so as to equip the church and every Christian on how to minister to people within the LGBTQ community without a judgmental spirit or compromise.

I must candidly say that reading this book has educated and empowered me to reach out to those struggling with this issue with a Kingdom wisdom and knowledge. I highly recommend this book to any Christian who loves Jesus Christ and loves all that He is to humanity.

—Dr. Kazumba Charles
Host of *Kingdom Insight TV*
founder of Christ Passion Evangelistic Network

Wilna's book, *When Gay Comes Home: Learning to Build Bridges*, is a must-read for people who are looking for insight and encouragement on same-sex issues. I have known Wilna for a number of years and have heard her teach and share her story of victory. She has amazing insights which can help individuals and families navigate through the journey of dealing with the gay lifestyle.

—Dave Wells
Team Leader, Life Links International Inc.

I applaud Wilna for tackling a subject so vital in this hour and yet so avoided. Because she shares her personal journey with such vulnerability, honesty, and transparency, it will bring much healing to all who open their hearts to her message. She has made what she has learned and walked through so clear and simple that anyone can benefit regardless of their struggles. Wilna communicates beautifully that the real issue is our heart condition—and that is what Jesus is after, first and foremost, in each one of us.

—Patricia Fraser
Founding Director of Saskatchewan House of Prayer

By sharing her experience of God's redeeming love and the ways in which the truth and grace of Jesus deeply transformed her life, Wilna gives us evidence that the Gospel is good news for gay men and women. The book helps us to respond to God's call to minister Jesus' truth and grace to others so that many more will come home to God's redeeming love.

—Bryan Kliewer
Director, Exodus Global Alliance

WHEN GAY COMES *Home*

Wilna van Beek

WHEN GAY COMES Home

LEARNING TO BUILD BRIDGES

WHEN GAY COMES HOME
Copyright © 2017 by Wilna van Beek

Front cover design and graphics by Jayna Snider
Image courtesy of Freestock

All rights reserved. Neither this publication nor any part of this publication may be reproduced or transmitted in any form or by any means, electronic or mechanical, including photocopying, recording or any information storage and retrieval system, without permission in writing from the author.

Scripture quotations marked (NLT) are taken from the Holy Bible, New Living Translation, copyright ©1996, 2004, 2007, 2013, 2015 by Tyndale House Foundation. Used by permission of Tyndale House Publishers, Inc., Carol Stream, Illinois 60188. All rights reserved. All Scripture quotations marked (MSG) are taken from THE MESSAGE, copyright © 1993, 1994, 1995, 1996, 2000, 2001, 2002 by Eugene H. Peterson. Used by permission of NavPress. All rights reserved. Represented by Tyndale House Publishers, Inc. Scripture marked (NKJV) taken from the New King James Version®. Copyright © 1982 by Thomas Nelson. Used by permission. All rights reserved. Scripture marked (NCV) taken from the New Century Version®. Copyright © 2005 by Thomas Nelson. Used by permission. All rights reserved. Scripture marked (ICB) taken from the International Children's Bible®. Copyright © 1986, 1988, 1999 by Thomas Nelson. Used by permission. All rights reserved. Scripture marked (The Voice) taken from The Voice™. Copyright © 2012 by Ecclesia Bible Society. Used by permission. All rights reserved. Scripture marked (AMP) taken from the Amplified Bible, Copyright © 1954, 1958, 1962, 1964, 1965, 1987 by The Lockman Foundation. Used by permission. Scripture marked (AMPC) taken from the Amplified Bible, Copyright © 1954, 1958, 1962, 1964, 1965, 1987 by The Lockman Foundation. Used by permission. Scripture marked (ERV) taken from the Easy-to-Read Version, Copyright © 2006 by Bible League International. Scripture quotations marked (HCSB) are taken from the Holman Christian Standard Bible®, Copyright © 1999, 2000, 2002, 2003, 2009 by Holman Bible Publishers. Used by permission. HCSB® is a federally registered trademark of Holman Bible Publishers. Scripture quotations marked (NASB) taken from the New American Standard Bible® (NASB), Copyright © 1960, 1962, 1963, 1968, 1971, 1972, 1973, 1975, 1977, 1995 by The Lockman Foundation. Used by permission. www.Lockman.org. Scripture quotations marked (NIV) are taken from the Holy Bible, New International Version®, NIV®. Copyright © 1973, 1978, 1984, 2011 by Biblica, Inc.™ Used by permission of Zondervan. All rights reserved worldwide. www.zondervan.com The "NIV" and "New International Version" are trademarks registered in the United States Patent and Trademark Office by Biblica, Inc.™ Scripture quotations marked (ESV) are from the ESV® Bible (The Holy Bible, English Standard Version®), copyright © 2001 by Crossway, a publishing ministry of Good News Publishers. Used by permission. All rights reserved. Scripture quotations marked (ISV) taken from the Holy Bible: International Standard Version®. Copyright © 1996–forever by The ISV Foundation. All rights reserved internationally. Used by permission.

ISBN: 978-1-4866-1577-3

Word Alive Press
131 Cordite Road, Winnipeg, MB R3W 1S1
www.wordalivepress.ca

Cataloguing in Publication may be obtained through Library and Archives Canada

This book is dedicated to my mother, Magdaleen, who passed away on June 10, 2015 after a debilitating battle with Alzheimer's disease. She gave me a Bible when I was eight years old, and the Word became a lamp to my feet and a light to my path (Psalm 119:105).

Mom, thank you for introducing me to Jesus! We will celebrate in heaven one day.

Contents

	Preface	xiii
	Acknowledgements	xvii
	Introduction	xxi
1.	I Have a Dream	1
2.	Born for a Purpose	3
3.	What Glasses Are You Wearing?	8
4.	Terminology and Factors Influencing Our Identity	10
5.	My Struggles with Identity	18
6.	My Struggles with Christianity	20
7.	A Revelation of My Identity	25
8.	Learning to Love	32
9.	How My Journey with Jesus Began	39
10.	My Attempts to Run Away from Myself	43
11.	The Sin Issue	54
12.	The Three Approaches	66
13.	The Jesus Approach (a.k.a. Wearing Jesus Glasses)	75
14.	The Temptations of the Flesh	94
15.	Unchosen Attractions vs. Chosen Identity	100
16.	Holy Sexuality	110
17.	What Is the Role of the Holy Spirit?	120
18.	The Stages of Grief	122
19.	Coping and Praying	130
20.	Cautions in Your Prayer	132
21.	A Very Simple Prayer	134
22.	Five Building Blocks for When Gay Comes Home	138
23.	Support Groups	142
24.	What Matters Most	144
25.	Cautions in Addressing Homosexuality	148

Appendix A: A Much-Needed New Approach	163
Appendix B: Questions and Answers	185
Appendix C: Who is Your Master? Study Guide	203
Introduction	209
Who is Your Master?	211
Conclusion	241
Reflection	243

Preface

"One day I am going to write a book!"

These words came out of my mouth often, and my friends would ask, "Why a book?"

"To tell my life story," I would answer.

They had no idea how scared I was. They had no idea what my story was really about—that I had been so afraid to openly acknowledge that I had been experiencing same-sex attractions and had lived a homosexual lifestyle. I was scared of being rejected.

Having been taught the Word of God from a young age, I felt ashamed for living a lifestyle I knew was not pleasing to the Lord. I know that some people may not like what I have to say, but it is my story and I need to be honest with myself about what is on my heart.

I felt guilty for living a double life. Fear, shame, and guilt kept me silent for too long, yet deep down I've hoped in some way or another that my story might someday be told.

Initially, I wanted to share my story to receive acceptance, both from myself and from others. However, it has unexpectedly expanded into a ministry of educating, equipping, and enlightening the body of Christ on how to better build bridges between the church and persons[1] within the Lesbian Gay Bisexual Transgender and Questioning/Queer (LGBTQ) community.

Our world is full of people who have been hurt by those who were supposed to love them, and I believe it is time for us to strive to undo that hurt, as best we can, by educating ourselves on the topic of homosexuality.

The reality is that many persons who experience same-sex attractions, just like the Israelites in Egypt, have endured various kinds of mistreatment. Often it has come from persons claiming to be Christian. The result of this mistreatment has been a gradual mass exodus from the church. However,

---

1   I personally prefer to use the phrase "persons within the LGBTQ community" rather than "people within the LGBTQ community." The reason? People seem so distant and far away. A *person*, to me, is one who has a *heart*. We must never forget this.

unlike the Israelites, this exodus was *not* led by God. Rather, it was led by persons who experience same-sex attractions who sought to find their own "promised land"—a land of belonging because they didn't find it in the church. Instead they found it in each other, because they could *understand* each other.

I know firsthand how this feels.

This pattern has greatly contributed to the LGBTQ movement we have today. They didn't get a sense of belonging in the church.

To begin to repair this, we need to learn how to love and accept all people, including persons within the LGBTQ community. God requires us to love, yet we must never compromise the truth of God's Word. We must remember that all are worthy of God's love. We have to be true ambassadors of Jesus, representing God's Kingdom well. In this way, we must hope that others will want to grow into a deeper relationship with Jesus Christ as well.

In my own life, I didn't fully realize what it would mean to be an ambassador for Christ. I only knew that I wanted to go deeper in my relationship with Him. Now I know that when things get exposed to the Light—to Jesus Himself—not only will darkness go, but we'll gain the strength to share our own painful life experiences to help others who are on a similar journey.

When I initially talked about sharing my story, I felt discouraged. I didn't know how I would ever be able to write it. I was fully aware of my poor English. In school, I never did well with writing essays, whether it was in Afrikaans or in English. Having received no formal training as a writer, I felt inadequate. I was only a farmer from South Africa. I had a degree in agriculture, and that was it.

Although I did have a desire to write a book, I never anticipated that publicly sharing my testimony would come first. The fact is, I had a debilitating fear of public speaking. I was terrified at the thought of even praying in front of two or three people. To stand in front of large audiences, as I have been doing for the past five years, went beyond anything I could ever imagine. Due to my fears and awareness of my inadequacies, writing and speaking about my journey remained an unreachable goal for many years.

Despite my fears, my shame in living a homosexual lifestyle, and my weaknesses as a person, I have come to learn how to recognize, hear, and listen to God's voice. My desire has always been to follow Him wholeheartedly wherever He is leading and sending me. He has a plan for all of us, and it is no different for my life.

But it is not about me! Looking back over my life, I can clearly see that now. In fact, recently hearing about the massacre in a Florida gay nightclub (June 12, 2016) has caused me to do a lot of thinking. I thought about those who died, those who didn't, and about second chances.

The concept of second chances made me think about my own life. I not only got a second chance once, but numerous times! I literally died at the young age of eleven from an electrical shock, and there were two other occasions when Jesus saved my life. I suffered an anaphylactic reaction when I was fifteen and was involved in a serious car accident at the age of twenty-one. These events are a personal affirmation to me that God has a plan and a purpose for my life, and for this I am grateful.

God has a plan, and He is not finished with me yet. I never signed up for this. I would never have chosen this path—to talk and write about my life, my shame, and my fears, and to be consistently addressing the very controversial and heartfelt topic of homosexuality so openly and honestly. This is a challenging task and I've come to learn that it requires persons of valor.

Silence was one of the tactics Satan tried to use in my life. In November 2011, as I walked on stage at a Women's Journey of Faith conference in front of 1,500 women, I was shaken to the core of my being. I did not feel brave, but I heard the prompting of the Holy Spirit, saying, "You are now starting to take back territory from Satan that he not only stole from you, but from thousands and thousands of others!"

This was not only the beginning of the ministry I am involved in, but also a personal experience of Acts 1:8, which says, *"But you will receive power and ability when the Holy Spirit comes upon you; and you will be My witnesses [to tell people about Me]…"* (AMP). This power remains the source I still so desperately need to sustain me in His work in and through me as a willing vessel.

People still ask me, "Wilna, are you getting better at speaking? Are you still nervous?" The truth is that I am still nervous, but I've learned that it is God who gives me the power, courage, and ability to do what He has called me to do. I have humbly accepted His calling. He empowers us when He calls us.

As Rick Yancey has said in his book *The 5th Wave*, "He does not call the equipped; He equips the called."[2] The only requirement on our part is complete surrender; we must lay down our own will and rely on Him to guide and lead us. Life is not about us. God has a plan:

> *[He] comforts (consoles and encourages) us in every trouble (calamity and affliction), so that we may also be able to comfort (console and encourage) those who are in any kind of trouble or distress, with the comfort (consolation and encouragement) with which we ourselves are comforted (consoled and encouraged) by God.*
>
> —2 Corinthians 1:4, AMPC

Like Moses in the desert telling God that he felt incapable of leading His people, I never thought God could or would use an ordinary farm girl from South Africa to tell the world, "This is who I was, but with the power of God and the work of the Holy Spirit I am a changed and a transformed woman. I no longer self-identify as a lesbian, but I have a new identity and I live it to the full as a daughter of the King of Kings." And in that, even as a person living celibately, I live the *joy of holy sexuality*.[3]

I don't know all the answers and I don't speak from a scientific standpoint. Nor could this book address every aspect of this topic. Rather, this is my journey and how the Lord has helped me to make sense of it. All I know is that my life has been transformed.

One of my favorite verses from the Bible is Esther 4:14.

---

2   Rick Yancey, *The 5th Wave* (New York, NY: Penguin Group, 2013), excerpted from *Goodreads* (https://www.goodreads.com/work/quotes/19187812-the-5th-wave).

3   Additional information on the term "holy sexuality" can be found in Chapter Sixteen.

For if you keep silent at this time, relief and deliverance shall arise… from elsewhere… And who knows but that you have come to the kingdom for such a time as this and for this very occasion? (AMP)

And as Boyd Hopkins writes in his book *Yes, Lord*,

> He scatters us, placing us where we can bring His message to those in need of it. Due to the way He has changed us, we are definitely a strange people. No longer able to endorse the values and practices of our world context, and contrasting with the society around us, we stand out like a light in a dark place. Those who are hungry for the light we carry will be drawn to us, seeking the message we bring through our words and by our lifestyle.
>
> In choosing to actively let go of who we were, and in embracing who we have become in Christ, we acknowledge that we don't belong here anymore, even though we still live and work here. We are strangers who have been scattered according to the Father's will. We are where He has placed us. We have a calling. We have a message.[4]

I know now, after a journey of about eighteen years during which literally everything in my life changed, that God has placed me here and now for a specific purpose. Not knowing the road ahead, I obeyed God. The journey took me from my home in South Africa to the United States (2000–2005), back to South Africa (2005–2006), and then finally to Canada. I arrived on November 13, 2006.

A prophetic word spoken through a friend just before I left South Africa has already come to be fulfilled: "God has plans to plant you in a specific place where you will bloom and belong. He has already gone before you and prepared the place. It will fit you like a glove. Do not allow your heart to be troubled." Since then, I not only became a Canadian citizen in 2012, but I now own a business, have my own home, and have a sense of belonging in my city. And though all my family live in South Africa, I now have many people who love and support me. I have a place prepared just for me.

Living here is yet another confirmation of how God has ordained my steps, as Acts 17:26 says, "… *having definitely determined [their] allotted periods of time and the fixed boundaries of their habitation (their settlements, lands, and abodes)*" (AMPC). God's plan was for me to not only receive healing and be fully restored back to Him, but also to help others.

My life story is yet another example of how pain in our lives can become a gain for others. As Joyce Meyer often says, "Our messes become our messages."

In sharing my journey, I hope that it will help others understand this complex topic better. And I truly stand amazed at how it all unfolded.

---

4   Boyd Hopkins, *Yes, Lord: A Surrendered Life* (Denver, CO: Westword Press, 2014), 19.

Acknowledgements

To God, my Heavenly Father, who is willing to use an ordinary farm girl with limited writing skills, who was utterly fearful of public speaking, thank You for continuing to give me the courage and boldness to speak about a difficult topic, and to be able to help others. When I fell apart and wanted to quit writing this book, which happened thousands of times, You gave me the endurance and inspired me to complete it in the right timing. Thank You. I love You passionately!

To the Church, the body of Jesus Christ whom I am part of, I am thankful for the biblical foundation I have received and for the ways in which I have been equipped to become a maturing member who is capable of sharing a message of hope and restoration. I exhort you to compassionately and lovingly uphold biblical principles in all manner of living, for His honor and glory. Particularly, I am grateful for Len and Hettie Deyzel, who kept pursuing me to attend a women's retreat, a life-changing event which became the starting point of following Jesus wholeheartedly. And to Danie de Bruyn, from my hometown in South Africa, who led us believers and motivated us to become and grow into mature believers in Christ.

To my home group in Delisle and Twyla Pearce, the Faith Story Coordinator for Women's Journey of Faith, who responded in love and grace when I shared my testimony with them for the first time ever. Your loving response changed everything and became a crucial building block in my personal life. You helped bridge the way for me to walk into the arms of Jesus. You also helped to build a bridge between myself and the church. If it was not for your loving response, I would not be where I am today, including being part of a ministry. Thank you!

To the forerunners who have addressed the topic of homosexuality over the years. You have shared your journeys and insights in various formats, and I am greatly indebted for the clarity your contributions have brought to my own life. I am grateful that I have not had to reinvent the wheel. Your materials have made this topic more accessible. I am fully aware that I am not the only voice out there. Your voices have been helpful to make all our voices stronger—stronger for the truth! I am also well aware that here in Canada very little has been written from a biblical perspective on the topic of homosexuality. I have been greatly influenced by the book *Out of a Far Country*, by Christopher Yuan and his mother Angela Yuan, and its focus on holy sexuality. I also wish to thank Jonathan DesRoches, who wrote the drama I use in my presentation, "The Much-Needed New Approach." To each of you and many others, I applaud your bravery and boldness to proclaim God's victory and His desire in your lives and the lives of your loved ones; I hope this book will help to make our voices stronger together.

To Pastor Bruce Martin, for his sermon "The Modern Family, Part Two." When I heard him use the words "what to do when gay comes home," it resonated deeply within me. Six months later, I felt a prompting in my spirit to write a seminar with the title "When Gay Comes Home." Martin also specifically addressed several approaches by which the church has been dealing with the topic of homosexuality. His Jesus approach has become foundational in my teaching and writing. His thoughts helped me form the outline for the fifteen different examples I offer to those who journey with a loved one who experiences same-sex attractions.

To Pastor Dave Wells, for his sermon in which I was inspired by the analogy of the Jesus glasses. I have used this concept to address how we view others regarding this topic.

To Carmen Bekkatla, whom I met "by chance" at a women's ministry in Saskatoon. Your selfless offer to help with this book, without knowing how much work it would entail, has blessed me beyond words. Your patience, support, friendship, and God-given skills as a phenomenal English teacher has blessed me. Thank you for sacrificing so many hours that you could have spent with your family and taking valuable time out of your busy schedule to sit with me. Neither of us knew how much writing a book entailed, and as both of us have said, we didn't know what we signed up for. Yet with God's help we did it. Words can never say how thankful I am. May your faithfulness be abundantly blessed by God!

To Jaime Schreiner, whom God provided miraculously during the last six months of finishing the book. Your dedication and commitment to get this book published goes beyond words. Thank you for the countless hours you put in to help me finish this project which took so many years.

To my friend Michael, a member of Courage International,[5] I thank you for your willingness to share your knowledge and wisdom about this topic with me. Your input brought tremendous value to the book. Your example of joyfully striving to live a virtuous life inspires me.

To my friend Jayna Snider, who did all the artwork for the book, including some editing. You are the best and most gifted graphic designer I know. Thank you for your friendship and willingness to do so many things for me. Your work is immaculate and your loving support is greatly appreciated. Thank you!

To the many individuals who have believed in me and played major roles in loving and supporting me since I started sharing my journey in 2009. If it was not for you, I would not be where I am today. God used you mightily, and in the process He gave me the courage to do what I do now. You will never know how much your love and support continues to inspire me. I would like to mention a few specific persons, including Deidre Havrelock and the board members of Women's Journey of Faith, specifically

---

5   His name has been changed to protect his identity. Courage International is a worldwide Catholic ministry which reaches out to persons with same-sex attractions. For more information, visit: https://couragerc.org/

the leadership of Sheri Deobald in 2011. You risked asking me to share my testimony in front of 1,500 women. Thank you for your obedience to the Holy Spirit.

To the many individuals who became wise counselors on this journey and who have given me much-needed perspective at times when I needed it most. Thank you.

To my late mother, who passed away on June 10, 2015 after a debilitating thirteen-year battle with Alzheimer's, you never got to see and share this exciting time of my life with me. Your example has always inspired me. Thank you for that. You have taught me the one and most important principle in life: to abide in Jesus daily despite storms, hardship, and pain. Your modeling of the Proverbs 31 woman will remain with me forever. I pray that your legacy will live on through me and the example I offer to those around me. I know one day we will celebrate in heaven together.

To my sisters, Anelie and Jeandri, even though you do not always understand my journey, you love me anyway. Thank you. I love you very much!

To my father, Gerard, who risked his own life to save me when I was electrocuted at eleven years old. I am grateful. Thank you and I love you.

To many of my friends and loyal prayer partners who kept supporting and praying for me when I was ready to quit, not only from writing this book but from continuing in ministry, and when I went through a major burnout in 2015–2016. Thank you.

Introduction

The church, of which I am a part, is in crisis. Too often I exchange conversations with Christians about the topic of homosexuality, and without intending to hurt me their many comments feel like a knife stabbing deeply into my heart. This is a dilemma, because I know there are others who feel this, too.

These comments come from a place of being poorly equipped to speak compassionately about the topic of homosexuality. For decades and decades, this topic has been shoved under the rug and not openly discussed.

Since persons within the LGBTQ community haven't been treated with love and compassion, it created a mass exodus out of our churches. Today, however, many churches realize the damage that has been done and have begun to try to "fix" it, many times errantly compromising the truth from God's Word. That is, they love and accept all persons within the LGBTQ community, but go even further to approve of same-sex sexual/romantic relationships. Compromising the truth wreaks great havoc amongst many churches around the globe.

This is a crisis! Neither of these two approaches are biblical, and both fail to fulfill the Great Commission.

I believe this can be changed by going back to basics. Scientific and theological seminars aren't alone sufficient; we need a desire to study and practice a pastorally minded Jesus approach. If we do this, I believe a crisis can turn into an opportunity, and in the process we can better fulfill the Great Commission. It remains our mandate from Jesus Christ Himself.

One key point is that we should strive to better know the hearts of persons who experience same-sex attractions or who are within the LGBTQ community. Even though I have chosen Christ above everything, and have been pursuing a heart of chastity while living celibate[6] for more than fourteen years, I find that most people have no idea about the struggles I've faced in making sense of the same-sex attractions I experienced earlier in my life.

This book is meant to help people understand persons like me.

It should be noted that as someone who speaks English as a second language, sometimes when I speak off the cuff, I use terms like "gay," "homosexual," and "LGBTQ" interchangeably. However, in writing this book I have tried to make the language more consistent for the purpose of greater clarity (and unity). I believe it's important to draw people toward clearer language so that we can understand this topic, and each other, more deeply. I also think that it's important for people to continue learning, long beyond what is contained in this book.[7]

As mentioned, getting educated about the topic of homosexuality is very important, but we must also equip ourselves to speak about it compassionately. We must care deeply about people's hearts.

Here is just a small portion of an article written by a father who has a son who chooses to self-identify as gay. This father preached to his son and told him the truth, but he forgot one key element. He writes,

> Yet I missed one key truth: knowledge is useful, but knowing our children's hearts is priceless. When my "right" answers didn't change my son's feelings or behaviors, I realized I was missing out on what was going on in his heart. I have begun to *ask more questions, seeking to understand, and listen more* instead of jumping to give advice or state my own opinions. I learned that though truth is important, it is our children's own perceptions that matter. I discovered there were times when my son actually felt rejected by my attempts to tell him the right way to go. Though I was speaking the truth in love, my son perceived that I was rejecting him through my attitude and approach. *Seeking to know his heart* has helped me be more loving, transparent and open in communication than my preaching ever did.[8]

---

6   Allow me to explain the difference between the words *chastity* and *celibacy*. The dictionary describes them as synonyms, but they have different meanings. Although I sometimes use them interchangeably, I'll explain the difference in simple language. Chastity has to do with our hearts being connected to God and loving Him deeply. We want to do the right things because we love Him and want to obey Him. We want to please Him in all we do. From this place, we also choose not to engage in any form of lust or sexual relations outside of biblical marriage, because we know that He won't be pleased; according to what the Bible teaches about virtue, we don't want to engage in any form of immorality. Practicing chastity in marriage is also important, as it implies that you don't use your spouse for your own selfish and lustful pleasures. In short, a chaste heart goes after virtue, and one of those virtues is to not participate in romantic or sexual relationships outside of God's will. Celibacy, on the other hand, is something any person can do, even without being in a relationship with God. This means that I can choose to not engage in any romantic relationship or participate in any form of sex whatsoever merely because I choose not to. With celibacy, God is not necessarily in the equation. I don't need to be a Christian or a Jesus follower to do this. The term celibacy is the most common word people use when they choose to not engage in sexual or romantic relationships, yet I want to emphasize in this book the importance of our hearts being connected to God first and foremost and doing all things from that place.

7   Also, with English being my second language, I have found it helpful at times to use quotes from the Amplified Bible, because of the extra clarification it provides.

8   Dr. Jerry Bassett, "Reflections from a Parent of a Gay Child," *The Fellowship Message*. September/October 2016 (https://www.portlandfellowship.com/newsletter/2016/sep2016.pdf). Emphasis added.

Introduction

Though homosexuality is a hot topic in our day, churches shouldn't cringe in fear when it comes up in conversation. We can educate, equip, and enlighten ourselves on this topic, ideally sooner rather than later. We need to not only learn the facts but learn how to speak, how to love without compromising the truth. This book addresses all that.

The reality is that Satan not only tried to kill, steal, and destroy my own life, but he is still at work. He will do anything to stop anyone and everyone from walking in the fullness of what God has for them. He draws people away from holiness and virtue.

A friend of mine, Michael, who is of Catholic faith, has remarked that Satan "draws people to reject the Order of Creation that God has authored into our bodies." Satan is not the "gay agenda" people sometimes speak about, but he *is* behind anything that draws people away from holiness. John Burton writes in his book, *The Coming Church, that* "the primary driver of the homosexual agenda is not same-sex *attraction*, but rather strong deceiving sprits of pride, self-promotion and identity and lust."[9] These spirits aim to drive people as far away from God as they possibly can, and they will use any means necessary.

Christians who don't read the Word of God on a daily basis are setting themselves up to be deceived. Satan will pump them full of lies, trying to convince them that to live an unchaste lifestyle, including a homosexual lifestyle, is okay. He will also convince them that God made them this way.

People and churches will cave in and compromise the truth from God's Word. We already see this happening, but hopefully by learning about this topic through my experience we can turn that around. We can love without compromising the truth.

As I mentioned in the preface, when I first stepped onto a stage to speak, I felt the assurance of the Holy Spirit that I was taking back territory from Satan. The church is His bride, and she is broken in many ways. When the bride is broken, He wants to heal and restore her. His bride can be a mom or a dad with a gay son, or a sister who has a gay brother, or it can be anyone whose friend is a person within the LGBTQ community. It could be a person wrestling with same-sex attractions, or even a person who experiences them but does not see them as any big deal. It could be you. Whatever the case may be, God wants to bring healing and restoration to wherever there is brokenness.

The intent of this book is not only to tell my story, but to teach a lesson from it in this time of need. I talk about what I have learned and how to apply it practically. More and more books are being published on this topic, and some are misleading people, but the voice of truth needs to be heard! We can't be silent. There is power in telling a biblical testimony, where Jesus always gets the glory.

I hope and trust this book will do just that. The principles in this book can also be used to address habitual tendencies towards sin of any kind.

Ephesians 5:16 says, "*[Make] the very most of the time [buying up each opportunity], because the days are evil*" (AMPC). We live in perilous times. Not only has right been perceived as wrong, and wrong perceived as right, but people are perishing because of a lack of knowledge (Hosea 4:6). Too many Christians don't read God's Word anymore. They are easily swayed by pressure from our now very worldly society.

---

[9] John Burton, *The Coming Church* (Branson, MO: Significant Publishing, 2013), 105.

And God is starting to sift His church. The time has come for pastors, mentors, parents, family members, and friends to take a stand between light and darkness. What will we choose? We can't have one foot in the world of Christ and the other foot in the world of darkness. We need to make a choice very soon. Lives are at stake. *Souls* are at stake.

When a person comes out, or comes home sharing their same-sex attractions, it often breaks bridges between loved ones. This book will help to navigate the possible restoration of those broken bridges. There are also broken bridges between persons within the LGBTQ community and the church, and it is time to learn how to repair these as well.

These broken bridges have contributed to people closing their hearts to Jesus Christ. I hear so many stories about people who "come out," who have a story of conversion to Christ as a young boy or girl only to hear they have chosen to walk away from Jesus and His teachings. Their wrestling and disappointments with same-sex attractions often creates distrust in God, making it an easy choice to walk away from Him.

The way the church and Christians have treated them has also caused some disbelief and discontentment. That's why persons who experience same-sex attractions have chosen to search for love and acceptance someplace else, because they couldn't find it in the church. This is not what God wants, and it must be a great disappointment for Him. I believe this book will offer practical tools for people to find that love and acceptance, while differentiating between acceptance of the person and approval of the behavior.

By repairing and building new bridges, hearts and souls can be restored back to the Father through Jesus. It's time that we repair what was broken and make things right. This book will point out the ways in which walls are built instead of bridges. After reading, you will be aware of these barriers and have the tools to move beyond them, if you so desire.[10]

Through being involved in ministry and writing this book, I have realized that there is a bigger picture. My story and journey with same-sex attractions has a purpose—and it is not just about me. It's about helping others. It's about building bridges. It's about sharing the gift—Jesus—with the world. I am not the gift. But Jesus, who lives in me, is.[11]

Are you comfortably able to speak with confidence, using the right language, when this topic comes up? Do you know how to speak the truth in love, using "Jesus glasses"? When a person tells you they're gay, what is your first reaction? Do you know without a shadow of a doubt how to lovingly respond? Do you accept and love them unconditionally when they tell you they experience same-sex attractions and or are LGBTQ? This book will help you communicate in a loving, respectful manner along your journey.

In the times we live now, the topic of homosexuality is coming at us from all directions. We don't ask for it. It is happening. Children in most public schools are subjected to new sex education programs, and everywhere we go we are bombarded with and exposed to everything pertaining to the advancement

---

10   These tools and resources are available on my website (www.wilnavanbeek.com) and they are incorporated throughout this book. My website also includes information about the seminars I give on this topic, among other topics.

11   I am fully aware that this book will expose a lot of my family life, which includes painful events. By telling my story, I pray that it won't bring more hurt, but healing. Truth hurts, but *the truth* also sets us free.

of the LGBTQ movement. It is not going away. This book will help teach how to resist and counter that movement with love and courage, while at the same time helping persons who experience same-sex attractions know that they do belong in the family of Christ.

This book contains my journey as a former lesbian, and how my journey brought me to a place of fully surrendering to the Lordship of Christ—with astounding results. It doesn't matter what you struggle with in life, this book will help you to understand that if you surrender your struggle to Christ, He can restore, redeem, and transform your life.

In saying that, I want to make it clear that this book is not intended to be a pastoral document in and of itself. It will help people with their pastoral responses, but the intended audience is persons who desire to become better equipped to respond to this topic. I wished so many times in my own journey that my family, community, and church were better equipped. I know it would have helped.

As the reader, you will be confronted with many challenges as I present my perspective on wearing Jesus glasses and how to love and accept those who have been marginalized for too long. When we have done something wrong, God requires repentance. This may be one of the challenges you'll face—the idea that we as Christians might need to say sorry on behalf of those who have mistreated others.

In the chapter where I address terminology and factors influencing the formation of identity, I discovered how crucial it was to discover my own true identity, which is in Christ. Not only was this a personal journey of discovery rooted in my pursuit of deeper self-honesty, but I came to realize that we must allow the Holy Spirit to work in people's lives so they can get to the same place. We can't control their journey.

This book will help you understand this process.

CHAPTER ONE

I Have a Dream

I have a dream! In fact, I have more than one. If you remember, Martin Luther King Jr. had a dream, too. Sadly, his dream cost him his life.

Yet his dream didn't die with him. Many others shared his dream. They took it and ran with it, and in the process his dream came true. But it wasn't accomplished without a lot of hardship and pain.

God can place dreams and visions in our hearts. I see it as a sovereign design and call, and I am undeterred by the cost.

I dream of the day when every Bible-believing church will be educated, equipped, and enlightened on the topic of homosexuality. When they will not cringe in fear of the day when gay shows up in their church. When pastors will grasp every opportunity to rebuild broken bridges between the church and persons within the LGBTQ community.

I dream of the day when church members will realize that every person within the LGBTQ community is worthy of God's love, and that our example as true followers of Christ needs to stir in them the desire for a deep and intimate relationship with Jesus.

I dream of the day when same-sex couples—or for that matter, any person who identifies as LGBTQ—will walk into our churches and not be rejected. When we will not turn our heads, but turn our eyes inward and look at our own hearts.

I dream of the day when church members won't judge, but instead show grace and unconditional agape love,[12] standing courageously and uncompromisingly for the God-authored truths upheld by the Bible and the teachings of Jesus Christ.

I dream of the day when family and friends who have gay-identified loved ones will engage every opportunity to walk alongside them towards the Lord.

---

12 *Agape* is a Christian term that references love, and not only love but "the highest form of love, charity [and] the love of God for man and of man for God" (*Wikipedia*, "Agape." Date of access: September 8, 2017 [https://en.wikipedia.org/wiki/Agape]).

I dream of the day when people won't judge hearts, but instead show love and compassion. When they'll demonstrate a listening ear and get to know the heart of their loved one, trying to understand what it means to journey through life while experiencing same-sex attractions while still courageously standing for biblical truths and values. In saying that, I don't minimize the reality of the pain and disappointment that some people experience. They have real hearts, too, and in the name of true compassion we should be open to hearing their voices as well.

I dream of seeing our young generation turn back to biblical values and truths—and I know many of them already are. I dream of the day when they pursue purity above fleshly pleasures. Our youth are bombarded with lies that have become "truths" for them. Sexual immorality is approved and practiced by the world around them, and by many churchgoing Christians. This only strengthens their belief in these lies.

I dream of the day when our youth stand up and say "Yes!" to Jesus and His plan for beautiful and joyful holy sexuality.

Dreams and visions are put into our hearts by God. He uniquely tailors a sovereign design and call for each of our lives. The ministry I'm involved in can certainly be classified in this way. In saying this, my aim is not to put myself on a pedestal. I honestly never desired to become involved in anything like this. In fact, I used to be terrified just thinking of telling my story as a former lesbian. But God had a plan, and I said yes when He called me.

I am not asking for your sympathy. I'm asking you to share these dreams and be a part of bringing them to fruition. This is something Jesus asks all of us to do. It is part of the Great Commission.

If you and I are born-again believers, it means that Jesus has already reconciled our hearts back to our Heavenly Father. He then commissions us to go and do likewise, by sharing His reconciliation and the restoration He offers. We do this not only by telling, but by the way we love. He gives you and me the ministry of reconciliation, that by word and deed we might aim to bring others into harmony with Him (2 Corinthians 5:18).

All of us can build bridges and be part of the reconciliation process. And we need not worry—God will give us the strength when we make ourselves available, when we say "Yes!"

You may say, "Wilna, your dreams are impossible." But I believe they are possible. When we do what we need to do, God will do what we cannot do. May I bring His words to mind: *"Is anything too hard or too wonderful for the Lord?"* (Genesis 18:14, AMPC) and *"What is impossible with men is possible with God"* (Luke 18:27, AMPC).

I have dreams… and I know the fulfillment of them. As they remain in line with God's will and word, they will bring beautiful results. Hearts reconciled to God Himself.

CHAPTER TWO

Born for a Purpose

Nothing in life happens by coincidence. This book is no coincidence. The events of my life that have brought me to this point are no coincidence. When I tell you how my life has played out, you'll see for yourself that God had a plan.

I was born and raised in South Africa, where we lived on a farm that belonged to my mother; she had inherited it from her father. On the family farm, we grew a lot of crops and also had cattle and sheep.[13]

I was only eleven when my family and I went with some friends to Hibberdene for a vacation on the coast. On this particular day, the wind was whipping fiercely and we could only tolerate being on the beach for a little while.

On our way back to the chalet where we were staying, something terrible happened. The high winds caused the overhead power lines to touch, with one of the lines melting and falling down. One end of the melted wire hit the ground and stayed there, while the other end remained attached to the pole. It looked like the pole had been anchored. In my excitement to be first to have a shower, I ran on ahead of my parents. When I saw the wire, I decided to grab on and swing myself around. The moment I touched it, seventy-five thousand volts entered my body and threw me to the ground. The live wire clung to my left arm like a magnet, the electric shock causing my muscles to contract. My hand and elbow came stuck to my body, making it impossible to pry the wire free.

When my parents and the people around us became aware of what had happened, they all wanted desperately to get the wire off—but if anyone touched me, the electrical current would flow through them, too. Everyone was wet from swimming in the ocean, and water and electricity do not go together.

Many people tried different methods to remove the wire, with no success. Finally, my dad took off his new tennis shoes and, risking his life, folded one in half and pulled the wire off me.

---

13 My heart was always to farm with animals. Later in life, after graduating from university with a bachelor's degree in agriculture, I purchased a big cattle and sheep farm and made it my livelihood.

But by this time, I was already dead. Our friends put a sheet over me and led my mom away, because I was gone.

When my mom entered the chalet, devastated and in shock, she suddenly remembered that she was trained in cardiopulmonary resuscitation (CPR). She immediately ran outside and began CPR. I didn't respond. She tried several times, but it wasn't until she told herself, "Just one more try!" that I finally gasped for air.

My parents took me to a doctor to have me checked over to make sure I was okay. The hospital staff figured I had been dead for about five minutes, but after extensive tests the doctor concluded I was totally fine. No brain damage after being dead for five minutes!

I had a second chance. God saved my life because He had a plan.

There's even more to the story. It was no coincidence that my dad had that tennis shoe he used to pull off the wire. After buying the new shoes, he'd told my mom that the shoe salesman had cheated him by selling him one shoe with a crack in it. Because of this crack, he had been able to fold it in half. The defect helped to save my life. God can use anything to save us.

A few years later, at age fifteen, I developed a headache one day. My mom always kept aspirin in a cupboard, and I had taken it many times before. I took two that day, hoping my headache would go away. This day, however, I had an immediate anaphylactic reaction. Instead of calling my parents, I hid from them. When they finally found me, I was blue in the face and needed oxygen right away.

On this particular day, a friend of my dad, a doctor, had taken the twenty-minute journey out to our farm for a visit. He came to visit often and never brought his doctor's bag with him.[14] But on this day, something—or Someone—had told him to put his bag in the car.

By the time my parents found me, there was no time to drive all the way into town. I needed help sooner. The visiting doctor was able to give me an intravenous injection of steroids, and I survived. But I wouldn't have if he hadn't been there with his medical supplies.

God saved me again, from physical and spiritual death, because He had a plan.

When I was twenty-one, I was in a very serious car accident. People who saw the accident said they couldn't believe anyone could survive it. The car had rolled seven times. I came out with only a scratch on my foot and a very sore head from hitting the roof of the car every time it rolled. My friend, who had been driving, and her husband walked away with only minor injuries as well.

I wasn't in a good place in my life at the time. There had been one hundred and twenty bottles of wine in the car (and less than a dozen of them broke). Though we hadn't been drinking and driving that day, I certainly loved wine more than I loved God.

But He saved my life again. He kept me from death, because He had a plan.

This plan eventually became very clear through listening, hearing, and acting in obedience to the voice of the Lord.

---

14   Years ago, doctors would do house calls and bring a bag containing their medical supplies.

Born for a Purpose

From the time I first became a born-again believer in 1991, on many occasions I heard the still, small voice of God very clearly in my heart. Each of these occasions changed the course of my life in profound ways. Today, I can look back with thankfulness for how He directed my path. And He still does.

I heard that still, small voice again in mid-1998. One morning while I was praying and journaling, I felt a prompting that I needed to sell my farm. At that point, I was a successful farmer and had just won an award for being the Young Farmer of the Year in the Free State Province. Being a woman, that was a huge accomplishment in South Africa—and I still marvel at it today.

God prompting me to sell the farm was not what I wanted to hear. In fact, my first reaction was to argue with Him. Farmers in general are very sentimental about their farms, and asking them to stop farming is almost asking the impossible. But God had done it anyway.

"God, if this is You, then all I'm asking is that you please take the sentiment away," I said.

Around the same time, South Africa was going through a very difficult time, not only with the economy but also with regard to people's safety. Many farmers went bankrupt and lost everything they had. Though I had been successful in many ways, I still struggled financially. When I heard God's prompting to sell the farm, I knew I needed to trust and obey Him, even though I had no idea what the future would hold for me.

I truly loved being a farmer, so following through with this was very difficult. Many people, including members of my family, were shocked and couldn't understand the decision I had made. I had little support as I went through the process of selling, but I knew it was what was best for everyone involved. I had loans from my parents and the bank, and it was important for me to pay them back.

I spoke with an auction company and we went ahead with the sale. On February 20, 1999, I sold everything. I was amazed that when the day arrived, I had absolutely no sentiment about it. I can honestly say that I was able to let go of everything I so dearly loved without feeling heartache and loss. I sensed that there had to be a plan and that this chapter of my life had come to an end. I knew it was time to turn the page, regardless of the cost.

I was able to pay back all my loans and begin the difficult journey of starting over. Somehow, I was okay with it. Today, I can look back and see God's hand. Even though people didn't understand the choices I made, today I know it was all a part of the path God had ordained for my life since the beginning of time.

Obeying God by selling my farm was the starting point of a journey I could have never anticipated. Truthfully, I never would have chosen to share my shame and guilt with the world. But I would never have guessed that God could use an ordinary farm girl from the small town of Reitz in the Free State Province for this task.

My life has taken me from South Africa, to the United States, back to South Africa, and then to Canada. I now stand in front of large audiences, educating, equipping, and enlightening the body of Christ.

In the story of Joseph (Genesis 37–50), the path his life was headed on was suddenly turned upside-down. This innocent man ended up spending many years in a dungeon. A man who was imprisoned with him, formerly the chief butler for the pharaoh, was let out and returned to his old life. One day, this man remembered to put in a good word for Joseph with the pharaoh, which led to Joseph being released from prison. He was then given charge *"over all the land of Egypt"* (Genesis 41:41, AMPC), a position in which he was able to save many people from starvation and death.

He was also given a wife. Two sons were born.

And Joseph called the firstborn Manasseh [making to forget], For God, said he, has made me forget all my toil and hardship and all my father's house.

And the second he called Ephraim [to be fruitful], For [he said] God has caused me to be fruitful in the land of my affliction.

—Genesis 41:51–52, AMPC

I'm sure Joseph questioned God many times. I have, too. Even though I never ended up in prison, discovering at the age of twenty-one that I was attracted to women felt like toil and hardship to me. I was ashamed, I felt guilty, but I kept silent. This was indeed my own prison.

But God has a plan. He never leaves us, and He will help us to forget our toil and hardship. He will cause us to be fruitful in the land of our affliction. Pain never has to be wasted.

As Rick Warren says in *The Purpose Driven Life*,

God never wastes hurt! In fact, your greatest ministry will most likely come out of your greatest hurt… God intentionally allows you to go through painful experiences to equip you for ministry to others… The very experiences that you have resented or regretted most in life—the ones you've wanted to hide and forget—are the experiences God wants to use to help others. They are your ministry. For God to use your painful experiences, you must be willing.[15]

Joseph was willing, and I continue to be willing.

As Rick Warren also wrote, "For God to use your painful experiences, you must be willing to share them."[16] By sharing, I am "making to forget" all my former struggles and pain, and now I can "be fruitful" in the land of my affliction. I can now bloom where God has planted me.

How can we doubt God? How can we doubt that we are His and our lives are not our own? Each life is one that is born and destined with a plan and a purpose, a purpose to bring Him glory.

My prayer for you is that this book will bring clarification to the topic of homosexuality and, most importantly, that you will recognize the importance of total surrender to Jesus Himself. He is the One who changes us all. He doesn't only have you and me on His mind, but *all* people.

As we surrender fully to Jesus, I pray that your life will be restored and redeemed, and that your example will be salt and light as you represent Jesus well. I pray that you will become a signpost that points others in His direction.

---

15 Rick Warren, *The Purpose Driven Life* (Grand Rapids, MI: Zondervan, 2002), 246–247.
16 Ibid., 247.

Our lives should build bridges, not walls. Reconciling others to Christ is a mandate from Jesus Himself. He personally reconciled us back to His Father and He calls all of us to do the same. We are to be bridge-builders through living lives of integrity, fully devoted to Jesus. 2 Corinthians 5:18 says,

But all things are from God, Who through Jesus Christ reconciled us to Himself [received us into favor, brought us into harmony with Himself] and gave to us the ministry of reconciliation [that by word and deed we might aim to bring others into harmony with Him]. (AMPC)

This is our ultimate calling: to become true followers of Christ and to point others in His direction. God told Abram,

Go for yourself [for your own advantage] away from your country, from your relatives and your father's house, to the land that I will show you. And I will make of you a great nation, and I will bless you [with abundant increase of favors] and make your name famous and distinguished, and you will be a blessing [dispensing good to others].
—Genesis 12:1–2, AMPC

This verse is clear. God had Abram on His mind, but not only him. He said, "[A]nd you will be a blessing [dispensing good to others]." God has many people on His heart. I left my home country twice, and even though the journey has been very difficult at times, God had me, and many others, on His heart.

He has His bride in mind. This includes you and me, and those who are willing to receive the message. I have been told that my story inspires and brings hope. For these reasons, I pursued writing this book. Even though it was hard and I wanted to quit numerous times, I know that it will bring a message of hope and restoration to others. This makes all the hardship and pain I've suffered worth it.

In this process, everybody wins. Jesus said, *"In this world you will have trouble"* (John 16:33, NIV). We can't let that stop us from the plans and purposes He has for us (Jeremiah 29:11). My prayer for this book is that it will be a blessing to many people for years to come. Nothing in my life is meant to be wasted, and like you, I was born and destined for a plan and a purpose!

CHAPTER THREE

What Glasses Are You Wearing?

I have lived a homosexual lifestyle, and this is my story. This is how I've made sense out of my journey. I speak for myself—you may not agree, but my ultimate prayer is that you will hear this message loud and clear: Jesus Christ redeems, heals, restores, and forgives us all—with Him, nothing is impossible (Luke 18:27).

I'd like to begin by asking you a few questions. If I tell you I experienced same-sex attractions, what is your first reaction? How do you see me? What kind of glasses do you have on? I have encountered all kinds of people on my journey and their reactions have been quite varied.

Do you wear the same kind of glasses the Pharisees wore? Will you bombard me with legalism and immediately remind me that the Bible says homosexuality is an abomination to God? Do you have hate glasses on? Will you justify calling me names? Will you respond by saying "I can't stand you" or "I hate you, and so does God"?

I will never forget a woman who came to me after I shared my testimony at a women's conference in 2011. I could tell she was very uncomfortable waiting in line to talk to me. When she got to me, she embraced me with a hug and begged me to forgive her.

"Ma'am, I don't even know your name," I told her. "What should I forgive you for?"

"I have hated gays. I have ridiculed them. I have judged them. Will you please forgive me?"

As an individual (I cannot speak for others), I was glad to forgive her. I will never forget the relief on her face.

Or perhaps your glasses indicate that you don't understand my experiences or you don't clearly understand God's standards. Maybe you would say, "I'm okay with how you live you life. You can marry another woman."

Or do you wear the kind of glasses that lead you to say, "You just need to choose not to be gay anymore"? Maybe you think it's merely a choice. But do you think I would have ever chosen to be gay, especially during the sixties when I grew up? I don't think any person would choose to be gay and be subject to ridicule and judgement.

Let me clarify: we can involuntarily experience same-sex attractions, but we must then decide what to do with those attractions. We must each decide whether we will orient ourselves first and foremost to gratify the desires of the flesh or pursue holiness of the heart (which of course leads us to holy behaviors).

Or do you have Jesus glasses on? These glasses look at the heart. They look at me with compassion and without condemnation, meeting me where I'm at and accepting me for who I am. Like Jesus, we are to speak the truth in love. God is love:

Beloved, let us [unselfishly] love and seek the best for one another, for love is from God; and everyone who loves [others] is born of God and knows God [through personal experience].
—1 John 4:7, AMP

God convicts us out of love, whereas the world, the flesh, and Satan often condemn. Jesus uses conviction to call us to action.

Doug Pollock, author of *God Space: Where Spiritual Conversations Happen Naturally* impels us:

When we start to notice others with our Jesus glasses on, something happens inside of us… His compassion melts away the coldness in our hearts. Our callousness towards others is replaced with a genuine concern.[17]

It is imperative that you understand how you initially respond to an individual who experiences same-sex attractions. How you answer these questions of perspective will highly impact your friends and loved ones.

---

17 Doug Pollock, *God Space: Where Spiritual Conversations Happen Naturally* (Loveland, CO: Group, 2009), 37.

CHAPTER FOUR

Terminology and Factors Influencing Our Identity

W<small>E NEED TO BE VERY CAREFUL WHEN WE USE THE TERMS LIKE</small> "<small>GAY</small>" <small>AND</small> "<small>HOMOSEXUAL</small>." When an individual says "I'm gay," we often assume she is living a homosexual lifestyle. She may mean that she experiences same-sex attractions but has chosen to live chastely or celibately. When someone identifies as gay, we have to be careful not to assume that they mean they're actively participating in a homosexual lifestyle. And above all, we must still love the person despite his or her personal choices in life.

Also note that the words "homosexual lifestyle" might mean different things to different people. When I use this phrase, I'm referring to my past choice to live unchastely in a same-sex relationship. It is important that we don't assume that a person lives a "homosexual lifestyle" like I did, based on their mere acknowledgement of the attractions they experience.

Another term people use a lot is the word "struggle," and we need to differentiate between its different meanings. Many persons within the LGBTQ community deeply struggle with the fact that they experience same-sex attractions. They know and perceive these feelings to be unnatural. They question it, they question God, and they wonder why it happened to them. They may feel it's unfair and don't want to feel those attractions, so it becomes a real struggle. This struggle is part of my own story. I deeply struggled with my same-sex attractions.

However, others don't seem to want to call this a struggle. Because they have accepted right off the bat that God "made them that way," this is not a struggle to them. They just live their lives the way they believe God made them to be. To them, hearing the word "struggle" in this sense can actually offend them. Therefore, we need to always use caution when we use the word struggle. It's always safer to say that a person *experiences* same-sex attractions rather than *struggles* with them.[18]

---

18   We'll get into lots of detail about these terms later in the book. But for our purposes, when I refer to persons within the LGBTQ community who "struggle," I have those in mind who truly are concerned about their same-sex attractions; they are trying to work through things and/or trying to change or accept themselves. In this struggle, we need to support them. You can read more about this in the Chapter Thirteen where I talk about the Jesus approach.

We need to clarify how we speak about this topic[19] while still being sure to love people, even if they're making behavior choices that don't adhere to biblical standards. We need to speak the truth in love (Ephesians 4:15). We need to love the individual and address their behavior respectfully and with dignity. Just because you choose to love an individual doesn't mean you accept or approve of his or her behavior. Acceptance does not imply approval.

Acceptance does not imply approval.

Another clarification that needs to be made has to do with people who identify themselves as gay Christians. Some might be merely acknowledging the attractions they experience. However, some of these people are living a homosexual lifestyle while declaring that they live for Jesus. This is a biblical contradiction. They are basing their identity on themselves (the attractions they experience) instead of God. This reflects the sin of idolatry, a state in which we, and our sexuality, become the idol.

We need to differentiate between experiencing same-sex attractions and acting on them. Many choose to place Christ at the center of their hearts and live a chaste life. They practice holy sexuality on account of their love for Christ and choose to identify themselves first and foremost as sons or daughters of God, not as gay Christians.[20]

When our hearts are fully open to Christ, they are fully open to growing in Christian virtue[21] and Christ-likeness. Peter declares,

> *For this very reason, adding your diligence [to the divine promises], employ every effort in exercising your faith to develop virtue (excellence, resolution, Christian energy), and in [exercising] virtue [develop] knowledge (intelligence), and in [exercising] knowledge [develop] self-control, and in [exercising] self-control [develop] steadfastness (patience, endurance), and in [exercising] steadfastness [develop] godliness (piety), and in [exercising] godliness [develop] brotherly affection, and in [exercising] brotherly affection [develop] Christian love. For as these qualities are yours and increasingly abound in you, they will keep [you] from being idle or unfruitful unto the [full personal] knowledge of our Lord Jesus Christ (the Messiah, the Anointed One). For whoever lacks these qualities is blind, [spiritually] shortsighted, seeing only what is near to him, and has become oblivious [to the fact] that he was cleansed from his old sins. Because of this, brethren, be all the more solicitous and eager*

---

19 In the book, I use the phrase "persons within the LGBTQ community" and "persons who experience same-sex attractions" interchangeably. The fact is that not all persons who experience same-sex attractions consider themselves members of the LGBTQ community. However, when I mention "persons within the LGBTQ community," I include *all* persons who experience same-sex attractions.

20 Additional clarification on the term "holy sexuality" can be found in Chapter Sixteen.

21 Virtue is defined this way: "moral excellence; goodness; righteousness… conformity of one's life and conduct to moral and ethical principles; uprightness…" (*Dictionary.com*, "Virtue." Date of access: September 8, 2017 [http://www.dictionary.com/browse/virtue]).

to make sure (to ratify, to strengthen, to make steadfast) your calling and election; for if you do this, you will never stumble or fall.

—2 Peter 1:5–10, AMPC (emphasis added)

I caution those who declare themselves to be gay that our human experience (attractions) should never define our true identity. Rather, our identity must be defined first and foremost in Christ.

Personally, I no longer self-identify as gay or lesbian. Instead I embrace the identity of being a daughter of the King of Kings. In that identity, I have found freedom beyond all measure; it reflects the greatest truth of who I am. Within this identity, I can be more honest with myself about who I am as a wholeheartedly accepted and beloved daughter of God.

Furthermore, many people seem to believe that an individual chooses the attractions they experience. Thus, they should be able to choose *not* to experience those attractions and instead simply choose heterosexuality. People need to understand that the counter to homosexuality is not necessarily heterosexuality but holy sexuality. People assume that a person's transformation comes from the pursuit of heterosexuality, and that by pursuing or practicing heterosexuality their same-sex attractions will "go away." This way of thinking is too small! It neglects the role and power of God's transformative love.

It is also important to understand that some people believe that if you just pray for a person or just lay hands on them, they will be "cured" or "fixed" from same-sex attractions. It is, of course, true that nothing is impossible with God, and He can remove those attractions in a moment. But the reality for many is that same-sex attractions may never go away. However, we can find meaning in the attractions we experience if we understand God's call to die to ourselves within this world with the promise of a greater world yet to come—in heaven. If we can remember this, while realizing that giving the gift of our sexuality back to God is truly a loving act of self-sacrifice to the Creator who loved us *first*, then we will be able to see how dying to ourselves in this way is life-giving.

How is it that people claim they have come into the world gay? Is it possible to be born this way? Scientists have had difficulty identifying a "gay gene" (and they won't find one), so why is it that I knew I was different for as long as I can remember? And why is it that thousands of other people like me relate to that feeling?

I've watched many videos from well-intentioned organizations who help people who identify as gay to encounter Jesus in a personal way. However, I cringe every time I hear them criticize those who claim they were "born this way." I understand that it's important for us to move beyond the genetic cause falsehood, but a genetic cause and being "born this way" are not the same thing.

In order to make sense of this, I need to describe how, for me, it all started in my mother's womb.[22] I do claim that I knew I was different for as long as I can remember. Many people react strongly to the declaration "I was born gay." Before you react, though, please hear me. I do not say that God made a mistake, and neither do I say that He created me gay.

---

22   I will explain this in greater detail in a later chapter.

I was born into a fallen, sinful world—as we all are; we all have our personal struggles with sin—and I needed Jesus as my Savior. But to get this revelation, I struggled for years with Psalm 139:

For You did form my inward parts; You did knit me together in my mother's womb… My frame was not hidden from You when I was being formed in secret [and] intricately and curiously wrought [as if embroidered with various colors] in the depths of the earth [a region of darkness and mystery]. Your eyes saw my unformed substance, and in Your book all the days [of my life] were written before ever they took shape, when as yet there was none of them.

—Psalm 139:13, 15–16, AMPC

How could God have created me wonderfully? Is it possible that He could have created me gay? I've read this psalm over and over again. I wanted to believe I was wonderfully made, but then the lies would creep in. How could I be wonderful if I experienced same-sex attractions? How is it possible that God created me in my mother's womb and I came out like this? I doubted Him so much.

Because we live in a fallen world, things sometimes happen in the mother's womb that are beyond her control. The human experience *begins* in the womb. Physiologically, some babies are born blind, and others are born deaf or without limbs. Some babies are born with both sex organs (hermaphrodite, although the preferred usage for humans is "intersex"), and some with none at all. Psychologically, the womb is our first relational environment, where we subconsciously learn our trust parameters.

In exploring questions about these complex issues, I came across a few important points:

Babies are not born with physical disorders to punish their parents in any way… From early on, the child should be taught how valuable, loved, and accepted he is by his family and also by God. He or she is not a victim of divine judgment but God has a plan for each one of us that will bring Him glory…[23]

A neonatal nurse once explained to me that until recently, when a baby was born in Canada without genitals they were all made into girls. Who knows if some of them should have been boys? Then how can we criticize that person when they experience attractions to someone who is of the same sex as the sex they were "assigned" by the hospital workers?

In John 9:1–3, we are reminded,

As He passed along, He noticed a man blind from his birth. His disciples asked Him, Rabbi, who sinned, this man or his parents, that he should be born blind? Jesus answered, It was not that this man or his parents sinned, but he was born blind in order that the workings of God should be manifested (displayed and illustrated) in him. (AMPC)

---

23 *Got Questions?* "What Does the Bible Say About Hermaphrodites?" Date of access: September 8, 2017 (https://www.gotquestions.org/hermaphrodites.html).

We all came into the world broken and fractured. This is why we need Jesus.

Regardless of how we came into the world, we were created by God, for God. And He has a plan and a purpose for each of us, a plan that will bring Him glory. If we fulfill it, it will draw others to the pursuit of holiness.

We all have a choice as to what we're going to do with our lives. I had a choice, too. I have come to the same place as the blind man in John 9, after Jesus healed him. If you don't know the story, I'll summarize. The Pharisees were upset and questioned his parents. They gave him a hard time over whether or not he had actually been born blind, and eventually this was his answer to them: *"But one thing I do know. I was blind, and now I can see"* (John 9:25, ICB).

All I know is that I used to live unchastely within a homosexual lifestyle, but now I live chastely for Jesus. I once was sexually attracted to women and drawn into unchaste pursuits (including my thoughts), but not anymore. As a result of striving to continuously abide in Jesus, I am more attracted to holy sexuality, and this has brought me to no longer desire a sexual relationship with another woman. I used to justify my unchaste homosexual behavior, but I can't justify it any longer. Nothing else matters anymore. Whether I was born gay or not is of no importance. All I want now is to leave a legacy of loving and living for Jesus. I quote Bill Hybels in his book *Just Walk Across the Room*:

> True followers of Christ who really get it right, give themselves to people. Most importantly, they give themselves to pointing people to faith in Jesus. That is the highest and best use of any human life—to have it serve as a signpost that points people toward God.[24]

I hope and pray that one day when I'm gone, people will not remember Wilna as the lesbian, but as the person who loved Jesus and pointed others in His direction. This is all I want to do! Like Paul said in Philippians 1:20, while he was in prison,

> *For I fully expect and hope that I will never be ashamed, but that I will continue to be bold for Christ, as I have been in the past. And I trust that my life will bring honor to Christ, whether I live or die.* (NLT)

When I came to the conclusion that I was born in a sinful state, as we all are, and God didn't make a mistake but rather created me for a reason and a purpose, I felt tremendous freedom. I could be myself. And I could share my journey with others in the hope that it may help them and those who love and care about them. I could live with who I was/am and not try to be somebody else. I've had to continually focus on choosing Christ. We all have to choose what we're going to do with our lives!

I have chosen to make Christ the center of my life. What do I mean by this? There's an illustration that explains this quite well—a bicycle wheel.

---

24   Bill Hybels, *Just Walk Across the Room* (Grand Rapids, MI: Zondervan, 2006), 28.

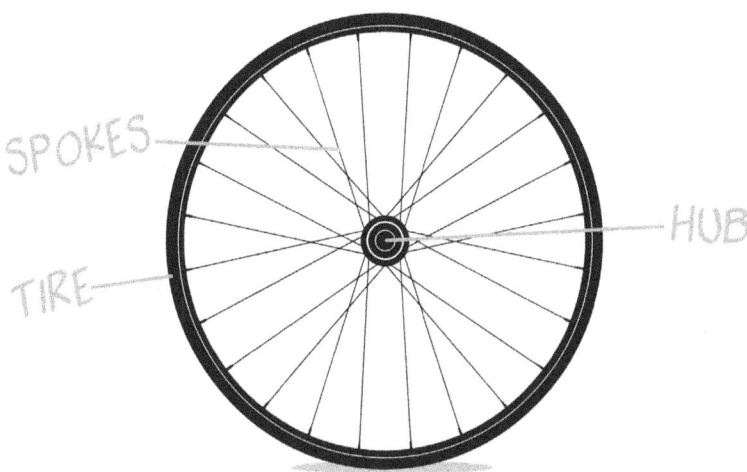

In the middle of this bicycle wheel is the hub which keeps all the spokes together. If you remove the hub, what will happen to the wheel? It will fall apart!

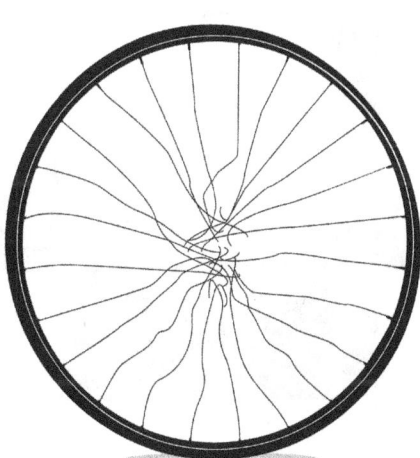

When we accept Jesus fully, He desires to become the hub of our life. He longs for us to surrender every area of our hearts to Him. The compartments between the spokes represent all the areas of our lives.

When I made Him the hub of my life, everything started to change, not only with regard to my sexuality but in every area of my life. This was key. I had to surrender and acknowledge that I could not change the things I wanted to in my own power, but things started to change slowly but surely through surrendering and allowing Him to do the work.

I like to explain it another way. As a Christian, when I accepted Jesus into my heart, I was essentially inviting Him into my house. Many pastors and Bible teachers use the same analogy, but this is how I've made sense out of it.

When I initially invited Christ into my life in 1991, I welcomed Him into my home. I showed Him around my house, telling Him where the bathroom was, the living room, kitchen, and the guest bedroom. I told Him not to go into my closet, though, as it is full of stuff, and I also told Him that I had locked the door to the basement. My basement had stuff in it I didn't want Him to see: sin, shame, and guilt!

This is a tactic of Satan, because he knows that when we allow Jesus in he must flee! By not allowing Jesus into the locked areas, I didn't experience victory in my life, not only with regard to my unchaste homosexual behavior, but in many other areas as well. Therefore, I experienced destruction in certain areas of my life, and I didn't understand why until I had the revelation of the house in 2003.

If I would ask Jesus why I experienced destruction, I believe this is what He would answer: "Yes, you have invited me into your home, and I'm excited to be here, but you didn't give me access to every room."

Inviting Jesus into the closet and basement of my house was the key as to experience change and transformation. That's how I started to have victory.

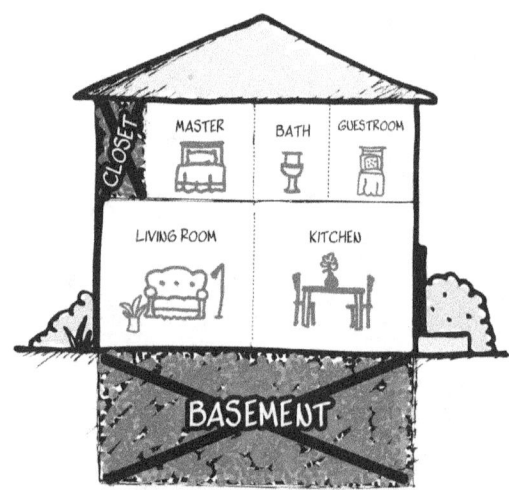

When we allow light to come, darkness must go. Psalm 18:28 declares, *"For You cause my lamp to be lighted and to shine; the Lord my God illumines my darkness"* (AMP). Isaiah 42:16 reminds us that God sees what we do not, and He will be a constant companion:

> *I will lead the blind by a way they do not know; I will guide them in paths that they do not know. I will make darkness into light before them and rugged places into plains. These things I will do [for them], and I will not leave them abandoned or undone.* (AMP)

John 1:5 informs us that the darkness doesn't win in the end:

The Light shines on in the darkness, and the darkness did not understand it or overpower it or appropriate it or absorb it [and is unreceptive to it]. (AMP)

When we allow the light of Jesus into our closets and basements, darkness has to go! But we can't do this on our own.

You see, prior to making Christ the center of my life—before inviting Him into the closet and basement of my house—I was caught in a state of guilt, shame, fear, and total silence… for too long. Though I wanted to share about myself and how different I was, my fear of people's reactions kept me silent. I had absolutely no courage to even mention homosexuality. It was a scary thought.

CHAPTER FIVE

My Struggles with Identity

Let me start from the beginning. When I grew up, there was a myth going around in South Africa that if I ran under a rainbow, my gender would change and I would become a boy. I tried to run under every rainbow I saw.

A rainbow, for me, was not merely a biblical symbol of God's faithful promise that He would never again send a flood to completely cover the earth. In today's society, the rainbow is used as a symbol of diversity, acceptance, and hope (while having significant political undertones). It's displayed on flags at LGBTQ pride parades. For me, it represented something I could never conquer—I would never be able to walk underneath it, even though I so longed to be able to do that.

As a young child chasing rainbows, what did I know about homosexuality? I used to chase rainbows, but I don't need to anymore because a rainbow now only reminds me of the promises of God, and they are "Yes" and "Amen" (2 Corinthians 1:20).

My strong desire to be a boy led me away from doing girlish things. I never wanted to play with dolls. The doll I had didn't even have a name, or if it had one I can't remember. I obviously had very little interest in it.

I preferred toy cars. I loved to play outside, making a "town" by building roads and then driving the little cars on it. I still have the first toy car I received as a gift. It's a plastic version of a Citroen. When I look at the toys kids play with nowadays, I can only laugh when I reminisce about innocently playing with the toys I grew up with. These days, children are over-occupied with electronic devices all day, and it's not helping them to grow into healthy relationships with one another through which they can discover God's amazing plan of joy and holiness.

I want to clarify here that interest in dolls or cars, whether society perceives these things as masculine or feminine, isn't necessarily an indicator that a child is inclined to experience same-sex attractions (or be transgender, for that matter).

Also, I hated wearing dresses. I remember that my mom made dresses so the three of us sisters would look the same. Bless her heart. She did what she thought was best—during the sixties and seventies, girls were expected to dress like girls.

On Sundays, we were expected to dress up for church. I couldn't wait to get home from church and change into shorts or pants. I never felt comfortable wearing dresses. Church represented another constraint on how I was expected to present myself instead of a time to meet with God. It felt like a set of rules I had to adhere to.

My school uniform was a dress, and again I couldn't wait to get home to put on pants. One thing I did like when I got to high school was the tie, shirt, and jacket we were allowed to wear. It felt more masculine, and I associated masculinity with being strong.

I wanted to be a boy so badly, and my family treated me as such and allowed me to be the tomboy I wanted to be. I loved to dress up like a man. I wanted to be a man—and a strong one, too. Men seemed so in control of everything. I would stand in front of the mirror and parade, putting on my dad's jackets or a tie. This made me feel the most comfortable. My mom tried her best to dress me like a girl, but I hated it.

Even though I wanted to be a boy—I dressed like a boy and had short hair like a boy—I wasn't a boy. It was painful to hear people call me *seuntjie*, which means "little boy" in Afrikaans.

It was a constant reminder of what I was not. I constantly felt conflicted about who I was and who I wanted to be. When people commented on my lack of femininity, and some would even laugh at me, I became angry. I wanted to run away. These comments didn't help me with my perception of my identity. It felt like they were mocking me.

It was a constant frustration. Later in life, when I learned of the concept of sex-change surgery, I had thoughts of pursuing it. My desire to be a boy ran so deep that I considered going this extreme process to make it happen.

I didn't know who I was. I was so confused. I was traumatized and paralyzed by fear. In my home, it was never safe or acceptable to express myself. I wasn't encouraged to think, speak, feel, or share about my identity struggles.

In fact, I often wasn't thinking clearly enough to be aware I was struggling with my identity at all.

CHAPTER SIX

My Struggles with Christianity

I grew up in a Christian home—or perhaps I should say, we went to church on Sundays. My dad farmed, working hard and long hours. In many ways, Mom was a Proverbs 31 woman. At some point in the morning, I would go looking for her and find her on her knees praying and reading her Bible. Her example inspires me to this day. She always put God and others first, lacking things herself. We never went hungry; we always had clothes, food, and shelter. I played competitive sports, and I never lacked any equipment. At our home in the mornings, my mom would help us get ready for school, but she didn't pack our lunches; she believed we had to learn how to do this ourselves. She believed in meeting our needs, but she also instilled in us a sense of personal responsibility. To this day, I am thankful for all I have learned from her.

Through my mom's example, I have learned the vital necessity of abiding in the Vine. Abiding in the Vine means spending quality time with the Lord each and every day. And it is best to do it at the beginning of the day. This is the time when I read my Bible, meditate on Scripture, journal, pray, and listen to God as He speaks to me.

The Bible teaches, *"The sheep that are My own hear My voice and listen to Me; I know them, and they follow Me"* (John 10:27 AMP). But because we live busy lives, we don't make time to listen to Him. I give every day to God and ask that He guides and leads me. I need Him, for without Him I can do nothing. I cannot successfully start a day without spending quality time with God (John 15:5). Today, I realize that my mom's relationship with God is what sustained her through the difficult times she faced.

At the age of eight, my mom gave me a Bible, and from that point on I felt a constant draw towards Jesus. In giving me the Bible, she underlined Psalm 119:105: *"Your Word is a lamp to my feet and a light to my path"* (ESV). This verse is significant. As I learned to put Christ first and genuinely invited Him into every area of my life, He truly became the light to my path. When I go off-track, He gently reminds me of my wrongdoing and directs my steps back to Him.

Psalm 32:8 reminds me, *"I [God] will instruct you and teach you in the way you should go; I will counsel you [who are willing to learn] with My eye upon you"* (AMP). God is interested in the littlest of details of our lives, but we need to continually allow Him to be the light that guides and directs us.

Throughout my childhood and teen years, I was a people-pleaser; I studied hard, got high grades, and did well in sports. I competed at a provincial level and I could tell my parents were proud of me. Mom never missed any of my competitions and matches. Dad attended the games he could.

However, I rarely felt loved. I never heard the words "I love you" from either of my parents. I also never heard them say it to each other or to my sisters. The only times when I did feel loved was on my birthday when I would get a card from my mom. She would write the words "I love you." But I never really felt loved by my dad, or at least I never felt like he expressed it. Now, looking back, I could have written a very similar experience as the one found in Melody Beattie's *Codependents' Guide to the Twelve Steps*:

> I received no nurturing and little love. From the time I was born, the people I expected to love me, disappointed me. I wasn't hugged. I wasn't told I was beautiful. I wasn't allowed to be afraid, to be angry, and of course, I didn't feel joy. I was told to be more, be better, try harder, and be stronger. Be in control. I learned that no situation merited falling apart or indulging in feelings. Feelings were a waste of time, a childish, weak, human, unnecessary display. By not feeling, I survived in this family. I survived life… I learned to treat myself as I had been treated —neglecting, avoiding, criticizing, demeaning, and berating myself for having feelings and needs, for being human.[25]

These were the ways I survived my upbringing. Even though I can't speak for my siblings, I know we each found our own way to cope. But my survival methods weren't helpful to me for dealing with conflict or for building healthy relationships throughout my life.

Today, after going through the very helpful twelve-step program for codependents, I continue to learn how to build and sustain healthy relationships. I've learned that if your childhood was not as you wished, you can take ownership over your decisions as an adult to move forward in life.

Looking back on my childhood, I realize that I behaved as I did because I was searching for love; I needed approval and to be loved. All people need to feel loved, and all want to belong. Even though I can't say I didn't receive any nurturing from my parents, the nurture that was shown in our home, I know today, is not full nurture.

To this day, I still long for my father's affection. I often envied my cousins. They seemed to have the perfect father. He took care of them, he lovingly disciplined them, and he was the one who made decisions and had authority. My own father would promise me things, but he would hardly ever follow through. Therefore, my trust in my earthly father never became a foundation on which to trust my heavenly Father.

I was often frustrated when I read in the Bible that how our earthly fathers wouldn't give us a stone when we had asked for bread, or a snake when we asked for a fish (Matthew 7:9). I couldn't relate to this.

---

25 Melody Beattie, *Codependents' Guide to the Twelve Steps* (New York, NY: Simon and Schuster, 1998), 20–21.

The Bible teaches that we can ask our heavenly Father for anything, and if it is according to His will it will be done. I never trusted God, because I likened His character to the character of my earthly father.

Though I went through a time of hating my dad, I realized later in life that he behaved as he did because he didn't feel cherished and valued. I understand many of his actions today, though I still don't justify them. I have learned that hurt people hurt others. I can only imagine that my father's actions came from a place of unresolved hurt.

There's much that didn't make sense to me in our home. There was a great deal of dysfunction. Although my dad worked hard and steadily, he struggled to lead the home and my mom did what was necessary to keep the home functioning.

My mom was the head of the house in every sense. Many times, she had to step up to save us from bankruptcy. This didn't help to create biblical balance in our home. She was the one who disciplined us, not my dad. This wreaked a lot of havoc. We would ask her for something, she would say no, and then we knew that if we only asked dad, he would say yes. These patterns generated much stress and contributed to the dysfunction. My dad was unwilling to follow through with necessary boundaries, and when he was frustrated he easily got angry. He was unpredictable.

I just wanted to be home with my mom. As children, we saw him physically abuse her numerous times and I took it on myself to protect her and be with her. I tried to never let her out of my sight, which of course was impossible because I had to go to school each day. I would rush home to be there in case she needed me. I lay in bed many nights, trying to stay awake, able to hear every word she and my dad spoke, every fight they fought. This happened almost every night. During those fights, my mom often said she was going to kill herself because of all the turmoil. This made me want to stay home all the time.

I was so scared he would take her life or she would take her own.

Too early, I took on the responsibility of being my mom's caretaker. This happens to many people, and it has devastating effects on one's personal life. For this reason, my life felt unmanageable after my mom was diagnosed with Alzheimer's. Because I lived far away in Canada, I felt helpless to care for her.

A few years ago, my dad and I had a huge disagreement. He told me that even as a baby I had pushed my grandfather away, and at the age of four I had pushed him away, too. Why would I have done this? I really didn't know. Perhaps it was out of fear of him. The anger he had demonstrated toward my mom would have made any child want to run away. But he took it personally that I pushed him away, and as a result we never had a healthy father-daughter relationship.

To this day, it saddens me to comprehend why my father would have taken a four-year-old so seriously, allowing an incident at such a young age to devastate our relationship. Oh, how I longed, and still long, for the blessing and affirmation of my earthly father, to have a loving and healthy father-daughter relationship.[26]

---

[26] With regard to my relationship with my father when I was young, I know now that I was afraid and angry. After a recent healing experience through prayer ministry, I've gained a greater insight into my emotions and the relationship dynamics I had with my father. This healing experience is explained in Chapter Seven.

In his book *Replenish*, Lance Witt writes, "Even though Jesus was fully God, in His Humanity I think he needed to hear the blessing and affirmation of his Father. That blessing of Sonship became an anchor in his life."[27]

Apart from my relationship with my mother, I didn't receive an unconditional sense of love and belonging from my church or family. The church we attended didn't preach salvation through belief in Jesus. Rather, they taught that He would punish us if we did something wrong. The church preached that we had to be good before Jesus would accept us. Man, did I try to be good.

I loved hearing sermons and they inspired me to go home and live out what I had learned. I would try so hard to be a good person, but my good behavior usually wouldn't last through to the next day. Then I would feel so condemned and disappointed—until the next good sermon, which could be months down the road, after which the cycle would start all over again.

I thought if I could just change and be a better person, God would love me. For some reason, I had the desire to become a preacher one day. I can relate to the apostle Paul when he shares that he struggled to do the good he wanted to do, and ended up doing the things he didn't want to do (Romans 7:18–19). In fact, I would go home many Sundays and parade in front of the mirror with a blanket over my shoulder, spreading out my arms as the minister would at the end of the sermon to give the blessing.

I am grateful today that God has brought me full circle. Though I don't consider myself a pastor, God has given me a platform. He has called me to speak to large audiences. He has blessed me with the courage to educate, equip, and enlighten through teaching and training the body of Christ not only on the challenging topic of homosexuality but also on many other subjects.[28]

These teaching opportunities have been the beginning of the fulfillment of another prophetic word I received back in 1998: "One day you will stand before pastors and leaders, training them." I certainly disregarded it back then. Today I travel around Canada speaking to many pastors and leaders of many Christian denominations.

Despite the calling on my life, I struggled to understand the love of God. Growing up, Jesus was God to me, but not a gentle God. He was this big man with a stick, ready to whip me when I did anything wrong.

I remember falling off my horse one day, breaking my tailbone. I had been swearing just before the incident and I thought God was punishing me for doing so. My mother used to say over and over again, "Always remember, God is watching you! And He will punish you when you do something wrong." So when I fell off the horse and injured myself, this was proof to me that God really *would* punish me.

For many years, I believed the lie that God was always waiting to punish me. Nobody ever told me that Jesus loved me just the way I am. I thought I had to be pleasing to God in order to be loved.

I was trying to work for the love of my parents by performing well, and I tried this with God, too. I had yet to understand that *"God shows his love for us in that while we were still sinners, Christ died for*

---

27 Lance Witt, *Replenish* (Grand Rapids, MI: Baker Books, 2011), 110.

28 My seminars include "When Gay Comes Home," "Abiding in the Vine," "Getting Dressed for Success: Putting on the Full Armor of God," "Who Is Your Master?" and "Holy Sexuality."

us" (Romans 5:8, ESV). In discovering my true identity, this passage helped me to understand that although I was born into a sinful state and a sinful world, God loves me just the way I am and He has a plan for my life.

In fact, He loves me so much that He doesn't *leave* me the way I am. He always draws me closer.

CHAPTER SEVEN

A Revelation of My Identity

The environment in the womb can play a factor in a child's development. We build our trust relationships in the womb, right from the beginning of our lives. I quote from the book *The Secret Life of the Unborn Child*:

> We now know that the unborn child is an aware, reacting human being who from the sixth month on (and perhaps even earlier) leads an active emotional life. The fetus can see, hear, experience, taste and, on a primitive level, even learn in-utero (that is, in the uterus—before birth). Most importantly, he can feel, not with an adult's sophistication, but feel nonetheless! A corollary to this discovery is that what a child feels and perceives begins shaping his attitudes and experiences about himself.[29] (Verny 12)

David says in Psalm 51:5–6, *"For I was born a sinner—yes, from the moment my mother conceived me. But you desire honesty from the womb, teaching me wisdom even there"* (NLT). This verse clearly states that from the moment we are conceived, we are already sinners: *"How then can man be justified and righteous with God? Or how can he who is born of a woman be pure and clean?"* (Job 25:4, AMP) We all came into the world broken and fractured.

Some people like to dismiss Christianity because of this. However, there is evil in this world. It didn't come out of the blue. It's actually the result of our ability to exercise free will, which was given to us by God because He loves us enough not to control us. Paul reminds us in Ephesians 2:3,

> *Among these [unbelievers] we as well as you once lived and conducted ourselves in the passions of our flesh [our behavior governed by our corrupt and sensual nature], obeying the impulses of the*

---

[29] Dr. Thomas Verny and John Kelly, *The Secret Life of the Unborn Child* (New York, NY: Dell, 1982), 12.

flesh and the thoughts of the mind [our cravings dictated by our senses and our dark imaginings]. (AMPC)

We are indeed very sensual creatures and we can react to things even in the womb. The reality is that while I was in my mother's womb, as a baby nearly ready to be born, I did make choices due to what I was experiencing. Those choices—to reject men—shaped my attitude towards them going forward. Why do I say this?

In 2014, some unwanted emotions surfaced from my childhood. These occurred after I had a visit from my two sisters who had come to Canada to celebrate my fiftieth birthday. While they were here, we did something we had never done before: we talked about our childhood.

After they left, feelings of anger started to manifest in me. At first I tried to control them, but they became unmanageable. I felt shame and guilt and didn't understand what was going on. I came to realize that I have buried a lot of things over my lifetime, and as these emotions surfaced I knew that I needed help—and I needed it fast. Unless I got help, I wouldn't be able to continue in ministry either.

I searched for help. I went to my pastor, and other trusted friends came to my house to pray for me, but things got worse. A friend recommended I read the book *Emotionally Healthy Spirituality*, by Peter Scazzero, and I realized that I needed to deal with some unresolved issues from my past.

Scazzero writes, "Sometimes we need to go back in order to go forward."[30]

I became desperate. A friend told me about prophetic prayer ministry and God provided a miracle—not only financially, but in every detail in regards to being able to get away for a week. The schedule of this ministry was wide open and the timing was perfect. Help was on the way. God had a plan.

Before I share the following, I want to remind you that God is the God of the impossible. He is the God of yesterday, today, and tomorrow (Hebrews 13:8).

Unfortunately, some people criticize me for sharing what Jesus has done. I wonder, is this not the same way the Pharisees responded in Jesus's day? After he healed the blind man in John 9, instead of praising God for the miracle the Pharisees questioned His healing and tried to discredit both the blind man and Jesus.

Our reaction should rather be like that of the people who witnessed Jesus healing a paralyzed man:

And overwhelming astonishment and ecstasy seized them all, and they recognized and praised and thanked God; and they were filled with and controlled by reverential fear and kept saying, We have seen wonderful and strange and incredible and unthinkable things today!

—Luke 5:26, AMPC

When I share publicly about my personal healing, it's because I believe God wants to use my story to help others. The reality is that we live in a broken world, and things happen to us that God never

---

30 Peter Scazzero, *Emotionally Healthy Spirituality* (Grand Rapids, MI: Zondervan, 2014), 93.

intended. I want others to know that help and healing is as close as reaching out to Jesus. He is even able to take us back to places where hurt and pain have taken root. He wants to heal us right there.

If you're unfamiliar with intensive prayer ministry, I urge you to be open to what I share in the next few paragraphs.

Usually the process begins with the counselor or prayer minister sitting with us. Then we quiet our hearts before the Lord and invite the Holy Spirit to enter. We ask that He guide and lead us, and we also ask Jesus to show us things in our life, but to take it further and specifically show us where He was during a particular past event or situation.

During the prayer ministry I attended,[31] Jesus not only addressed and healed me in several areas of my life where I was so broken, but He also took me back into my mother's womb. I saw there what happened to me. I was aware of what was happening to me, and I also saw how I responded. I saw Jesus there in the womb.

Jesus says, *"I will never leave you nor forsake you"* (Hebrews 13:5, NKJV). Psalm 139:13 reminds us that He formed us, which also means that He was there, present with us.

I saw how afraid I was in the womb. I was not in a relaxed fetal position, but rather I was standing, with my fists held up—I was ready to fight! My color was pitch black, and I was screaming, "I want out… I don't want to be in this place." I held my fists close to my ears, covering them. I even heard my mom say that this wasn't a good time to have a baby.

Then the most significant thing happened: Jesus took both my clenched hands away from my ears, removed something from my ears, and said, "Now, I make you to hear My voice." Since then, I have come to hear Him very clearly. Jesus says in John 10:4 that His sheep hear and know His voice. Next, He took my fists, opened them,

> *Painful life experiences, right from the time of being in the womb, can tempt us to believe lies and make vows that cause us hardship later on.*

and said: "I now write My name on the palms of your hands."[32] Then He took me out of the womb and changed my color from black to transparent. He covered both of us in a rainbow and said, "May this always remind you of the promises that I am with you and I will never leave or forsake you."

When we asked the Holy Spirit to continue to guide us during my prayer ministry time, He revealed to me the vows I had made way back then. The emotional wound I'd received had caused me to make these vows, and they created bitter roots which bore bad fruit from the moment I was born!

---

31   Elijah House (www.elijahhouse.org) was founded with the mandate to restore the hearts of the fathers to their children, and the hearts of the children to their fathers (Malachi 4:5–6). This is being accomplished by equipping the saints with biblical tools founded upon universal laws in the Word of God, to enable the discernment of root issues and allow true healing.

32   Note that Revelation 3:12 talks about how God writes His Name on us.

Painful life experiences, right from the time of being in the womb, can tempt us to believe lies and make vows that cause us hardship later on.

In my mother's womb, I chose that I would resist, fight, and keep all men at a distance for the rest of my life. I was ready to fight my dad and other men. I came out of the womb pushing men away. I wouldn't let them near me.

The fear and anger I experienced in my mother's womb caused roots of resentment, bitterness, and hatred. And the fruit of the bitter roots resulted in defilement—even when men came near me, they sensed a wall. These bitter roots caused me to push men away—that is, the wound I received not only created bitter roots but it conditioned me to keep all men at a distance.

Is it any surprise that this fear drove me into the arms of women? I found safety and refuge in women on an emotional level, and that became sexualized over time. This was Satan's aim. He is the father of lies. The bad roots—fear, anger, bitterness, and unforgiveness—started to bear bad fruit. In my case, the bad fruit was same-sex attractions. Can you see how Satan was behind it all?

There are many root causes underlying the experience of same-sex attractions. In my case, my fear of getting close to men became the root, and the fruit was that I found myself becoming more and more drawn to women. I grew to trust these women and allowed myself to become intimate with them. In short, I didn't specifically choose to be gay, but the fruit of the bitter root was my later experience of same-sex attractions.

Even though I did not specifically choose it, I acknowledge that I made choices in my life about who I would let get intimately close to my heart. God didn't make me this way; He did not "give" me same-sex attractions. These attractions emerged within me as a result of sin and the fallen world we live in—not my particular sins, but sinfulness itself.

Regardless of how the sexual attractions I experienced came to be, my response to them can be used for God's greater glory, as with anything else.

Bad roots bear bad fruit. If a tree has bad roots, that means it is sick. But the Bible has the answer for these bad roots. It is clear what happens to sick trees; when the roots are bad, it will produce bad fruit. Luke 6:43–45 declares,

For there is no good (healthy) tree that bears decayed (worthless, stale) fruit, nor on the other hand does a decayed (worthless, sickly) tree bear good fruit. For each tree is known and identified by its own fruit; for figs are not gathered from thornbushes, nor is a cluster of grapes picked from a bramblebush. The upright (honorable, intrinsically good) man out of the good treasure [stored] in his heart produces what is upright (honorable and intrinsically good), and the evil man out of the evil storehouse brings forth that which is depraved (wicked and intrinsically evil); for out of the abundance (overflow) of the heart his mouth speaks. (AMPC)

Remember, God wants to heal us. When He exposes these roots in our lives, it is not to hurt us but to heal us. Healing helps us not to blame others. I'm not sharing my prior experiences to blame my parents or anyone else, but I share them so that we can recognize the spiritual battle we are in. Satan will do anything to turn our roots bitter, so they can bear bitter fruits.

A few years ago, I had a conversation with a friend of mine. She is a beautiful woman who had recently lost her husband, and a lot of men were showing interest in her. I had tears in my eyes as I shared with her my wonderment that men would show interest in her, but not me. I know that I am a beautiful woman and it's kind of hurtful when men don't "see" me or show interest in me. Today I have come to know the truth about why they don't "see" me. Isn't it wonderful? When we know the truth, we are set free (John 8:32).

The truth is, fear of men became a bitter root in me, causing me to build a wall to keep men at a distance. When men came near me, they could sense this barrier as though it were a literal wall.

Hebrews 12:15 cautions us, *"See to it that no one falls short of the grace of God and that no bitter root grows up to cause trouble and defile many"* (NIV). I can see now that the walls I had built were in some way a form of me defiling these men. Have you ever been in a room where you felt "invisible"? Or have you been at a place where you felt like nobody could "see" you? This could mean you don't want to be seen. Perhaps you have built a wall around yourself.

My tree needed to be healed. My bad roots needed to be severed and dealt with. And none of this was possible without the marvelous work of the best heart surgeon of all: Jesus. Lance Witt writes in his book *Replenish*,

God put me up on the operating table and did spiritual surgery. He shined the light on broken areas and went to work on them. And even though it was sobering, and painful, it was good and helpful.[33]

---

33   Witt, *Replenish*, 155.

I can also say that the Vinedresser from John 15, God the Father, has been working diligently on this tree for a while now, as I let Him! And I'm grateful for the changes, and for those dead roots and branches He cut off.

I had to renounce these vows and acknowledge the bad roots, which included my rejection of men. And I had to ask for forgiveness.

In the process of dealing with bad roots, the fruit in my life began to change. In fact, I called my dad in 2015 and for the first time we had a talk that involved real depth. This was something I prayed over for weeks. I needed to make amends with him. I told him how sorry I was for rejecting him. I asked for his forgiveness. We both cried and he said it was the best day of his life.

I still desire a more complete restoration with him. I've offered what I can to bring about further restoration, and I hope and pray for our restoration to continue.

A healthy relationship involves work from both sides, not just one person. But I know today that forgiveness is the beginning of restoration, and I believe this with all my heart. Martin Luther King Jr. said, "Forgiveness is not just an occasional act, it is a constant attitude."[34] Jesus Himself forgave us and reconciled us back to a restored relationship with our heavenly Father, and this is no different! 2 Corinthians 5:18 reminds us,

> *But all things are from God, Who through Jesus Christ reconciled us to Himself [received us into favor, brought us into harmony with Himself] and gave to us the ministry of reconciliation [that by word and deed we might aim to bring others into harmony with Him]. (AMPC)*

Many people tell me that I have the right to feel angry towards men. Yes, I know. But we all have a responsibility to take ownership over our own lives. Consequently, I desire to make godly choices based on biblical principles. I made vows, and these vows kept me in bondage. Since I've started to own my stuff, to take responsibility for my part and stop living in denial, I have become healthier and more whole.

I know with certainty that my life has changed since my prayer ministry experience. Shortly after, while on holidays. I went for a few massages. What makes this significant is that my massages were given by a male therapist, something I would never have previously allowed. During my massage, I was able to relax and I felt absolutely no more fear, anger, or bitterness towards that man or any man. There has been a huge shift. I am eager to see what God has in store for me now.

Nothing is impossible with God. God wants to heal us. He wants to help us to sever the bad roots so we can start to bear healthy and desirable fruit, the fruit He wants us to bear. He says, *"Therefore, you will fully know them by their fruits"* (Matthew 7:20, AMPC).

Having chased rainbows as a young girl, I can now ask, what did I know at the time about homosexuality? And do you think I would ever have chosen to be gay? Would you? I don't think any person

---

34   Martin Luther King, Jr., *Goodreads*, "Quotable Quote." Date of access: September 17, 2017 (https://www.goodreads.com/quotes/57037-forgiveness-is-not-an-occasional-act-it-is-a-constant).

would choose to be gay in order to be ridiculed and judged! I didn't choose to be gay, but the fruit of those bitter roots became same-sex attractions.

In coming to know and understand myself, I don't blame others for my behavior. I believe that by sharing my experiences, I can help many others to understand why they might feel they were born that way. When a person shares a similar statement with you, please don't disregard it. They have struggled long enough, and it's painful and hurtful for them to hear dismissive things like "It's not possible," "There is no gay gene," or "You're wrong." Instead they need to hear that Jesus was there, they are loved, and they belong in His loving arms. He wants to restore us from our wounds, whether they occurred in the womb or later in life. He will forgive and take away the bitter roots. He will bring about beauty from ashes:

To grant [consolation and joy] to those who mourn in Zion—to give them an ornament (a garland or diadem) of beauty instead of ashes, the oil of joy instead of mourning, the garment [expressive] of praise instead of a heavy, burdened, and failing spirit—that they may be called oaks of righteousness [lofty, strong, and magnificent, distinguished for uprightness, justice, and right standing with God], the planting of the Lord, that He may be glorified.

—Isaiah 61:3, AMPC

Our churches and societies are full of broken people and they need to know that help and healing is as close as choosing to reach out to Jesus. He is even able to take us back to places where hurt and pain took place. He wants to heal us right there, even when it means going back in time.

I ask you, do you still believe what is said about Jesus? That He can still heal today? We all come into the world broken and fractured. This is why we all need Jesus. Transformation *is* possible—when we give Jesus permission to work in our lives. Our sense of identity and self-concept can change as we open our hearts and die to ourselves and the attachments of this world. This can—and does—transform our entire perspective of what we perceive to be fulfilling.

> *Transformation is possible—when we give Jesus permission to work in our lives.*

Because I have chosen Christ above everything else, I no longer self-identify as gay, but I can say today that my embraced identity is that of a beloved daughter of the Most High God. The joy I have experienced as a result of my choice to more profoundly let God into my heart has inspired me to continue to pursue holiness in all I do. I practice holy sexuality through chaste living. I have tasted the joy of this and I am never turning back!

I was only able to get here through a daily and intimate relationship with Jesus as I put Him first and at the center of my heart. I have invited Him into every area of my life. Placing Jesus at the center of our lives doesn't only apply to the topic of homosexuality, though. I have come to realize that God's love is truly the greatest love of all.

CHAPTER EIGHT

Learning to Love

My first experience with love outside of my family came at a fairly young age. When I was thirteen, I dated a young man whom I fell in love with—but we didn't have a physical relationship. We were too young for it, but I know I loved him deeply, inasmuch as I knew how.

He ended the relationship by declaring his love for someone else. My heart was broken. I had no one to talk to and I had to deal with this painful experience all alone. This deeply impacted me, and even though he came back to me a year later to try again, I would not. I believe I made vows then about whom I could trust and whom I could be with.

Because I was already carrying such brokenness and a tremendous fear of men, this experience only served to make things worse. It aided in the destruction of even the possibility of heterosexual relationships.

I couldn't pinpoint the onset of my desire for same-sex sexual and romantic intimacy. Although God had created me a girl, my identity was distorted from experiencing so much hurt and pain. This was the devil's plan.

Following this dating experience, I always felt uneasy around men, until my healing experience in 2014. Though I had many boyfriends, I never felt comfortable around them. I always dreaded the moment when they would say good night to me after a date, because it was customary to get a kiss or a hug at that point. This was scary to me. I preferred to push them away, though I never understood why. I thought it was because I wasn't in love with them yet. I always told them I wouldn't kiss until I could say "I love you."

I never fell in love with another man.

I did, however, fall in love with women! It wasn't hard to kiss or hold hands or give hugs to women. Being close with women felt so good. I know it's hard for some people to imagine how it's even possible to feel attracted to a person of the same sex, but this is a reality for people who experience same-sex attractions. I had to come to terms with it, whether people understood it or not.

From the moment I started feeling same-sex attractions, though, I was already fighting them. Today, it is my passion to try to explain to people how hard a fight this is.

I started engaging in same-sex sexual and romantic relationships when I was twenty-one. I dated women and men at the same time; I really had no clue what I was doing. At that time in my life, I understood that sin included any sex outside of marriage. However, I also sensed that my same-sex attractions were unnatural (Romans 1:26).[35]

I dated some wonderful men, but I never felt towards them the same way I felt towards women. It was very frustrating. I felt so guilty for hurting the men I dated. They truly loved me and I really tried to feel the same way, to change myself. I wanted my heterosexual relationships to work. They never did.

My mom greatly desired for me to get married. This was a source of tension between us.[36] Even in my mom's final stages of Alzheimer's, her expressions and wishes remained the same.

I remember a funny incident that occurred when her mind wasn't functioning properly anymore. On my birthday, she said, "Wilna, I hope you find a husband this year."

"What would I do with a husband?" I asked.

She commented, "He will cook for you!"[37]

I could never understand why my heterosexual relationships never worked. I would wake up one morning and realize it wasn't going anywhere and we had to break up. It was hard breaking up, and it hurt knowing that my decision would hurt another. But how could I go on, without any physical attraction?

Physical attraction is certainly a driving force in any romantic relationship. Here's how I understood it: when two people kissed or held hands, it meant that they liked each other. Affection for me was very important; it showed that another person cared for me. However, I never saw my mom and dad show any affection toward each other. In fact, on the rare occasions when I did see my mom showing affection to my dad, I noticed he was resisting it, and vice versa.

The strong physical attractions I had towards women were extremely difficult to bear. Imagine, for one moment, that you had to resist the attractions you experience to your handsome husband or beautiful wife (or the person you are currently in a relationship with). Imagine that even though you love this person, and want to hug or kiss them, you *have to* fight and suppress your attractions towards them. That would be very hard, wouldn't it? This is the reality of what I felt.

Having sex with a person of the opposite sex will not change a homosexual person into a heterosexual one.

Same-sex attractions exist without you specifically choosing them, but you can make the choice whether or not to act in unchaste ways.

---

35   The terms "natural" and "unnatural," in the Christian sense, refer to what is structurally evident in nature itself, both visibly and invisibly. They do not refer to what someone might perceive to "feel" within their human experience, which may include attractions and inclinations which arise without one's specific choice.

36   In Chapter Nineteen, I'll provide a caution to parents of children who self-identity as gay about how to pray for them.

37   In her last year of living at home, my dad was the one who did all the housework, and he obviously became her cook as well.

Some people believe that if I could just have sex with a man, I would be forever "cured." Well, I've been there and done that. It didn't work and it isn't true. Having sex with a person of the opposite sex will not change a homosexual person into a heterosexual one. For me, sex with men did bring physical gratification, but it didn't cure my sexual attraction towards women.

For this reason, I struggle to fully endorse organizations who guarantee to have the ability to "fix," "cure," or "change" everyone. They guarantee they can change a homosexual person into a heterosexual person. There really are programs out there doing this kind of work that have done a lot of damage. We can't promise change, but we can share with people the fact that God is able. It is all His doing. Total healing does happen for some—as is true of any issue—but no one can guarantee that total healing will happen for everyone. Some people are so devastated by the failed promises of such programs that they have committed suicide. The reality is that although inner healing can diminish same-sex attractions—and for many the change is dramatic—the reality is that some people's same-sex attractions may never completely go away.

> *The reality is that some people's same-sex attractions may never completely go away.*

Though with God, anything is possible. He could remove or diminish these attractions in a moment. In my case, He has done both, although this happened over the course of a number of years. It wasn't due to suppression, but rather filling my heart with something better: the love of God.

The fact that God permits (not wills) these attractions to exist might be His sign to us that people in this age deeply need a witness to joyful chastity, and persons who experience same-sex attractions might be that profound witness. I humbly choose to offer God my sexuality by living chastely. If there is anyone who does experience transformation, it is all by the grace of God, coupled with that person's choice to cooperate with Him. Keep in mind that only God is able to transform an individual. It is His work.

In preparing to share my story with you, I remembered a very painful event. I was dating a wonderful young man whom I really liked, and I hoped our relationship would work. He was already talking about getting engaged. We spent a lot of time together. He adored me and I so badly hoped to reciprocate his affection.

He had a brother who was very skeptical about our relationship; he openly showed hostility towards me. One morning, his mom called me and in an unfriendly and forceful manner told me not to see her son anymore because I was a lesbian and I would never change. She mentioned that she'd spoken with psychiatrists who had told her that "gay people never change." This resonated with me because I had tried to change on my own for so long.

This confrontation showed me how much people talked about me behind my back. I had not yet come out of the closet, and this confirmed to me that people "knew" I was a lesbian. This was a very painful experience. It didn't help me with regard to speaking up. In fact, it created more shame, guilt, and fear. I didn't want to hear, nor did I need to hear, all these hurtful comments. So I did what she asked me to do—I broke up with him.

Today, however, I know that part of what that woman said to me was true.

In a recent study, fifteen men who used to live a homosexual lifestyle but have chosen to live celibate were asked what kind of night dreams they have. One hundred percent of them answered that they still have dreams of being sexually active or romantically involved with men. This is also true in my own personal life, despite the fact that I have chosen to pursue chastity and live celibately and no longer experience same-sex attractions in my waking hours. These dreams have diminished over time, especially since my healing experience in 2014. However, in the mornings after I wake up from one of those dreams, I am very upset. I can remember fighting the attractions while in the dream, resisting physical and sexual participation. This always makes me feel more at peace and I know God is still at work. Much healing has taken place over the years and I expect more to come. Keep in mind here that there are also many who, because of inner healing, no longer dream of sex and romance.

I never wanted to be in homosexual relationships. From the very first one, I tried to fight it. Looking back, I was fighting the relationship because I knew in my heart that something just wasn't right. As Paul states in Romans 1:26–27,

For this reason God gave them over and abandoned them to vile affections and degrading passions. For their women exchanged their natural function for an unnatural and abnormal one, and the men also turned from natural relations with women and were set ablaze (burning out, consumed) with lust for one another—men committing shameful acts with men and suffering in their own bodies and personalities the inevitable consequences and penalty of their wrong-doing and going astray, which was [their] fitting retribution. (AMPC)

Honestly, I had no clue what I was feeling during my first relationships. I didn't understand the fact that I'd rather be with a woman than with a man. I had nobody to talk to. There were trust issues in my family; we hardly talked about anything, and when we did it usually ended up in a fight. Nothing got resolved, so it seemed better to keep things inside.

It is a tactic of Satan to keep people silent. Silence and deception keep us in a state of torment. In this state, we don't experience freedom.

Talking about these things involved finding people I could trust, but I had no one at the time. I would lie to my family and friends. I never had the courage to admit that I was in a homosexual relationship. I always denied everything. I made excuses. But deep inside I knew I was lying, and I didn't feel good about myself.

Denial and dishonesty quashed my feelings of frustration for a time. However, not knowing or understanding myself still caused a great deal of fear, guilt, and condemnation.

It wasn't until 2008 that I had the courage to disclose to my family that I had lived a homosexual lifestyle.[38] Nonetheless, it eventually became obvious to people that I was in a homosexual relationship. My mother's first response was to take me out of her will. She was the primary influence in our home and made key decisions for our family. She held a lot of power. When things didn't go her way with me or my sisters, her first reaction was to disown us. Her occasional harshness was a tender spot in her relationship with all her loved ones. She had money and owned the farm. She was a Proverbs 31 woman in many ways, but she still had struggles like everyone else.

Parents often don't realize that when they draw hard lines like this, their children will most likely choose their loyalty to other people in their lives. For instance, I chose my partners above everybody else. All I can say is that I wish my mother hadn't made such significant decisions while being so angry. She simply didn't know how to deal with the reality of my experience. Disowning me was her way of saying, "If you continue on this path, you will inherit nothing."[39]

In my mom's anger and helplessness, she decided to send me to psychiatrists. She hoped they could "fix" me. However, this desire to fix someone doesn't help the relationship.

Back then, in the mid-seventies and eighties, there were no resources about homosexuality, and nobody talked about it. It was a taboo subject in South Africa. It certainly wasn't talked about in church, as the Bible clearly forbids homosexual behavior.

My mom did what she thought was best, but none of the psychiatrists she sent me to were helpful at that time in my life. In saying that, there are also psychiatrists who are very helpful, and I am in no way minimizing the impact their expertise can have. However, many of my experiences with psychiatrists were scary. They not only used hypnoses but they tried to brainwash me.

I remember the day when a male psychiatrist gave me an injection. I'll never forget it. They tied me down to a bed and I felt my head start to spin. He and the nurse then urged me not to fall asleep while they asked me very personal questions. Though I didn't want to answer the questions, the hypnotic state of mind made me willing to talk. I felt empty and frustrated after the session and told myself I would never allow anyone to do that to me ever again.

The psychiatrists gave me books to read. To tell you the truth, most of them had a condemning message. Their message was that as a homosexual, I was going to hell. Most didn't differentiate between same-sex attractions and the practice of homosexuality, let alone speak about the chaste or unchaste state of the heart. The authors of the books I received declared that I was going to hell if I practiced homosexuality, and also if I claimed to experience any same-sex attractions at all.

I have since come to make a differentiation between the attractions I experienced and the way I chose to respond to them. However, the books I was given didn't make this distinction.

---

38   Again, note that my homosexual lifestyle did not, and does not, define who I was.

39   This was my mother in grieving. I write more about this in Chapter Eighteen, which covers the five stages of grief. One of the stages is anger, and it can be very destructive!

Other books I read were about parents who discovered their kids were gay and how they tried to cope by praying for them to just find the right opposite-sex partner in order to be cured or fixed.[40]

I also read books to try to understand myself. Because I had no one to talk to, I would buy books that approved of the homosexual lifestyle, although they were very limited at the time. I hid them from people because I didn't want them to know what I was reading.

None of these books helped me either. They only allowed me the liberty to justify my choices of behavior.

There was a time in my life when you wouldn't have been able to convince me that living a homosexual lifestyle was sinful and displeasing to the Lord. Realizing this required me to invite the Holy Spirit into my heart; out of that place of total surrender, my thoughts, desires, and behavior patterns began to change.

No man, psychiatrist, self-help book, or my own efforts to change myself could do for me what the Holy Spirit has done. I see a struggle in the church today to accept the work of the Holy Spirit. The role of the Holy Spirit is not only to declare the truth of Scripture but to instruct us to live lives that are holy and pleasing to the Lord.

Today, biblical standards seem to be up for interpretation and subject to relativism. It seems people are concerned with pursuing their own agendas regardless of what the Bible says. This could be rooted in the desire to try to please people, or pacify them. Nonetheless, to their detriment, people are trying to make the Bible fit their own agendas or ways of thinking. Rick Warren from Saddleback Church in California said in an April 8, 2012 interview with ABC News on the topic of same-sex marriage, "Accommodating culture will weaken the church." I feel that the church should be influencing society and not the other way around.

> *No man, psychiatrist, self-help book, or my own efforts to change myself could do for me what the Holy Spirit has done.*

I am deeply concerned for the church of Jesus Christ. So much has changed, even since I started writing this book. I feel things are changing at an accelerated pace, often not in a good direction. Many churches not only adapt and accommodate our immoral culture, but they approve and condone many unbiblical practices God prohibits and hates.[41] I use the word "hate" only to imply that something is rejected by God, being counter to the order He established and counter to His plan for us to live in union with Him. Again, God doesn't hate people, and neither should we; it's simply that God "hates" the things we do that separate us from Him, that remove us from being in harmony with Him.

---

40 Again, please refer to Chapter Nineteen for a further understanding about how to bring children before the Lord in prayer when these circumstances arise.

41 The word "hate" here is used to imply that something is rejected by God, being counter to the order He established and counter to His plan for us.

Out of the desire to accommodate, some have become fearful to preach difficult messages on the reality of sin, hell, and the necessity of the full gospel which includes repentance. Many people like to hear messages of cheap grace rather than be confronted with difficult messages which require change and dying to self. Some people's fear of losing church members, along with a lack of fear of God, is weakening the church overall. So many are deceived by these lies and there will be devastating eternal consequences. Lies take people away from God instead of bringing them closer to Him. This is another aim of Satan.

CHAPTER NINE

How My Journey with Jesus Began

I began a personal relationship with Jesus in 1991 at a Christian women's retreat. Friends had invited me to attend the retreat for years. I finally gave in and took my older sister and partner with me. My relationship with my partner hadn't been publicly disclosed, as we were both unwilling to let anyone, including ourselves, acknowledge it. If we were accused of living a lesbian lifestyle, we would vehemently deny it.

I wasn't very serious about the weekend. On the way there, we stopped at a liquor store to buy beer, as we thought we could drink it between sessions. Needless to say, we never got to drink the beer. In the first session, the facilitators asked us to divide into groups where no one knew each other. They sat us down and asked this question: "Do you know that you know that you know that if you died tonight, you would go to heaven?" I couldn't answer yes, and I realized I needed Jesus in my life.

Immediately, a softness came into my heart, I regretted all my past sins. My life literally changed 180 degrees that day—Jesus totally transformed me. I felt heavily convicted about my same-sex relationship.

I tried hard to give up this sexual relationship in response to my spiritual renewal. However, my spirit was willing but the flesh was weak. This was the beginning of my awareness of the constant battle between the flesh and the spirit. Genesis 4:7 warns us that *"sin crouches at your door; its desire is for you, but you must master it"* (AMPC).

You wouldn't have wanted to know me before I met Jesus. I had anger issues, and I couldn't speak two words without cussing. I would use the name of Jesus in vain. I wasn't a giver. People didn't like me and I didn't like people either. I was verbally and emotionally abusive to my staff at the farm. In our South African culture at the time, it was not customary for a farmer to ask her workers for forgiveness. But I knew that God was prompting me to do it. After I did this, one by one my staff surrendered their lives to Jesus.

A few months after my salvation experience, the Holy Spirit also convinced me to get baptized, which I did. It was the most exciting experience and I will never forget it. I had been baptized as an infant in the Dutch Reformed Church, but this time I chose to be baptized as an act of obedience.

I again attended a ladies retreat, this time in the middle of winter. We had a baptism service in the middle of the night, and because we used a swimming pool the water was freezing. As I walked into the water towards the lady who was going to baptize me, I felt warmth run through my body as she held me, getting me ready to go underwater. That warmth, I know, was the presence of God and I will never forget it.

I went home excited about my baptism and made an appointment to share my experience with my minister. He was upset. He told me that I had sinned by choosing baptism when I had already been baptized. He gave me a choice: I could ask for forgiveness from the church or I could leave the church.

I chose to leave the church.

It was difficult to be rejected and abandoned by the church. However, I began attending Spirit-filled churches, because I knew there had to be more to my life of faith. I found deeper relationship with Christ rather than remain in a state of living out rules and regulations. Religion itself does not satisfy, but an intimate relationship with Christ does.

Many people ask me if I'm religious. I say no. However, I have a daily, intimate relationship with Jesus Christ. That comes first.[42]

Despite the fact that I had invited Jesus into my heart, it didn't prevent me from choosing to live a homosexual lifestyle. My spirit was willing, but my flesh was weak. I am no different than any other person. I also want to be loved and to belong, but we all struggle between answering the conviction of God and succumbing to the temptation of Satan. It was difficult for me to understand that there was a war going on between my flesh and spirit.

> *My spirit was willing, but my flesh was weak.*

Though I had no intention of entering into a gay relationship, I still struggled with these temptations and I gave into my flesh in many ways. Though I never intentionally put myself in a position to experiment with a gay relationship, Satan knows our weaknesses and he will do everything in his power to exploit them. Remember, Satan seeks to devour and destroy:

> *Be well balanced (temperate, sober of mind), be vigilant and cautious at all times; for that enemy of yours, the devil, roams around like a lion roaring [in fierce hunger], seeking someone to seize upon and devour.*
>
> —1 Peter 5:8, AMPC

---

[42] In saying that, I do recognize that many people have intimate encounters with Christ in their religion and in their church.

I am not abdicating responsibility. I take ownership for my own actions and choices. However, I hadn't been discipled. As a baby Christian, drinking spiritual milk, I now realize, as Paul teaches,

...I could not talk to you as to spiritual [men], but as to nonspiritual [men of the flesh, in whom the carnal nature predominates], as to mere infants [in the new life] in Christ [unable to talk yet!] I fed you with milk, not solid food, for you were not yet strong enough [to be ready for it]; but even yet you are not strong enough [to be ready for it], for you are still [unspiritual, having the nature] of the flesh [under the control of ordinary impulses]. For as long as [there are] envying and jealousy and wrangling and factions among you, are you not unspiritual and of the flesh, behaving yourselves after a human standard and like mere (unchanged) men?
—1 Corinthians 3:1–3, AMPC

I wasn't prepared for this battle. As a new Christian, I was confused when Paul stated in 2 Corinthians 5:17,

Therefore if anyone is in Christ [that is, grafted in, joined to Him by faith in Him as Savior], he is a new creature [reborn and renewed by the Holy Spirit]; the old things [the previous moral and spiritual condition] have passed away. Behold, new things have come [because spiritual awakening brings a new life]. (AMP)

After my born-again experience, I made the assumption that I was going to be okay and wouldn't do bad things ever again. When that didn't happen, it was a big disappointment. Baby Christians should be taken by the hand by mature Christians who are striving for holiness, who can tell them about the reality of life. They can tell them, through both words and the way they live, that sanctification is a lifelong process and that Satan will try anything to make us fall and go back to our old, sinful lives which in many ways seem "easier" than following the narrow road.

Even the Israelites wanted to go back to Egypt, even though the Egyptians had mistreated them. That was a place of familiarity. At least they had food there and didn't starve. Their wilderness experience had become too hard.

> *Baby Christians should be taken by the hand by mature Christians who are striving for holiness, who can tell them about the reality of life.*

Soon after my born-again experience, I sinned, and as a result I doubted my salvation. This didn't help me to live a victorious life. It tripped me up in my Christian walk. I relied on my own strength, which didn't go so well. I had yet to learn to abide in the Vine.

Thankfully, within the following nine-year period, I encountered members in my church fellowship who were intent on discipleship. Together with them, I went through an intensive course entitled "Welcome to Your New Family: Your First Process in Becoming an Equipped Disciple." In this course, we learned about spiritual formation, the validity of spiritual battle, evangelism, and leadership characteristics. It was then that I learned to eat solid spiritual food. This course has been foundational in my personal faith, in my walk with the Lord, and in ministry.

We are truly in a constant battle. We are in a war, both spiritually and in our flesh and in the world. It is a war for our souls, and it will go on until the day we die. 1 Peter 2:11 reminds us,

Beloved, I implore you as aliens and strangers and exiles [in this world] to abstain from the sensual urges (the evil desires, the passions of the flesh, your lower nature) that wage war against the soul. (AMPC)

The fury of Satan is declared and prophesied in Revelation 12:17,

So then the dragon was furious (enraged) at the woman, and he went away to wage war on the remainder of her descendants—[on those] who obey God's commandments and who have the testimony of Jesus Christ [and adhere to it and bear witness to Him]. (AMPC)

The good news is that even though Satan and his cohorts are warring against us, Revelation 17:14 declares that *"the Lamb will triumph over them; for He is Lord of lords and King of kings"* (AMPC). Revelation 19:20 states, *"And the beast was seized and overpowered…"* (AMPC)

CHAPTER TEN

My Attempts to Run Away from Myself

Shame, guilt, and fear brought me to a place of running away from the life I'd built for myself in South Africa. I thought if I could just start fresh someplace else—someplace where nobody knew about my past—my problems would go away.

I ran to the United States in 2001. I was very confident in joining a mission to save lost souls and start a new life. Unfortunately, within four months I was in my next gay relationship. Why? Because unless our problems are brought under the transformative power of Christ, they will follow us wherever we go.

My other problem was that I still relied on my own power. I thought I was strong enough by myself. I had a "Peter attitude." When Jesus told Peter he was going to deny Him, Peter argued… but it didn't take long for that rooster to crow (Matthew 26:34–75). The same thing happened to me. I thought I was strong enough to fight the temptation and that I, Wilna, would never enter into a gay relationship again. This was short-lived. As I've said many times, my own efforts didn't go so well. I just wanted to be loved and to belong!

The same thing happened each time I entered into a gay relationship. The moment it started, a wall would go up between me and God. Although I tried to pray or stay close to Him, He would feel so distant. As Isaiah 59:2 says, *"But your iniquities have made a separation between you and your God, and your sins have hidden His face from you, so that He will not hear"* (AMPC). I've experienced this firsthand. Being separated from God is not a good feeling.

I tried to pray. I tried to go to church. I tried to stay connected with Him. I did all the right things, but He felt far away. I attended church just to say that I attended church, but I had no relationship and definitely no intimacy with God. I tried hard to restore it, but while in a same-sex relationship, I couldn't experience closeness with the Lord.

I've come to see that once a person enters into or starts practicing a homosexual lifestyle, their relationship with God withers. They transform God to fit into what *they* want instead of pursuing the holiness that *God* wants. I fully agree with Boyd Hopkins of Spoken Word Ministries,[43] who has said many times, "If it is a biblical lifestyle, it should draw you closer to God." Any habitual sin in our lives will create distance in our relationship with God.

My partner and I attended church as a couple, even though we never told anyone we were a couple. She had a four-year-old daughter. I actually led them both to the Lord, but deep down everything felt wrong. We had done our own research and came to the conclusion that we weren't harming anybody while in our relationship, so our relationship was okay. I never felt it truly was okay. I felt a dryness and leanness in my soul. As it says in Psalms,

But they hastily forgot His works; they did not [earnestly] wait for His plans [to develop] regarding them, but lusted exceedingly in the wilderness and tempted and tried to restrain God [with their insistent desires] in the desert. And He gave them their request, but sent leanness into their souls and [thinned their numbers by] disease and death.

Psalm 106:13–15, AMPC (emphasis added)

God is a gentleman; He will never force us to make the right choice (the choice that's best for us), but we will lose our closeness with God when we choose sin. We also won't have any peace. In Luke 7, Jesus was anointed with oil by a "wicked" woman—wicked according to the Pharisees. They judged Jesus for allowing her to do that, but Jesus knew her: *"But Jesus said to the woman, Your faith has saved you; go (enter) into peace [in freedom from all the distresses that are experienced as the result of sin]"* (Luke 7:50, AMPC). She didn't have peace in her life when she lived in sin. But when she was forgiven, she experienced true peace. So it is with all of us. When we indulge in sin, we have no peace.

God puts before us the choice of life and death. He wants us to choose life.

I call heaven and earth to witness this day against you that I have set before you life and death, the blessings and the curses; therefore choose life, that you and your descendants may live…

—Deuteronomy 30:19, AMP

When I chose to live a homosexual lifestyle, I wasn't living a life of abundance.

As I think back, I hope and pray the damage I've done to her daughter won't have long-standing consequences. She and I were in constant competition for her mother's love. I was jealous if my partner spent too much time with her daughter, and vice versa. It was selfish of me to engage in that relationship and to treat them as I did, and I have asked God to forgive me.

This was not a healthy situation. We showed affection towards each other—not in public, but at home, and her daughter saw much of it. I am fully aware today of how much confusion that created for this young girl. Although I know God has forgiven me, I still struggle with the web of shame and guilt

---

43 I heard Boyd Hopkins say this at a seminar called "Biblical Sexuality in a Sexualized World."

I feel today—shame from the church, from society, and from knowing my same-sex relationship was wrong. I believe Satan uses shame and guilt to keep us from freedom and victory in our walk with God.

Despite the fact that I experienced a leanness in my soul and a separation from God, our relationship went on for two years. It paralyzed me completely in my walk with God. After almost two years of being in a very dry and desolate spiritual place, I came to the point where I cried out to God, "Please change me!" I couldn't live without His presence in my life any longer. If I had to choose between physical love and the presence of God, I wanted God more. I wanted Him desperately.

> *God is a gentleman; He will never force us to make the right choice (the choice that's best for us), but we will lose our closeness with God when we choose sin.*

It may be hard for some to understand, but I had to make this choice in order to move forward with God.

I also chose celibacy at this time, out of my love for Jesus and because I wanted to please Him in everything I do. Living celibately was the fruit of growing in my desire for holiness. By the grace of God, I have been joyfully living celibately since 2003.

By inviting God into my closet and basement, He started to transform me. Having Jesus at the center of my life profoundly changed my core identity and my whole perspective. Previously, other people's hurtful or judgmental comments didn't convince me to change. Not even being told that I was going to Hell would motivate me, and yes, I heard these comments numerous times. They were meant to make me feel ashamed, but it was the Holy Spirit who gently and softly convinced me that the presence of God is what I needed. He satisfies all my needs. To know Him intimately and personally is to experience true joy. I don't need to be married to experience true joy.

I love what it says in Ecclesiastes 12:13:

All has been heard; the end of the matter is: Fear God [revere and worship Him, knowing that He is] and keep His commandments, for this is the whole of man [the full, original purpose of his creation, the object of God's providence, the root of character, the foundation of all happiness, *the adjustment to all inharmonious circumstances and conditions under the sun] and the whole [duty] for every man.* (AMPC, emphasis added)

Being in a daily relationship of surrender and abiding in Jesus gives me the strength to live for Him. Can I say that I will never be in a homosexual relationship again? *Yes.* But only if I abide in the Lord daily. What does this mean? Jesus says in John 15:5,

I am the Vine; you are the branches. Whoever lives in Me and I in him bears much (abundant) fruit. However, apart from Me [cut off from vital union with Me] you can do nothing. (AMPC)

When we cut ourselves off from our vital union with the Vine (Jesus), we wither.

I once tested this and picked green bean leaves from their vine. I took pictures on the first day and every subsequent day. I watched as they started to wither and eventually die after about twenty days.

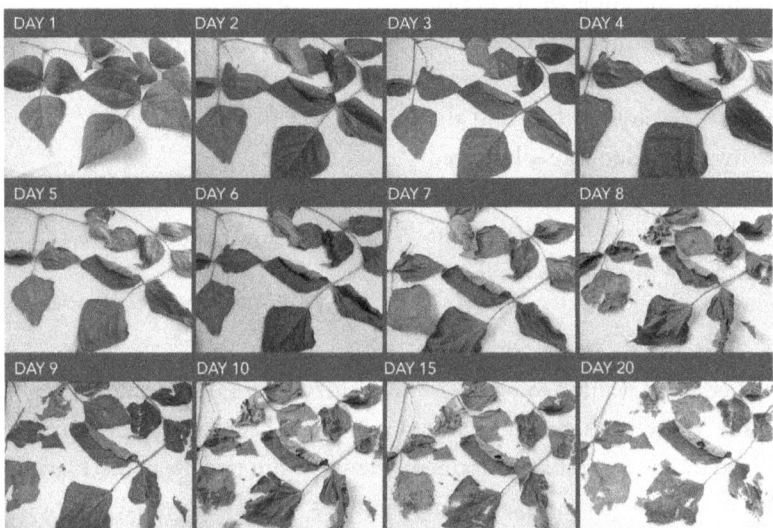

When you look at the leaves in the first few days, the withering isn't so obvious. At the end of twenty days, however, the leaves are dead and of no use. If we distance ourselves from God and don't stay connected to Him daily, the same will happen to us.

Did you know that to start a day with God is the single most important habit we must develop in our lives? If we don't do this, we may end up *"like an oak tree with all its leaves falling off, like an unwatered garden, withered and brown"* (Isaiah 1:30, MSG).

When we don't stay connected to the life-giving sap that flows from the Vine, our ability to bear good fruit dies over time, just like the leaves. We will have zero power to overcome and live a life of victory unless we abide in Jesus. It's vital to pursue a *daily* relationship with Jesus, otherwise it doesn't take long for us to go back to our old sinful nature.

That's what happened to me! I tried to succeed in my own strength and power, but thank goodness for God's grace and mercy. He was willing to forgive me for such things when I came to Him with a repentant heart. I am so

> *We will have zero power to overcome and live a life of victory unless we abide in Jesus.*

thankful for Jesus. He met me in my dry and desolate place, forgave me, and took me in just the way I was.

All He asks is for our willingness to surrender. As I surrendered, Jesus started to transform my heart. I finally stopped trying in my own power!

We cannot fully change ourselves, and neither can we change anybody else; only God can make the transformational changes in our lives. As Joyce Meyer reminds us, and I paraphrase, "If we will do what we can do, God will do what we cannot do." It is a daily necessity to intentionally engage in spiritual growth. This is our part to play:

Train yourself toward godliness (piety), [keeping yourself spiritually fit]. For physical training is of some value (useful for a little), but godliness (spiritual training) is useful and of value in everything and in every way, for it holds promise for the present life and also for the life which is to come.
—1 Timothy 4:7–8, AMPC

Shortly after choosing celibacy, my work permit in the United States was denied and I was forced to return to South Africa in early 2005. This was one of the hardest things I've ever had to do. The circumstances required me to return to the place I had been running from. Although I loved and deeply missed my family, I had hoped to never return. I wasn't ready to face my family, friends, or the culture from which I had run away.

But God had a plan. As you read on, you will see the continued faithfulness of God and His plan for my life. He allows hardship and pain, trials and tribulations, to build our character and transform us into the image of His Son Jesus, who modeled the truest form of dying to self for us to emulate.

Just before I received notice from my lawyer that my work permit had been denied, I'd been on holiday in Florida. One morning on the beach, I was praying and asking God for direction. I said these words to Him: "I need to know what 2005 is going to bring." Up until this point, I had been so frustrated with my permit. I was never sure if the government would allow me to stay in the United States. This is what I wrote down in my journal and what I felt God say: "2005 is going to bring a lot of changes in your life, but I will be with you!"

Less than three weeks later, my lawyer contacted me to say that my work permit had been denied and that I had twenty-one days to leave the country. At that moment, I remembered God's words. Though I was devastated, I told Him that I was going to hold Him to His words.

I cried night and day. I didn't want to return to South Africa. I didn't even inform my family that I was going back, as I wasn't capable of sharing in their joy.

I asked a friend to pick me up at the airport and drive me to my hometown. My mom almost had a heart attack when I walked into their home with my dog. They were, of course, happy to see me, but I wasn't happy to be back.[44]

Not long after my return, I started a new job and fell in love with the first woman I met at my new job. This time, however, by God's grace and mercy, I was able to keep Jesus as my focus. Although she never knew I had feelings for her, it brought me to a total emotional breakdown. I was in a deep pit of despair. I knew this time what would happen that if I entered into that relationship: the lack of God's presence in my life.

I was devastated that my same-sex attractions hadn't gone away. After all, I had begged God to change me.

This made me desperate, and for the first time I reached out for help. My pastor and his wife didn't judge me when I shared with them my deep secret. They lovingly spent lots of personal time with me. We prayed for hours and shared deeply. I felt I could trust them, and I was able to open up my heart.

Through hours of prayer, loving support, God-centered counseling, and lots of tears, I can say today that I have never felt sexually or romantically attracted to any woman since that time. Though I'm not attracted to women in that way anymore, I can't say that I am attracted to men either, as I have not engaged in any relationships with men since the nineties.

If attraction to a man is God's plan for my life, I believe He will transform me even more. I am willing to enter into a relationship with a man, if this is God's desire for me. However, I have been very content with being single and do see it as a gift many days. As Paul teaches in 1 Corinthians 7:7–9, I agree that singleness is not a bad thing:

Sometimes I wish everyone were single like me—a simpler life in many ways! But celibacy is not for everyone any more than marriage is. God gives the gift of the single life to some, the gift of the married life to others.

I do, though, tell the unmarried and widows that singleness might well be the best thing for them, as it has been for me. But if they can't manage their desires and emotions, they should by all means go ahead and get married. The difficulties of marriage are preferable by far to a sexually tortured life as a single. (MSG)

When Paul speaks of marriage in this passage, it is between a naturally born man and a naturally born woman.

As a single person for most of my life, I sometimes stop at a traffic light and watch how people drive together, and I feel envious about the conversations they have. I often observe others in their relationships and think that it would be nice to have somebody to love and to do things with.

---

44   I've had lifelong struggles with feeling accepted, understood, and loved by my family. And I've had a deep desire to become really close with my siblings. The fact that I live abroad and only see them every few years hasn't been helpful in creating the bond I so deeply desire.

This is when I must remember the acronym HALT, which I've heard many speakers explain. When you are *hungry*, *angry*, *lonely*, or *tired*, you must use caution in making decisions. I'm well aware that a heterosexual relationship won't fulfill all the needs I have—or anyone has, for that matter. As I've heard it said, a person's spouse is intended to complement them, not complete them.

Though I received help and God started to transform me, people continued to ridicule and judge me for who I once was. Fear and my own silence kept me in bondage and on the run.

When I received notice that my work permit had been denied in the United States, I immediately applied for permanent residency in Canada. I left the United States in January 2005, went to South Africa, and twenty-one months later the paperwork came through to go to Canada, where I arrived in November 2006 to start fresh again.

I am totally amazed at how God's plans have unfolded. The prophecy my friend shared with me has come to pass. God has prepared a place for me, and I've since become a Canadian citizen.[45] I own a home and run a successful business. God has brought many people and friends into my life who make me feel that I do belong. Therefore, I can bloom where He planted me. He has proven Himself faithful; the prophetic word has come full circle.

Not long after my arrival in Canada, I went through extreme loneliness, and one day I received an email from my best friend announcing her engagement. She had recently gotten divorced for the second time. Though I wished her all the best, her email brought me to a complete standstill. I started fighting with God, telling him how unfair it was that my friend could divorce and find another man in less than six months. I had tried so hard to change, to be accepted as "normal" or "straight." I desired to be accepted for who I was by family, friends, and society. I desired to have somebody I could love unashamedly, without the need to hide my feelings and affections.

This state of frustration went on for weeks, until I got to the point of just throwing in the towel. Until then, I had never realized who I was.

One morning, a thought struck me: *Wilna, you truly are same-sex attracted!* I was shocked at first, but then the freedom came—the freedom to understand myself and why I acted the way I did. I understood why my relationships never worked and why I wasn't attracted to men. I received an instant answer to some of the lifelong struggles and questions I'd had.

This was huge for me. It was as if weights had been lifted from my shoulders.

Once the silence had been broken and the fear subsided, I felt greater freedom. I finally understood myself. It took forty-four years to get to this place of bravery where I openly and willingly acknowledged my lifelong struggle. It wasn't coming out, per se, but more identifying what my struggle was about.

> *Coming out is necessary to start talking, to acknowledge who you are, and to begin accepting reality.*

---

45   More specifically, I am dual citizen between Canada and South Africa.

Can you see how many years Satan has stolen from me? Coming out is necessary to start talking, to acknowledge who you are, and to begin accepting reality. However, it can have long-lasting effects on how people see you. For that reason, I'll caution you that if it must be done, it should be done prudently with trusted persons. Otherwise, people who don't understand might never see you outside of that identity. People might put you in a box and never let you out.

I needed to get to this place of acceptance. I needed to acknowledge myself as same-sex attracted and simply be content while being honest with myself about this facet of my being. I needed to acknowledge that I was born into sin and one of my primary struggles was refraining from a homosexual lifestyle.

I had known from my first homosexual relationship that practicing homosexuality wasn't what I was created for. From a fleshly standpoint, it felt good. It was wrong. I am a daughter of God, but living a homosexual lifestyle is outside of His will, outside of how He created us. For that reason, it is against nature itself. It is against the order of creation that God established. It counters the art of the Divine Artist, in which we as humans are part of His masterpiece. That is why it's a sin—it's a rejection of God's artwork, as written into our very bodies!

What a wonderful place it is now to be living in truth, identifying myself as a beloved daughter of God: *"I will give thanks to You, for I am fearfully and wonderfully made; wonderful are Your works, and my soul knows it very well"* (Psalm 139:14, NASB). The truth of God's Word has not changed; my perspective has.

Not long after my "Aha!" moment, I attended a Women's Journey of Faith Conference (WJOF) in 2008. The speaker, who had been responsible for killing someone, was still able to talk about being the bride of Christ! From this, I completely understood God's forgiveness for the first time. I thought, *If God can love her and forgive her sin, He can love me and forgive me, too.* I realized that He wanted to satisfy all my needs, and I didn't need to be married to experience this satisfaction.

Two weeks after the conference, I shared my story with my home group for the first time. I was leading the group in a small town and I was terrified to share about my former life as a lesbian. Fear, guilt, and shame had kept me silent for so long. I was scared of being rejected due to the reality I faced: *many Christians will judge persons within the LGBTQ community.* I know this is changing, but back then it was the norm.

Even though I had been living celibately for five years at the time, I was still terrified to talk about the lifestyle I had previously lived. Deep down, I hoped that in some way or another my story would be told. I wanted to bring it out into the open, yet I feared and expected that I would be rejected and pushed away.

I wrote it out, told them I was going to read it to them, and that I would leave right away afterward because I thought they would despise me once they heard my story. When I was finished reading my story, their response stunned me and changed the course of my life. They didn't shun me. I will never forget the unconditional love, care, and acceptance I received from them. They all stood, formed a circle around me, and thanked me for being open, honest, vulnerable, and brave. They laid hands on me, prayed with and for me, and *told me they loved me.* They also asked for forgiveness for judging other persons like me in the past. This part was huge for me. They showed humility. They acknowledged their own wrongdoing and the wrong that so many churches have done in the past.

At that point in my life, I had been ready to give up everything—including my faith in God. But their loving response changed everything. This was a crucial building block in my life, and it bridged the way for me to walk right back into the arms of Jesus. When we respond in love and grace, it may just become the crucial step for a person to be able to walk into the arms of Jesus.

I couldn't believe it. It had taken me so long to be honest, open, and authentic about my life. Their response not only gave me the courage to share my story with others, but it's the reason I am in ministry today. If they had responded differently, I don't think you would be reading this book.

Showing unconditional love and acceptance is key. By loving and accepting others, listening to them and not condemning, and genuinely caring about them, you will allow them to experience acceptance in the struggle.

I experienced a valuable biblical principle when I was open, honest, and authentic about my struggle. As Proverbs 28:13 says, *"He who covers his transgressions will not prosper, but whoever confesses and forsakes his sins will obtain mercy"* (AMPC). By sharing my story with the group, they showed me mercy. This experience removed the shame I had carried for so long.

The amazing response I received from my home group motivated and encouraged me to share my story with others. I had allowed Satan to steal so many years from my life while he kept me silent. Part of what God has called me to do is to take back territory Satan has stolen, in His power and strength.

Revelation 10:11 explains that we overcome adversity by the blood of the Lamb and the word of our testimony. Joyce Meyer has said that when we share our testimony, we give Satan a big black eye. When we testify, we take back territory. A biblical testimony glorifies God and not self. God is the center of the story. It is His story. In sharing our testimonies, we must remember the limitations of Satan's power—God already has the victory.

The life-changing WJOF conference, and sharing my story with my home group, profoundly impacted my life and truly is the reason for writing this book. When 1,500 women during another WJOF conference in 2011 gave me a standing ovation, it didn't make me feel special or impress on me that I was a good speaker. Rather I recognized for the first time in my life that I had been heard. This alone brought freedom and empowerment for me to continue to share on the topic of homosexuality.

> *We need to support anyone who struggles with anything and brings that struggle out and into the light.*

My need to gain freedom and the recognition of others' need to embrace freedom has been a motivation for this book. I know my story is one of hope, and with God nothing is impossible. I will be forever grateful to the board members of WJOF who risked their reputation for allowing me to share my testimony at their event.

I want you to know that when people come out of the closet, they are finally at a place of honesty and clarity. They are addressing the reality of their lives. You may not agree with or desire to hear their declaration, and you may be in a state of shock and disbelief, but trust me: this is a great place for them to be and it is a good starting point to move forward. You can't address what you don't acknowledge.

We need to support *anyone* who struggles with *anything* and brings that struggle out and into the light. "Coming out" can apply to many scenarios, not only announcing being gay.

Today, many churches acknowledge the need to love, accept, and come alongside persons who self-identify as LGBTQ. Churches didn't have that same willingness or perspective when I was young. I believe if this topic is more openly addressed in churches, as long as they remain faithful to the truth of Scripture, the person who is struggling will find the road less lonely.[46]

People quite often ask me, "Wilna, how do you identify? Who are you now?" Today I can say with boldness that I do not self-identify as being gay. My true identity is a daughter of God Most High. I was formed by His hands, dreamt up in His heart, and placed in this world for a purpose. God created me *"for such a time as this"* (Esther 4:14, AMPC) to share about His redeeming love, and also to openly and honestly address this very controversial topic, in order for people to understand, learn, and show compassion and love towards others like me. I share my story so God can get the glory. How can I keep silent any longer?

Nothing is too big for or beyond the redemptive power of Jesus Christ. If He can transform me, He can and will do the same for you and for the person you are praying for. Jesus looks at us through His glasses of compassion, love, acceptance, and forgiveness.

May I remind you of the story of the woman caught in adultery recorded in John 8? Many gathered to stone her and Jesus said to them, *"Let him who is without sin among you be the first to throw a stone at her"* (John 8:7, AMPC). One by one, they all left and Jesus looked at her with compassion and said, *"I do not condemn you either. Go on your way and from now on sin no more"* (John 8:11, AMPC).

Notice the acceptance Jesus offered her, how He showed her compassion and yet gently convicted her, then sent her away with the expectation of how He wanted her to live from then on.

My life has been transformed by God. He has put a tremendous passion and desire in me to talk, teach, and train about this topic, especially in the church. If you would have told me ten years ago I would stand in front of large crowds, speaking about my life and the topic of homosexuality, I would have dismissed you as crazy. This is how I know God is working in me. I did not set out to do this, neither can I do it in my own strength. I want to give God all the glory for redeeming me, for changing me, for wanting to use me, and for using my pain for gain.

Like Rick Warren, I feel that my greatest ministry came out of my greatest hurt. I am passionate about helping to train the church, parents, or friends of persons who self-identify as gay but who don't understand the struggles, pain, and fear we go through. We need more people of courage who are willing

---

46 Please refer to Appendix A, where I talk about a much-needed new approach for pastors and church leaders to address the topic of homosexuality.

to share their journey with regards to this controversial topic in the church. We need compassion and love from others, not condemnation.

I hope my life story will inspire and explain that there is only one way to freedom, truth, and victory. There is only One who can do the work in our hearts. If we're willing to surrender to God, if we're willing to make Him the hub of our wheel, He can and will do far more than what we can ever think or dream. He can do impossible things.

If God can transform me, He can and will transform anybody else. Running away doesn't solve anything. Running to God does.

> *Running away doesn't solve anything. Running to God does.*

CHAPTER ELEVEN

The Sin Issue

I'VE HAD TO DIFFERENTIATE BETWEEN EXPERIENCING SAME-SEX ATTRACTIONS AND PHYSICALLY living and practicing a homosexual lifestyle. Throughout my whole life, guilt and condemnation overpowered everything. Whether I was practicing a homosexual lifestyle or simply experiencing same-sex attractions, I felt guilty and condemned.

That's why it is so important when someone tells you that he's gay that you ask him what this means. Is he practicing a homosexual lifestyle or is he merely acknowledging that he's experiencing same-sex attractions? It was not, and is not, God's original intent for same-sex attractions to be a reality. But because sin entered the world, this became a reality for some.

We can choose not to give in to this temptation. Just as all of us struggle with sin, God requires we choose holiness over sin. It's important to set one's mind and heart at ease; despite experiencing same-sex attractions, one does not have to give in to it.

> *Just as all of us struggle with sin, God requires we choose holiness over sin.*

This being said, it was just recently that I discovered I don't have to feel guilt or condemnation about experiencing same-sex attractions. Rather, it is my choice what I do with this temptation. My word of caution on this: it is vital to put Christ at the center of your heart, because out of the heart all else flows: *"Watch over your heart with all diligence, for from it flow the springs of life"* (Proverbs 4:23, NASB).

If experiencing same-sex attractions isn't the sin, what is? The Bible is very clear about practicing sexual sin. Though it never talks specifically about the mere experience of unchosen same-sex attractions, it is very clear that we ought to choose not to practice unchaste behavior (with homosexual behavior being only one type of unchaste behavior out of many). In 1 Corinthians 6:9–10, Paul explains,

The Sin Issue

Do you not know that the unrighteous and the wrongdoers will not inherit or have any share in the kingdom of God? Do not be deceived (misled): neither the impure and immoral, nor idolaters, nor adulterers, nor those who participate in homosexuality, nor cheats (swindlers and thieves), nor greedy graspers, nor drunkards, nor foulmouthed revilers and slanderers, nor extortioners and robbers will inherit or have any share in the kingdom of God. (AMPC)

Note here that any form of sin we choose to engage in will lead to unrighteousness. Sin will separate us from God. Sin is sin, which is why the Bible says that *"all have sinned and fall short of the glory of God"* (Romans 3:23, NASB).

For many years, I've been carrying the following piece of paper in my Bible as a reminder of what the Bible says about homosexuality. All these scriptures are underlined in my Bible and I've included them below. They are a reminder to me of what the Bible says about practicing a homosexual lifestyle. These scriptures are often the same ones that are quoted to condemn and point a finger at people living a homosexual lifestyle.

The reason I include this paper here is as evidence of what the Bible says about living and practicing a homosexual lifestyle—including the practice of all abominations, of which living a homosexual lifestyle is just one. These verses don't say that the *person* is an abomination.

I offer these verses as a means of conviction and not condemnation. I have read them over and over and over. I have squirmed from the harshness of their words, and in the past I have certainly tried to justify my behavior too. The truth is, we all need Jesus and His forgiveness. I have needed Jesus and He took me in just the way I was, ultimately transforming me.

These are the Old Testament passages:

The woman shall not wear that which pertains to a man, neither shall a man put on a woman's garment, for all that do so are an abomination to the Lord your God.
—Deuteronomy 22:5, AMPC

Personally, I can relate to this passage because as a child I did want to dress as a boy. I wished I *was* a boy. Trying to be someone I was not didn't help me become the woman God created me to be. I can see the love behind these words now: God does not make mistakes and He desires that we accept who He created us to be. I believe He is grieved when we, as the clay, tell the Potter that He should have created us differently.

Growing up, being confused about my sexuality, I now realize that my identity is not based in my sexuality but rather in being a child of God. My identity in Christ supersedes all other ways of identifying who I am.

As for the practice of homosexual behavior, the Bible is clear:

You shall not lie with a man as with a woman; it is an abomination. Neither shall you lie with any beast and defile yourself with it; neither shall any woman yield herself to a beast to lie with it; it is confusion, perversion, and degradedly carnal. Do not defile yourselves in any of these ways, for in all these things the nations are defiled which I am casting out before you. And the land is defiled; therefore I visit the iniquity of it upon it, and the land itself vomits out her inhabitants. So you shall keep My statutes and My ordinances and shall not commit any of these abominations, neither the native-born nor any stranger who sojourns among you, for all these abominations have the men of the land done who were before you, and the land is defiled—[do none of these things] lest the land spew you out when you defile it as it spewed out the nation that was before you. Whoever commits any of these abominations shall be cut off from among [his] people. So keep My charge: do not practice any of these abominable customs which were practiced before you and defile yourselves by them. I am the Lord your God.
—Leviticus 18:22–30, AMPC

In the many years I've been carrying this paper in my Bible, I have seen numerous political, educational, and cultural changes both within the church and society—and I am deeply concerned. This passage not only convicted me about not practicing a homosexual lifestyle, but it's a continuous reminder even today of what our righteous God is compelled to do when we participate in any of the above-mentioned abominations.

We have been forewarned about the consequences of sin. God does not relish in punishing us, but He will correct us out of love. I'm concerned and care deeply about how the practice of these abominations will take us further from intimacy with the Lord.

The Sin Issue

Growing up, the following verse brought about a deep sense of fear in me.

If a man lies with a male as if he were a woman, both men have committed an offense (something perverse, unnatural, abhorrent, and detestable); they shall surely be put to death; their blood shall be upon them.

—Leviticus 20:13, AMPC

I believed that God would certainly do to me what this verse said. I was so fearful. I was taught that God was watching me and that He would punish me. I now have a healthy sense of fear, of reverence for who God is. I understand that God corrects me out of love, not out of a desire to punish. But even with that, my primary motive is my love for Christ, not my fear of God.

We need to understand who God is, who He says He is, and have an appropriate frame of reference before we consider what a particular scripture is saying. This is especially true with this verse.

We need to remember that the Book of Leviticus is where God establishes all of the rules for His people. They were to be separate from all other nations, and it was to be evidenced in how they lived. Until then, they had no written rules from God about appropriate conduct in order for them to live holy lives. He laid it out plainly for them to understand just how serious sin is.

The fact remains that society has forgotten the severity of sin before God. By God's standards, our sin requires the death penalty. That's why, being a gracious, loving God, He sacrificed His own Son on our behalf.

But God's grace and mercy is no excuse for continuing in that which is an abomination before Him. Conversely, although we deserve death, Jesus paid the price. Those churches and individuals who spew hate and attempt to take on the role of God in punishing others are out of line—they are building walls rather than bridges.

Scripture is clear about what the Lord will and will not bless:

For the perverse are an abomination [extremely disgusting and detestable] to the Lord; but His confidential communion and secret counsel are with the [uncompromisingly] righteous (those who are upright and in right standing with Him). The curse of the Lord is in and on the house of the wicked, but He declares blessed (joyful and favored with blessings) the home of the just and consistently righteous.

—Proverbs 3:32–33, AMPC

I not only felt it to be an abomination when I lived a homosexual lifestyle, but it also created a separation between God and me. Once I walked away from a homosexual lifestyle, I found a renewed intimacy with the Lord.

He is true to His Word: light and darkness don't go together. Practicing any abomination and expecting intimacy with the Lord isn't compatible. Some people disagree with this stance, but when we follow God wholeheartedly, choose obedience to the Lord, and practice holy sexuality, the result will be greater intimacy with Him. We should not wrongly interpret this passage to mean that when we walk in righteousness we are better than others; we all need Jesus. We need to be appreciative of God's mercy and grace in our own lives and extend it to others. We also need to love others enough by speaking the truth in love as we ourselves walk in truth.

> *Practicing any abomination and expecting intimacy with the Lord isn't compatible.*

The practice of homosexuality is consistently addressed in Scripture. God's standards and His stance have not changed.

The New Testament verses listed on my sheet are as follows:

> *For this reason God gave them over and abandoned them to vile affections and degrading passions. For their women exchanged their natural function for an unnatural and abnormal one, and the men also turned from natural relations with women and were set ablaze (burning out, consumed) with lust for one another—men committing shameful acts with men and suffering in their own bodies and personalities the inevitable consequences and penalty of their wrong-doing and going astray, which was [their] fitting retribution.*
>
> —Romans 1:26–27, AMPC

Even though there was a time in my life when I tried to justify practicing a homosexual lifestyle, deep down I knew that it wasn't natural, in terms of nature. The realization that same-sex attractions are not natural causes many to ask: "Why me? How did this happen? Am I a freak?" We question God, especially when He doesn't "take away" our same-sex attractions.

The fact is that even though many people do experience same-sex attractions, acting on them remains displeasing to the Lord. This feels unfair. Satan would love for us to dwell on the fact that life is unfair. He wants to continue to deceive us. He wants us to believe that we will always be lonely and without companionship, that God made a mistake. He would love for us to remain in this deception. The deception can at times feed our own emotions, and sometimes it seems easier to dwell in misery than to do the hard work of looking at what God desires instead.

Although God desires abundant life and promises that the truth will set us free, Satan keeps eroding truth to the best of his ability.[47] We often feel God's vision is too far away and don't think it will come to fruition, so we settle for less-than. When we settle for the lie, one thing leads to another: what seems enticing becomes a tangled mess. Deception, if left rooted, can run deep and bear bad fruit. Why? Because we act on what we believe.

---

47   Although, remember that his ability is limited in comparison to God's.

The Sin Issue

We must uproot deception and replace it with God's truth. Instead of blaming God, we must remember the reason that this unnatural tendency happens. It is a result of the fallen world, and Satan is behind it. The flesh wants to justify the unnatural and the world wants to condone it.

Not only is Satan willing to use deception, he is more than happy to use division. Many churches today are so divided on the issue of same-sex marriage that it has caused a split. We are cautioned in Scripture about the destruction of division:

Why, the very fact of your having lawsuits with one another at all is a defect (a defeat, an evidence of positive moral loss for you). Why not rather let yourselves suffer wrong and be deprived of what is your due? Why not rather be cheated (defrauded and robbed)? But [instead it is you] yourselves who wrong and defraud, and that even your own brethren [by so treating them]!
—1 Corinthians 6:7–8, AMPC

Please note in the following passage that the practice of homosexuality is mentioned as one of many sins, all requiring repentance:

Do you not know that the unrighteous and the wrongdoers will not inherit or have any share in the kingdom of God? Do not be deceived (misled): neither the impure and immoral, nor idolaters, nor adulterers, nor those who participate in homosexuality, nor cheats (swindlers and thieves), nor greedy graspers, nor drunkards, nor foulmouthed revilers and slanderers, nor extortioners and robbers will inherit or have any share in the kingdom of God. And such some of you were [once]. But you were washed clean (purified by a complete atonement for sin and made free from the guilt of sin), and you were consecrated (set apart, hallowed), and you were justified [pronounced righteous, by trusting] in the name of the Lord Jesus Christ and in the [Holy] Spirit of our God.
—1 Corinthians 6:9–11, AMPC

The fact that we are forgiven doesn't give us license to continue in our sin. When we repent, we are to turn fully from our sin. We know God's love contains mercy, but we can't forget that it also contains justice for our choice to reject Him.

Practicing homosexual behavior separates us from God, because it is counter to virtue and how God created us. This is why it is seen to be immoral.[48]

I include the following passage because it reminds me of what Jesus said: He did not come for the healthy, He came for the sick. This passage doesn't specifically name homosexuality; it talks about all kinds of sin. We all sin and we all need Jesus:

Knowing and understanding this: that the Law is not enacted for the righteous (the upright and just, who are in right standing with God), but for the lawless and unruly, for the ungodly and sinful,

---

48 Forms of heterosexual sex that are outside the bounds of virtue are also immoral.

for the irreverent and profane, for those who strike and beat and [even] murder fathers and strike and beat and [even] murder mothers, for manslayers, [for] impure and immoral persons, those who abuse themselves with men, kidnapers, liars, perjurers—and whatever else is opposed to wholesome teaching and sound doctrine…

—1 Timothy 1:9–10, AMPC

Although we are prone to sin, we are called to holiness. Practicing any sexual sin, homosexual or otherwise, is not God's will:

For this is the will of God, that you should be consecrated (separated and set apart for pure and holy living): that you should abstain and shrink from all sexual vice, that each one of you should know how to possess (control, manage) his own body in consecration (purity, separated from things profane) and honor, not [to be used] in the passion of lust like the heathen, who are ignorant of the true God and have no knowledge of His will, that no man transgress and overreach his brother and defraud him in this matter or defraud his brother in business. For the Lord is an avenger in all these things, as we have already warned you solemnly and told you plainly. For God has not called us to impurity but to consecration [to dedicate ourselves to the most thorough purity]. Therefore whoever disregards (sets aside and rejects this) disregards not man but God, Whose [very] Spirit [Whom] He gives to you is holy (chaste, pure).

—1 Thessalonians 4:3–8, AMPC

I don't want to disregard or reject what God is asking. We are to live chaste and pure. Practicing homosexuality, however, simply doesn't fall into this category, even in the case of stable or monogamous relationships. The following passage is another confirmation about immorality and the pursuit of intimacy with the Lord above all else:

> *We are to live chaste and pure. Practicing homosexuality, however, simply doesn't fall into this category, even in the case of stable or monogamous relationships.*

Do not love or cherish the world or the things that are in the world. If anyone loves the world, love for the Father is not in him. For all that is in the world—the lust of the flesh [craving for sensual gratification] and the lust of the eyes [greedy longings of the mind] and the pride of life [assurance in one's own resources or in the stability of earthly things]—these do not come from the Father but are from the world [itself]. And the world passes away and disappears, and with it

the forbidden cravings (the passionate desires, the lust) of it; but he who does the will of God and carries out His purposes in his life abides (remains) forever.
—1 John 2:15–17, AMPC

This scripture reminds me not to cave into worldly views or fleshly desires. Where at first it brought fear, it has since become a reminder to me to keep an eternal perspective:

But nothing that defiles or profanes or is unwashed shall ever enter it, nor anyone who commits abominations (unclean, detestable, morally repugnant things) or practices falsehood, but only those whose names are recorded in the Lamb's Book of Life.
—Revelation 21:27, AMPC

I am daily conscious of my need to remain vigilant in my faith.

We need to be conscious of our focus and who or what we are serving, or else we will become a slave or servant to that which we serve. The following passage reminds me that living a homosexual lifestyle will create entanglement. It's not life in abundance as God intended it to be. In fact, re-engaging in the sinful condition is so repugnant that it's referred to as a dog returning to its own vomit. Nobody wants to live like that.

They promise them liberty, when they themselves are the slaves of depravity and defilement—for by whatever anyone is made inferior or worse or is overcome, to that [person or thing] he is enslaved. For if, after they have escaped the pollutions of the world through [the full, personal] knowledge of our Lord and Savior Jesus Christ, they again become entangled in them and are overcome, their last condition is worse [for them] than the first. For never to have obtained a [full, personal] knowledge of the way of righteousness would have been better for them than, having obtained [such knowledge], to turn back from the holy commandment which was [verbally] delivered to them. There has befallen them the thing spoken of in the true proverb, The dog turns back to his own vomit, and, The sow is washed only to wallow again in the mire.
—2 Peter 2:19–22, AMPC

Because I've tasted and seen that God is good, going back to living and practicing a homosexual lifestyle isn't something I desire for myself or anyone else who has chosen to walk away from the lifestyle.

This concludes all the scriptures I've carried and cherished in my Bible for so many years. At first, their effect on me created unhealthy fear. But after such a long journey and keeping the Word close to my heart, the above scriptures helped me understand that sin is sin and that God loves me. His grace and mercy are new every morning (Lamentations 3:23).

I am not the only one to come to such realizations.

Christopher Yuan formerly practiced a homosexual lifestyle and became HIV positive in the process. He and his mother wrote the book *Out of a Far Country* which shares his journey, and consequently hers, of transformation through Jesus Christ. In a YouTube video, Christopher shares how devastated his mother was when he broke the news to his parents about being gay. She was not yet a Christian at the time, but God changed her through the words of a small pamphlet that stated, "We are all sinners and yet in spite of our sin, God still loves us." Christopher also shares in his video, "God opened the eyes of her heart to see, just as God loves her, she could love me."[49]

God first loved us, we are to love others. 1 John 4:7–10 clearly confirms love comes from God and we are to in turn love others:

> *My beloved friends, let us continue to love each other since love comes from God. Everyone who loves is born of God and experiences a relationship with God. The person who refuses to love doesn't know the first thing about God, because God is love—so you can't know him if you don't love. This is how God showed his love for us: God sent his only Son into the world so we might live through him. This is the kind of love we are talking about—not that we once upon a time loved God, but that he loved us and sent his Son as a sacrifice to clear away our sins and the damage they've done to our relationship with God.* (MSG)

I have wondered many times why and how it happened that the issue of being gay reached the highest category of sin. I'm not sure why people who identify as gay have been marginalized and not welcome to come and sit alongside other sinners in church pews. The church—we, the body of Christ—have often done more harm than good by not inviting, accepting, or allowing persons within the LGBTQ community to come into our churches. On the whole, we can do a better job of inviting all people to become part of our church family. This doesn't imply that we ought to change our church teaching to suit differing viewpoints.

When you talk to many persons within the LGBTQ community, they will say that they don't feel welcome. This resonates with a quote I heard a long time ago: "If it wasn't for Christians, there would have been more Christians." Author Brennan Manning has also said, "The greatest single cause of atheism in the world today is Christians who acknowledge Jesus with their lips and walk out the door and deny Him with their lifestyle. This is what an unbelieving world simply finds unbelievable."[50]

Recently, a person shared with me how "nasty" her Christian co-workers were towards a self-identified gay person at work. This reminds me of what Gandhi once said: "I like your Christ, I do not like your Christians. Your Christians are so unlike your Christ."[51] As Christians, we need to remember to always represent Christ well:

---

49 Christian Yuan, *YouTube*, "I Am HIV+." March 29, 2008 (https://www.youtube.com/watch?v=ivcfw2vJF1M).
50 *Wikipedia*, "Brennan Manning." Date of access: September 11, 2017 (https://en.wikipedia.org/wiki/Brennan_Manning).
51 Mahatma Gandhi, *Goodreads*, "Quotable Quote." Date of access: September 11, 2017 (https://www.goodreads.com/quotes/22155-i-like-your-christ-i-do-not-like-your-christians).

The Sin Issue

So we are Christ's ambassadors, God making His appeal as it were through us. We [as Christ's personal representatives] beg you for His sake to lay hold of the divine favor [now offered you] and be reconciled to God.

—2 Corinthians 5:20, AMPC

During some of my presentations, I often get this question: "Wilna, but what do we do about the homosexual couple who comes to church on Sundays and sits in the church pews? How do we tell them that what they're doing is wrong?" I always answer by asking another question: since when do we have the right to judge the heart of *any* person who walks in the door? What about the adulterous, the overeater, the one participating in pornography? And don't forget the gossipers! Are we to decide who can sit in church pews and who cannot?

> *Judgment and differentiating between sins was not Jesus's intention. That's why He called sin, sin.*

Yes, within the context of a relationship there may be a time and place to say something—to help them fall more deeply in love with the pursuit of virtue and holiness. But that is best said not with words but with how we live our lives. We have to understand that transformation of the heart is God's business. How about we allow all sinners to sit under the teaching of the truth and let the Holy Spirit do the work that only He can do?[52]

Don't we all tend to differentiate between sins and categorize it to minimize our own? Judgment and differentiating between sins was not Jesus's intention. That's why He called sin, sin. James 2:9–11 states,

> *But if you show servile regard (prejudice, favoritism) for people, you commit sin and are rebuked and convicted by the Law as violators and offenders. For whosoever keeps the Law [as a] whole but stumbles and offends in one [single instance] has become guilty of [breaking] all of it. For He Who said, You shall not commit adultery, also said, You shall not kill. If you do not commit adultery but do kill, you have become guilty of transgressing the [whole] Law.* (AMP)

In the Message Bible, Jesus is clear about how we shouldn't judge others, as it will boomerang back on us. Matthew 7:1–5 gives us a simple guide for behavior:

> *Don't pick on people, jump on their failures, criticize their faults— unless, of course, you want the same treatment. That critical spirit has a way of boomeranging. It's easy to see a smudge on your neighbor's face and be oblivious to the ugly sneer on your own. Do you have the nerve to say, "Let me wash your face for you," when your own face is distorted by contempt? It's this whole traveling*

---

[52] And let's hope the pastor is preaching the truth from the pulpit.

road-show mentality all over again, playing a holier-than-thou part instead of just living your part. Wipe that ugly sneer off your own face, and you might be fit to offer a washcloth to your neighbor. (MSG)

Barbara Johnson, a Christian comedian and author who was the mother of a son who practiced a homosexual lifestyle, has said that we all need to repent, especially of judgment. In a video that was taped during a Women of Faith conference, she quotes Dr. Richard Loveless:

Most of the repenting that needs to be done on the issue of homosexuality needs to be done by straight people, including straight Christians! By far the greater sin in our churches is the sin of neglect, fear, hatred, and just wanting to brush these people aside… We have wanted to brush these people aside! We have wanted to push these people under the rug, and now the rug has become so lumpy. And we need to decide what we are going to do with these people.[53]

Johnson mentions a marvelous pastor who decided he would welcome homosexuals into his church, including those who were HIV positive. One of his church board members said, "Oh no, then you will be bringing in hordes of homosexuals!" The pastor answered, "Well, wonderful! Then they can come in and sit next to the adulterers, slanderers, and the others in the church!"[54]

Johnson continues,

We have to realize what unconditional love is—not sloppy agape, or "Oh, I love you, but do your own thing!" No, I am going to love so much, I am going to pray for you! And love, unconditional love, is what is going to bring people back. Condemnation will not work. It is only conviction from God that changes any of us… A lot of parents bring their children to me and want me to fix them. I can't fix anybody! You give your kids to God! When your kids are little, you talk to them about Jesus and when they get older, you talk to Jesus about them… We are living in a broken world. I don't have the answers. I don't get into political things, because my job is to help parents love their kids![55]

I take a similar approach in ministry, agreeing with Amy Carmichael, who said, "If I can easily discuss the shortcomings and the sins of any; if I can speak in a casual way even of a child's misdoings, then I know nothing of Calvary love."[56]

---

53   Barbara Johnson, "David—Gay Son & Family Restoration." March 13, 2008 (http://www.youtube.com/watch?v=x-l62XmuyBsk).

54   Ibid.

55   Ibid.

56   Amy Carmichael, "If—Part 2 (Calvary Love), *Women of Christianity*. May 4, 2011 (http://womenofchristianity.com/if-part-2-calvary-love-by-amy-carmichael/).

Many people are eager to quote scripture declaring homosexuality as an abomination to God. But there are other abominations and things God hates. These have nothing to do with homosexuality. These sins seem to be considered "lesser," but they are not. In Proverbs 6:16–19, homosexuality isn't even mentioned:

These six things the Lord hates, indeed, seven are an abomination to Him: a proud look [the spirit that makes one overestimate himself and underestimate others], a lying tongue, and hands that shed innocent blood, a heart that manufactures wicked thoughts and plans, feet that are swift in running to evil, a false witness who breathes out lies [even under oath], and he who sows discord among his brethren. (AMP)

When we look at a person within the LGBTQ community and overestimate ourselves and think or act as if we are better, it is an abomination to God. Have you ever thought about it this way? So, telling them how sinful they are definitely isn't the approach Jesus wants us to use. It won't make them feel loved and valuable.

They need to know that Jesus loves them and cares deeply about them. Jesus wants to be in an intimate relationship with them. Jesus will take them as they are and do the work of the heart. It's the Holy Spirit's job to convict hearts, it's not our job to condemn.

In saying this, we are always called to draw people to greater holiness and virtue in some way. This is best done by our lived example of humility, and can best reach hearts when we have a relationship with others.

And yes, this will take us beyond our comfort zones.

CHAPTER TWELVE

The Three Approaches

Unfortunately, Christians can get in the way of God's work. The reality is that the church, and Christians in general, have approached the LGBTQ community in a way that has created a crisis in the body of Christ. This was not God's way.

Not only do we as the church need to realize how we have stood in the way of God's work, but I believe it is time we go back to basics and know and practice what the Bible teaches. His Word is the ultimate measuring stick; it is our best GPS (God's Perfect Solution) for how we need to address the topic of homosexuality. We often want to make it complicated, but it's really not.

In this chapter, I'll cover in detail the different approaches people take towards the LGBTQ community. In addressing this topic, I believe we need to see homosexuality the same way that Paul saw the issue of new Christians needing to be fed milk, in 2 Corinthians 3. They weren't ready to eat solid food. I believe that the church has remained an infant in this area, and it needs to mature. The church has naively looked at persons within the LGBTQ community, seeing their lifestyles and not their hearts. Many believed they were like lepers and outcasts and pushed them away.

We need to grow beyond this, go back to the basic truths, and learn from scratch how to approach the LGBTQ community. The answer isn't complicated, if only we are willing to acknowledge what we have done wrong, then repent and walk away from doing it again. It's time to do things differently. That's what I dream about.

In Chapter Three, we talked about the various glasses people wear. Those who wear Pharisee glasses bombard me with legalism and no love. Others wear glasses of hate. Some are wearing glasses that lead them to say, "I don't understand gays, so I agree with them if they want to live this way." Still others believe that sexuality is a choice, and therefore a person can choose not to be gay any longer.

I once listened to a beautiful sermon by Pastor Bruce Martin of Calvary Temple in Winnipeg, Manitoba. It was called "The Modern Family, Part Two." In it, he described three approaches by which people tend to respond towards persons within the LGBTQ community. I was so encouraged by hearing his sermon. At the time of hearing it, I thought he was very brave.

Martin acknowledged the reality of unwanted approaches in the church. Because I've never met him personally, I'm not sure what the stance of his church was prior to his sermon. The mere fact that Martin addressed the topic of homosexuality, and that he was willing to share it from the pulpit in addition to mentioning that the extreme conservative and liberal approaches are both wrong, demonstrated to me that he, too, desires to reach LGBTQ persons with the Jesus approach.

For so long I have desired to hear sermons like this, for more pastors to be willing to address the topic from the pulpit. When congregations are offered this type of information, they will be educated, equipped, and enlightened on this challenging topic. By avoiding it, we don't learn, and therefore we fail to understand the journey of persons in the LGBTQ community.

Avoidance has been the approach of most churches for decades. Through our collective unwillingness to approach homosexuality through the lens of Jesus, we have neglected biblical teaching and been one of the reasons why persons who experience same-sex attractions have left the church. They felt unloved and oppressed by the people and actions of the church, thus creating a mass exodus.

In hearing Martin's sermon, I almost felt like I was entering the Promised Land. I saw light in the dark tunnel, bring hope and shining much light on a difficult topic. I will always applaud him for presenting an excellent and compassionate approach towards addressing homosexuality. It resonates with me.

Martin identified three different approaches: the conservative approach (radical rejection), the liberal approach (affirmative acceptance), and the Jesus approach (intentional incarnation). I have been asked in some of my seminars, "Do these approaches reflect real politics?" No. I don't see Martin's sermon as a political statement. Rather, I believe his intent was to explain why certain people behave in certain ways towards the LGBTQ community.

Looking up the word *conservative* helped me to understand why extremist Christians act the way they do. It refers to "one who adheres to traditional methods or views."[57] Next, I looked up the word *liberal*: "one who is open-minded or not strict in the observance of orthodox, traditional, or established forms or ways."[58] This, in turn, has helped me to understand why liberal Christians act the way they do.

Finally, Webster's defines the word Jesus this way: "the highest human corporeal concept of the divine idea rebuking and destroying error and bringing to light man's immortality… the Jewish religious teacher whose life, death, and resurrection as reported by the Evangelists are the basis of the Christian message of salvation—called also Jesus Christ."[59]

In pondering Martin's different approaches, I have added my own personal views on them, yet I remain in debt to him for naming the approaches so well. In his explanation of the Jesus approach, he

---

57 *Merriam-Webster's Collegiate Dictionary*, Eleventh Edition, "Conservative." Edited by Frederick C. Mish (Springfield, MA: Merriam-Webster, Inc., 2004).

58 Ibid., "Liberal."

59 Ibid., "Jesus."

mentions three very important points. In my journey of understanding what Jesus might do, I have included twelve additional examples which I believe can be helpful for the body of Christ.

First, let's look at the two extremes, conservative and liberal. Right off the bat, I'll say that neither these first two approaches are biblical, even though those who practice them believe them to be.

1. The Conservative Approach—Radical Rejection

Many conservative Christians will take passages of Scripture and apply them literally. Those who have extreme views sometimes want to force, rather than invite persons in the LGBTQ community to adhere to their methods or views. They forget that Jesus came to *fulfill* the law and that practicing *"[e]ye for eye, and tooth for tooth"* (Matthew 5:38, NIV) is no longer applicable.

How can we agree to stone persons within the LGBTQ community and think it's God's will? The Bible teaches us that God doesn't rejoice in the death of sinners, and that His heart is to see every person come to Him: *"For the Son of Man did not come to destroy men's lives, but to save them [from the penalty of eternal death]"* (Luke 9:56, AMPC).

Some very extreme conservative Christians want to see persons within the LGBTQ community killed as punishment for the lifestyles they choose to live.[60] They believe and profess the following statements regarding the LGBTQ community: "God hates you. We hate you and you are not welcome here!"[61] They believe these statements in their hearts and even demonstrate during public events. They "go around with slogans and flyers, calling persons within the LGBTQ community 'faggots'… They shout, 'Kill gay people,' 'All gays go to hell,' etc."[62]

I was appalled when this extremist approach became so evident during the funerals of the victims of the mass killing at the gay nightclub in Orlando, Florida on June 12, 2016. The family members of the victims had to ask for police protection from these "Christian" protestors whose signs and words spewed hatred and judgment. What a disgrace for Christianity! I was ashamed on behalf of Christendom at how certain "believers" chose to act. How dare they not be compassionate towards family members who just lost loved ones?

Personally, I experience this approach quite often when I speak. And keep in mind that I only speak to Christian groups. There are individuals in my audiences who look at me with resentment, judgment, and in some cases hate. I also find that some Christians avoid me once they know my story. Even though I try not to take their behavior and words personally, it still feels like "radical rejection," like a knife piercing through my heart. It hurts, especially when it comes from professing Christians. This is why the conservative approach is such a very dangerous, destructive, and sad approach. Instead of drawing people to Christ, it pushes them away. Instead of building bridges, it builds walls.

---

60   This goes beyond the mere attractions they experience.
61   Bruce Martin, "The Modern Family, Part Two," Cavalry Temple, Winnipeg. April 22, 2012.
62   Ibid.

History has proven the failure of this approach and how destructive it is. It has created an exodus from our churches by persons like me, who as a result help *build* the LGBTQ community. It has created a non-loving atmosphere for generations and brought about the current dilemma that all churches now face: we lost them for Christ and failed to fulfill the Great Commission, so what now?

Our wrong approaches have discouraged their attendance and aided their departure. We oppressed rather than loved. They must have felt the same way the Israelites did in Egypt.

You may feel appalled that the LGBTQ community can be included as God's chosen people, but God loves every one of us. He desires that every individual should choose an intimate relationship with Him. Keep in mind that God continually addressed the stubborn nature and rebellious acts of the Israelites. They wandered for forty years in the desert as a result of their disobedience. God is a righteous judge; it is His job to judge, not ours.

Although conservative Christians may base their views on biblical principles, their literal approach is often exceedingly harsh, judgmental, and full of hatred. Their approach has driven, and will continue to drive, the LGBTQ community so far away that they won't have the desire to engage in a relationship with Jesus.

We can't afford this approach any longer. The LGBTQ community has become a large marginalized group of people and God's heart is to see them come to Him. His heart is to see the captives set free. The conservative approach can't accomplish that. It is an incorrect interpretation of biblical truths.

In making all these statements, I'm not disregarding everything these Christians believe. Rather I'm taking issue with the way they go about it.

2. The Liberal Approach—Affirmative Acceptance

This approach is marked by compromise. Christians in many churches will take passages of scripture and try to apply them liberally, creating an open-minded view of the LGBTQ community. Many of these people have seen the damage done by the extremist conservatives, so they lean more towards love—but this is often interpreted to mean that people ought to do whatever *feels right* to them. It is entirely about following one's own conscience instead of pursuing a heart of holiness as exemplified by our Lord Jesus Christ.

The liberal approach can lead people into false charity, or false accompaniment. As my friend Michael from Courage International has said,

> Sometimes following our hearts leads us to counter the order of Creation (God's design), and thus by merely following our hearts we can easily fall into sin. However, we are called to model our lives after Jesus Christ, which means we are called to die to ourselves and our own attachments to this world. This is beneficial for the sanctification of our souls, for it helps us to grow in holiness.

We have seen the pendulum swing to the other side, thus people have made the decision to compromise truth. They believe that compromising will undo the problem that extremist conservatives created.

Liberal Christians change Scripture to fit their plan to support, accept, and approve of lifestyles that are not pleasing to the Lord. They believe that affirming persons within the LGBTQ community in their choice to live and practice a homosexual lifestyle is the right thing to do. Many do not fully understand this journey themselves, so they end up compromising God's truth by trying to please men rather than offend.

They feel the pressure to be politically correct. In our society today, being politically correct is one of the enemy's favorite ways to hide the truth. These liberal Christians will use these phrases: "God loves you, we love you, and we will affirm you in your choice of living a homosexual lifestyle... Please come to our church. We won't oppose or intrude in the choices you have made. In fact, we want you to just be yourself and live out how God made you to be."[63]

They will cave in to the pressures of the world, pleasing men rather than God and minimizing or throwing away His teachings altogether. The crisis today is that so many church denominations and leaders have fallen into this trap, baited strategically by Satan himself.[64]

The lie is that God made them this way, that it is in their nature to be gay, so they can love whoever they want and it is okay with God to enter into a same-sex marriage. Taking this bait is a cause of tremendous division amongst Christians all over the world.

This liberal approach is putting the church at risk of falling apart. In fact, it has already done much damage. Many churches have split after voting to approve of same-sex marriage. This suggests that the liberal approach is destructive rather than constructive. It won't build bridges like they believe it will, because they are replacing truth with a lie. It's not a building block, it's a hindrance to reconciling people with Christ. Scary thought. I am convinced that this approach hurts God's heart, since He wants to see all people come to Him.

> *Same-sex marriage was never God's original plan, and therefore it is not His will for our lives.*

This approach has wreaked great havoc in the religious domain. It is a topic of much controversy. The topic of same-sex marriage is arguably one of the biggest dividers of churches in the world today. Same-sex marriage was never God's original plan, and therefore it is not His will for our lives. Approving and affirming this lifestyle is biblically incorrect and wrong, and God is going to require leaders and pastors to stand before Him one day and give account for what they taught their congregations.

Paul cautioned the Christians of Rome to be aware of those who create dissensions, cause divisions, and oppose the original teachings of God (Romans 14:17–18). There is also a passage in Daniel which

---

63   Ibid.
64   For more details on specific leaders who have fallen into this trip, see Appendix A: The Much-Needed New Approach.

predicts that this will happen. There will come a time, and we're living it now, when leaders will cave in and approve of unbiblical values. This is actually a test.

> *And some of those who are wise, prudent, and understanding shall be weakened and fall, [thus, then, the insincere among the people will lose courage and become deserters. It will be a test] to refine, to purify, and to make those among [God's people] white, even to the time of the end, because it is yet for the time [God] appointed.*
>
> —Daniel 11:35, AMPC

This is what liberal Christians do. Being open-minded, they don't hold strictly to the views of the Bible and are easily swayed. Believing the lie and preaching it from the pulpit causes others to stumble and fall. Instead of getting a reward from God one day, Jesus says in Mark 9:42 that *"it would be better (more profitable and wholesome) for him if a [huge] millstone were hung about his neck, and he were thrown into the sea"* (AMPC).

Confirming this is another scripture where Jesus firmly warns, *"And [Jesus] said to His disciples, Temptations (snares, traps set to entice to sin) are sure to come, but woe to him by or through whom they come!"* (Luke 17:1, AMPC) Being open-minded by affirming a lifestyle that is not pleasing to the Lord is a trap, and it can entice or lure others into sin.

The liberal approach is dangerous, not just for instilling lies, but by preventing persons of the LGBTQ community from learning the truth. We must remember that God loves the individual, but He will not tolerate the sin.

One of the best books about same-sex marriage is *The Truth About Same-Sex Marriage* by Erwin W. Lutzer. It addresses in detail what is really at stake. I endorse this book with all my heart. Lutzer strongly cautions,

> Before our eyes, we are witnessing a cultural revolution that, if successful, will have ongoing repercussions for our children, our grandchildren and ourselves. There is a reason to believe that this revolution to remake the family has the potential to destroy the very concept of marriage along with freedom of religion. If God's people do not act now, it might be too late.[65]

This book was written in 2009. How much has come true since then? I am deeply concerned.

The first churches to embrace marital compromise have been the Anglican and United churches. Many of these churches have embraced and performed same-sex marriages, even ordaining ministers who actively live a homosexual lifestyle. These churches use the rainbow flag to symbolize their support of the LGBTQ community.

Today, more and more denominations are debating the necessity of such compromise. In the Christian community, there is great pressure to embrace and engage in advocating and endorsing the practice

---

65   Erwin W. Lutzer, *The Truth About Same-Sex Marriage* (Chicago, IL: Moody, 2004), 14.

of a homosexual lifestyle. Biblical Christian principles are becoming less popular, less acceptable, and more marginalized. Many churches think that if they choose not to offend or marginalize, thus compromising the truth, they will grow.

The result is the opposite of growth. In today's world, church attendance is dwindling. There is no *life*. We have compromised a lot.

One of the reasons for low church attendance is that people are tired of "religion." Another reason may be that many pastors don't address today's hot topics. Out of fear of stepping on toes, they silently approve of unbiblical sexual practices. By doing this, they lose the power and presence of God.

Those who still want to hold to the truth of God and His Word will choose to go somewhere else, or not attend any church at all. I know many strong Christians who don't attend a church any longer. Could it be that we have become a club rather than fulfilling what God originally intended for the church to be? Could it be that we're all about programs, excluding the leading of the Holy Spirit? Is it still as Paul describes in 1 Corinthians 14:26?

> *What then is the right course, believers? When you meet together, each one has a psalm, a teaching, a revelation (disclosure of special knowledge), a tongue, or an interpretation. Let everything be constructive and edifying and done for the good of all the church.* (AMP)

Many of these churches have tried to accommodate culture, and it has weakened them.

Regarding homosexuality, the sad reality is that many people believe Christians are hostile towards those who identify as LGBTQ. With the practice of the conservative approach, it is no surprise the LGBTQ community believes that Christians are hostile towards them—because they have been. By swinging the pendulum to the other extreme, liberal Christian believe they can fix the dilemma the church is in. They will not.

The reality is that our churches and societies are full of broken people who need healing and restoration. But by introducing compromised truth to the church, there is no life to be found there, so people search elsewhere. Thus the exodus of persons who experience same-sex attractions will continue. We have lost them.

So what is the church going to do about it?

I believe we have come to the place where we need to take the church to the world, since the world is not coming to us anymore. Lorna Dueck, a television personality who for decades has examined the juncture of journalism and Christianity, states,

> Churches are beginning to ask tough, new questions—marking an age of introspection rarely seen before… We go to the grocer for our food, to the tech store for our phones, the mall for our clothes, and my favorite, to the shoe store for shoes. But where do you pick up what you need for the ability to love? Where do you source forgiveness? Who has had a sale lately on facing fear? These are spiritual necessities I really need. I also need them from a source outside

my own limitations. So for that, I look for trustworthy ideas about having a relationship with God, and that information must be found in our churches. It's the most important information I ever source. So I am not an advocate of ditching organized religion, but I am a fan of discerning it. It was Jesus who said, "I am the way, the truth and the life, no one comes to the Father except through me.[66]

It is time the church stops to ponder Lorna's words. This is the dilemma the church faces today. The conservative approach chased the LGBTQ community away, and the liberal approach leads us to believe and teach a lie so that they won't hear the full truth.

In neglecting the full truth of God's Word, liberal Christians fail to share the importance of being obedient to God and His ways. They aid persons within the LGBTQ community in following their hearts, not guarding their hearts as the Bible commands. When a church does this, its people fail miserably in reconciling people with Christ. They fail to fulfill the Great Commission. They can never bring people into harmony with God, and fail to build the bridges God requires them to build. And God will hold them accountable: *"Woe to those who call evil good and good evil, who put darkness for light and light for darkness, who put bitter for sweet and sweet for bitter!"* (Isaiah 5:20, AMPC)

This is what God says will happen to us if we embrace these lies:

Therefore, as the tongue of fire devours the stubble, and as the dry grass sinks down in the flame, so their root shall be like rottenness and their blossom shall go up like fine dust—because they have rejected and cast away the law and the teaching of the Lord of hosts and have not believed but have treated scornfully and have despised the word of the Holy One of Israel.

—Isaiah 5:24, AMPC

These liberal churches falsely believe that their approval and affirmation is what the LGBTQ community needs. Yes, they need our love. But as true disciples of Jesus who are called to make fishers of men, we forget that we are called to share the full gospel of Jesus without compromising it. This includes making people aware of His full teachings and warning them when they are on a path that displeases the Lord.

Approving and affirming a homosexual lifestyle serves to separate them from God instead of bringing them into a closer relationship with Him. Sharing this lie breaks down spiritual bridges instead of building them. Speaking the truth is the keystone of the bridge we are called to build, and this is how persons within the LGBTQ community will eventually walk across into the arms of Jesus.

If only liberal Christians could see this. So many talk freely of God's grace and how it is enough! I, too, am grateful for His grace and mercy in my life, but people have used God's grace as an excuse to justify living and practicing a homosexual lifestyle—or, for that matter, any unbiblical behavior. Jude shared his concerns with the church. He was compelled to remind them about his concern when he noticed

---

66 Lorna Dueck, "God's PR Problem," *Context with Lorna Dueck.* November 28, 2014 (http://www.contextwithlornadueck.plujoextended.com/episodes/gods-pr-problem).

certain believers perverting grace and changing it into *"lawlessness and wantonness and immorality,"* and by doing so they *"disown and deny our sole Master and Lord, Jesus Christ"* (Jude 4, AMPC).

We can never use God's grace to promote, accept, or affirm a behavior that is not pleasing to Him. When we do this, we actually join them and God will hold all of us accountable.

By following the unbiblical liberal approach we will lose the opportunity for persons within the LGBTQ community to get to know Jesus personally, to follow Him wholeheartedly and live in obedience to His requirements as a child of God. We need our churches to uphold and defend biblical values without compromising truth.

Both of these approaches are extreme, though, and neither are ultimately effective. That's why we need to find a third approach—the Jesus approach.

> *We can never use God's grace to promote, accept, or affirm a behavior that is not pleasing to Him.*

CHAPTER THIRTEEN

The Jesus Approach (a.k.a. Wearing Jesus Glasses)

This is the *only* correct approach, the one we should all follow. This approach is biblical. Jesus modelled it, leading by example when He walked the earth. He experienced the same temptations and feelings we all go through, yet He never stumbled. He never fell.

When Christians use the Jesus approach, they will intentionally ask themselves, "What would Jesus do?" Have you ever pondered this phrase? We all face difficult situations in our lives, and I think for most Christians it's quite natural to wonder how Jesus would do it. They will ponder, reflect on, and study the Bible to learn His ways and how He interacted with people. They will keep in mind the meaning of His name—"the highest human corporeal concept of the divine idea rebuking and destroying error and bringing to light man's immortality... His life, death, and resurrection are the basis of the Christian message of salvation."[67] Then, when they are confronted with the issue of homosexuality in their lives, following His ways and example will hopefully be their desire and the foundation of how they will approach it.

> When Christians use the Jesus approach, they will intentionally ask themselves, "What would Jesus do?"

In my own personal search for answers, studying and digging into the Word of God, I found a classic example of how Jesus would do it in Mark 8. Before you continue reading, I strongly encourage you to read the entire chapter from the Amplified Bible, Classic Edition. Read it slowly and prayerfully, paying attention to the amplifications in the verses. Read it with an open and teachable mind. If you are sincere in your efforts to be educated, equipped, and enlightened on the topic of

---

67 *Merriam-Webster's Collegiate Dictionary*, Eleventh Edition, "Jesus." Edited by Frederick C. Mish (Springfield, MA: Merriam-Webster, Inc., 2004).

homosexuality, and if you desire to practice the Jesus approach, Mark 8 contains all the guidance you need in order to do it.

Some of the aspects of this approach will come naturally, while others will take "intentional incarnation," as Martin has described it. Some will take courage and boldness. Whether you are a parent, friend, or family member with a loved one who experiences same-sex attractions and or who self-identifies as gay, whether you are a pastor or leader in your church, realize that Mark 8 contains all the tools and guidelines to do just that.

I am fully aware that nothing I write can change your view of how to approach persons within the LGBTQ community, but I know that the Word of God contains all the answers. It is our only trustworthy measuring stick. When we are open to the instructions in the Word, poison will turn into perfume. Ashes will turn to beauty. Our actions will become an invitation for others to come into harmony with Jesus!

In Mark 8, you won't find a trace of either the extremist conservative or liberal approaches. It contains several examples of Jesus approaching tough situations, though. The reality is, when gay comes home (or to your church), you will be faced with challenging conversations—and you'll need to approach it the way Jesus would.

In this section, I'll go over His examples in chronological order, not necessarily in the order of which should come first. At the end, I've included a diagram to summarize them.

Example 1: Jesus Shows Compassion

The story in Mark 8 plays out with a large crowd of about four thousand gathered to hear Jesus speak. When they had been there and listened to Him for three days, they ran out of food. He said, *"I have pity and sympathy for the people and My heart goes out to them…"* (Mark 8:2, AMPC) Jesus showed compassion towards them. He was genuinely concerned for their well-being and was worried that they might faint on their way home.

When we meet gay people in the course of life, we need to have and show compassion, even if we don't understand. Having and showing compassion will show that we care and build trust. Even though we may not understand what the person is going through, compassion will pave the way for conversations to happen, helping us to gain clarity. Open dialogue is the key to building a bridge; it can be a bridge between a child and his parents, but it can also be a bridge between that child and God.

Example 2: Jesus Is Concerned for Our Well-Being

In Mark 8, Jesus was concerned that the people might faint on their way home. When the Israelites were oppressed by the Egyptians,

...God heard their sighing and groaning and [earnestly] remembered His covenant with Abraham, with Isaac, and with Jacob. God saw the Israelites and took knowledge of them and concerned Himself about them [knowing all, understanding, remembering all].

—Exodus 2:24–25, AMPC

We need to be concerned for the well-being of each person, whether it be a physical or spiritual concern. Many struggle deeply with the reality of experiencing same-sex attractions. Some feel as though they are in an Egypt all their own. This is a tough journey and we must be concerned for anyone who's on it. Having experienced it myself, I wouldn't wish for anyone else to have to go through the journey, and especially not alone.

For those who choose to practice the lifestyle, our concern is about the consequences of their choices, whether they are physical (sexually transmitted diseases which could harm or kill them) or spiritual. Many persons within the LGBTQ community who grew up in Christian homes and have made choices earlier in their lives to invite Jesus into their hearts as their personal Savior will walk away from Him when they choose this lifestyle. In their struggle to understand this challenging journey, they will blame God. The result is often that they walk away, creating a separation between them and God.

We must be deeply concerned when a person walks away from the Lord. Jesus's concern moved Him to action. He fed them. He performed a miracle, multiplied the bread, and *"they ate and were satisfied"* (Mark 8:8, AMPC). His concern for their well-being helped them to be in a better situation physically. They wouldn't die of hunger on the road back home.

When gay comes home, our concern will feed them. They will know that they're not alone. They will know that they are loved. This is a building block in the bridge between us and them, and between them and God.

Be aware that some won't take our concern to heart. This, too, is a reality, but it shouldn't discourage us from showing concern.

After Jesus performed the miracle of feeding the four thousand, the Pharisees started to argue and question Him. Mark 8:12 goes on to say that He *"groaned and sighed deeply in His spirit and said, Why does this generation demand a sign? Positively I say to you, no sign shall be given this generation"* (AMPC).

These verses bring up several examples of how Jesus would respond to difficult situations.

Example 3: Jesus Is Willing to Engage in Tough Conversations

Finding out that a child has same-sex attractions is a likely scenario for some, so we shouldn't be afraid to engage in such difficult situations. Jesus was willing.

Challenging issues may come to the discussion table. The issues will vary from trying to figure things out after a loved one comes out to dealing with the shock and disbelief—especially when this person chooses to embrace a lifestyle that is not biblical.

These discussions may involve arguments, anger, and any number of other unloving responses. In my own personal experience, growing up in a home where none of us learned how to deal with tough or challenging topics, we always ended up in severe conflict, leaving us with scars of pain and hurt. Unless both parties use caution, the same scenarios will happen in other families, and people will get hurt.

Example 4: Jesus Is Careful Before He Speaks

We need to learn how Jesus approached and dealt with similar situations, and be encouraged. Jesus got frustrated, too. It's okay to feel frustrated, as long as we remember the key: responding the way Jesus would.

He didn't voice His frustrations when *"he groaned and sighed deeply in His Spirit"* (Mark 8:12, AMPC). He kept His feelings in check.

Example 5: Jesus Responds Respectfully and Assertively

Note that when Jesus finally opened His mouth, His words were respectful and assertive. As He says in Mark 8:12, *"Why does this generation demand a sign? Positively [assuredly] I say to you, no sign shall be given this generation"* (AMPC).

He didn't bash them. He didn't voice His deep frustration. The answer He gave was assertive and uncompromising, yet respectful; He was declaring a consequence.

Keep in mind that one type of conversation will create a lot of frustration: your loved one will try to argue and change your views. In acknowledging his own same-sex attractions, he may try and make you believe that God made him that way, making it seem right for him to subsequently act on his feelings. We, in turn, get frustrated and try to change his mind or convince him that his views are wrong. And it goes on and on.

This can be a very challenging conversation, and it's a futile one. The discussion goes back and forth, creating division, tension, and heated debate. Giving a gentle and calm answer remains the challenge. And if this is something we just can't do, it may be time to consider something else Jesus did.

Example 6: Jesus Goes to a Place of Solitude

According to Mark, Jesus then *"went away and left them"* (Mark 8:13, AMPC), going to a place of solitude.

Walking away doesn't mean that the conversation is over or that you are rejecting, pushing away, or hating the other person. When we walk away, we create a time for reflection and give each other space. It can be a time to ask the Lord for guidance and wisdom. This time can be used to examine your own heart to ensure you aren't carrying grudges, unforgiveness, bitterness, or anger.

We must always keep in mind that it's not our job to change anybody. That remains the work of the Holy Spirit, as it is He who convicts us if our ways are displeasing to the Lord. This is why I say that no man, psychiatrist, or my own efforts could do more for me than what the Holy Spirit has.

When Jesus walked away from the Pharisees, He chose not to engage them on that issue any longer. He knew He would have to face them again, but for that day He chose to walk away and have no further conversation with them: *"He went away and left them and, getting into the boat again, He departed to the other side [of the sea]"* (Mark 8:13, AMPC).

Sometimes when we find ourselves in the middle of a frustrating conversation, the best thing we can do is walk away for a while. It may just mean that we need to rest. It may mean choosing to find solitude to pray and regain our strength to continue the difficult conversation.

Practicing this principle shows how important it is for us to spend time alone with God, during which we pray, rest, and are replenished for the journey ahead. During these spiritual pit stops, our time alone with God allows Him to guide us, and to gain not just His wisdom for the situation but His peace as well.

There are numerous examples in the Bible where Jesus went away to be alone with His Father. He not only did it Himself, but He invites us to do the same. Mark 6:31–32 says, *"And He said to them, [As for you] come away by yourselves to a deserted place, and rest a while… And they went away in a boat to a solitary place by themselves"* (AMPC). This is a powerful principle. When Jesus walked away from the Pharisees, He freed Himself from further frustration and allowed the fire to die down.

Example 7: Jesus Doesn't Get Involved in Politics

When Martin spoke about this approach in his sermon, he said that Jesus "would not get involved in the politics of the issue."[68] So when He walked away from the Pharisees, He chose not to get involved in the politics of the issue, which He knew would create more tension.

If we continue arguing, this is an indication that we are too interested in the politics of the issue, and that isn't helpful. It can make our lives unmanageable and insane. Addressing an issue like homosexuality on a regular basis creates a lot of tension just for the sake of debate, or to prove that we're right, which is not how Jesus would do it. The elephant in the room may be huge, but we don't always have to acknowledge its existence, as hard as this may sound.

This is something many parents face when their child comes out. In hosting a parent support group, I try to encourage them to resist getting involved in the politics, as this is a huge stumbling block in journeying well with their loved one. Getting involved in the politics can break down existing healthy relationships. It builds walls, not bridges.

But how do we avoid getting involved in the politics? Martin explains in his sermon, "Jesus would always depolarize things, meaning

> *The elephant in the room may be huge, but we don't always have to acknowledge its existence, as hard as this may sound.*

---

68   Ibid.

He would go back to the Word. He would address it as sin, but then explain that sin is sin."[69] In the depolarizing process, we don't categorize sin and label homosexuality as the biggest sin out there.

Living a homosexual lifestyle was never and should never be a standalone sin issue. James 2:9–11 explains that if we fail to obey even one aspect of the Law, we have failed in keeping the whole Law, revealing to us that it doesn't matter what kind of sin we commit, because sin is sin.

Yes, we must show concern when a person engages in homosexuality, but we can't treat them as if they are the only person in the world who sins. We all sin and fall short of the glory of God (Romans 3:23). When we name homosexuality amongst other sins, we depolarize it. This is the Jesus approach.

After Jesus left the Pharisees in Mark 8, He and the disciples sailed to the other side of the sea. While in the boat, they realized that they had forgotten to take food with them. They only had one loaf of bread. How ironic. Jesus had just fed four thousand people, and here they found themselves in a similar dilemma.

I love how Jesus responds. He doesn't criticize them for forgetting. Instead He gently and lovingly continues to teach them truth: *"And Jesus [repeatedly and expressly] charged and admonished them, saying, Look out; keep on your guard and beware of the leaven of the Pharisees…"* (Mark 8:15, AMPC).

The word *admonish* means "to give friendly earnest advice or encouragement… to express warning or disapproval to—especially in a gentle, earnest or solicitous manner."[70] When gay comes home, this can be one of the most difficult things to do. How do we share with a person who is living this lifestyle that it is not God's will? And how do we do it in a loving, non-condemning way?

Example 8: Jesus Warns in a Gentle, Encouraging Way

When we share the truth from God's Word, and when we warn about the consequences of living in disobedience to God's teachings, the goal must always be to do it in a gentle, loving, and encouraging way. We must think carefully before we speak and ask the Holy Spirit for the right words.

The fact is that He does warn. We need to do the same, just not in the wrong way. When I think about the slogans and flyers that extremist conservative Christians use to demonstrate their beliefs, I can only shake my head in disapproval. That is not how Jesus did it. Their warning is done with hate. They show no gentleness and their message is discouraging.

Example 9: Jesus Meets Us Where We're At

In the meantime, Jesus and His disciples arrived at the other side of the sea to the town Bethsaida and He immediately healed a blind man who was brought to Him by the people. He stopped and took the

---

69   Ibid.
70   *Merriam-Webster's Collegiate Dictionary*, Eleventh Edition, "Admonish." Edited by Frederick C. Mish (Springfield, MA: Merriam-Webster, Inc., 2004).

time to hear about the blind man's condition. Look what He did next: *"He caught the blind man by the hand and led him out of the village"* (Mark 8:23, AMPC).

Jesus not only cared and showed compassion, but He met the man where he was—blind and desperate for healing. And by leading him outside the village, Jesus spent time with him.

Jesus would encourage us all to meet the LGBTQ community right where they are. He always attracted those whom religious people didn't want to interact with. For example, sick people, tax collectors, prostitutes, etc. Not only was He willing to meet them where they were at, regardless of whether they had a spiritual or physical condition, He stopped what He was doing and spent time with them. In some cases, He healed them; in others, He listened. There were also times when He called them to a higher standard, inviting them to walk in truth and holiness.

This should be our approach as well. Meet all persons within the LGBTQ community where they are at. Stop and spend time with them, listening to them and getting to know them better. Be compassionate towards them, and if they're not at the same point in their spiritual journey as you are, show patience. Don't force them to heed what you say. Leave the heart work to God. Our role remains to meet them where they are—to accept, love, listen, pray, and respect everyone.

When and if a person has a true encounter with the living God, they will transform over time. This is not our doing, but the work of God. God alone can change a heart of stone into a soft, pliable heart (Ezekiel 36:26). Consider Paul's road to Damascus experience. His whole life changed, and he went from being a persecutor and killer of Christians to a true Christ follower, reaching the lost. Did he change by the influence of a person? No, it was a divine work of God.

I ask you, has Jesus met you where you were at? Has your life changed or transformed in an instant, or have the changes only become evident after years of journeying with Him? How can we expect sudden changes from the LGBTQ community if our own journeys have taken time? Certainly, none of us have arrived yet.

We remain in a state of ongoing and daily surrender and submission to God's authority. If we are unwilling to understand and practice Jesus's powerful approach of meeting people where they're at, we fail to build effective bridges.

We must use patience in the process and build true friendships. We can't force people to open their hearts further to Christ.

The process might take a long time. Jesus never gave up on people, but we humans do tend to give up, especially when we don't see any change. But who knows? God is working behind the scenes, and it's not for us to judge this process. Another benefit to meeting persons within the LGBTQ community where they're at is that relationship allows us to be aware and sensitive to where others are spiritually. This only comes through building relationships and trust. Never quote scripture bluntly or harshly, or try to hit them over the head with the Bible if they're not a believer yet. Jesus didn't chase after people if they were unwilling to receive truth.

After Jesus healed the blind man, He and His disciples continued on to the village of Caesarea Philippi. On the way, He asked His disciples, *"Who do people say I am?"* (Mark 8:27, AMPC) Then He asked them a more personal question:

But who do you yourselves say that I am? Peter replied to Him, You are the Christ (the Messiah, the Anointed One).

—Mark 8:29, AMPC

Jesus went on to explain how He would be *"put to death, and after three days rise again [from death]"* (Mark 8:31, AMPC). Peter wasn't happy when he heard that. He took Jesus by the hand, led Him aside, and rebuked Him for saying those things. Peter was being influenced by his own fleshly desires as a human being and blinded by Satan from knowing the full purpose in Jesus's coming to earth. In his own mind, he thought it crazy that Jesus should die. He didn't know or understand the plan of God.

Example 10: Jesus Deals with the Real Enemy

But Jesus saw things for what they were. Peter's reply made Him do something very powerful.

But turning around [His back to Peter] and seeing His disciples, He rebuked Peter, saying, Get behind Me, Satan! For you do not have a mind intent on promoting what God wills, but what pleases men [you are not on God's side, but that of men].

—Mark 8:33, AMPC

Jesus knew who had blinded Peter's spiritual eyes. Satan was influencing Peter to try and prevent Jesus from dying to set us all free.

Jesus knew that Peter would be hurt to see Him angry, and He didn't want Peter to think He was angry at him, so He turned His back. Jesus's anger was at Satan, not Peter.

We, too, need to see things for what they are. Getting angry at your son or daughter for coming out is the wrong approach. We need to recognize who is behind it, the one who has started these attractions, and our anger should be aimed at him—Satan. He is the enemy, not the person who succumbs to sin by choosing to practice a homosexual lifestyle.

The LGBTQ community is not our enemy. Your son or daughter who experiences same-sex attractions is not the enemy. When we have conversations with them and try to find solutions, we must be aware who the real enemy is. Experiencing same-sex attractions is due to the fallen nature of man. It started in the Garden of Eden when Eve caved in and chose to believe Satan's lies. As a result, things happen—things God never intended to happen to us.

The Jesus Approach (a.k.a. Wearing Jesus Glasses)

Ever since the fall of man, people come into the world with various forms of brokenness, drawing them towards desires that aren't pleasing to God. We cannot blame God for that. God *permits* everything, but this does not mean He necessarily *wills* everything.

The brokenness we experience is because of the work of Satan. Unchaste desires of any type, which includes same-sex attractions, have a spirit behind them—the spirit of Satan himself, working alongside other fallen angels.

Please don't misunderstand what I'm saying here. I am *not* saying that persons who experience same-sex attractions or who are within the LGBTQ community are demon-possessed. That idea sometimes comes from extremist conservative Christians; they like to share this viewpoint through abrasive flyers and slogans. In saying that, we must recognize that the further we choose to reject God in any facet of our lives, the further we open our hearts to the demonic realm. This may lead anybody into a state of demonic oppression, and then possibly demonic possession.

We must understand that it is Satan and his cohorts who draw people away from upholding and honoring the order of creation, as revealed in nature. He draws people in many ways, one way being the draw to behave in ways that lead us to use the precious gift of sexuality in unvirtuous ways that counter who we truly are as men and women. Being able to see the true enemy enables us to look at persons within the LGBTQ community with love and compassion, not criticizing and condemning them for having to journey with the weight of same-sex attractions. Understanding Satan's role will bring clarity.

> *God permits everything, but this does not mean He necessarily wills everything.*

Example 11: Jesus Invites People to Follow Him

The story in Mark 8 moves along.

> *And Jesus called [to Him] the throng with His disciples and said to them, If anyone intends to come after Me, let him deny himself [forget, ignore, disown, and lose sight of himself and his own interests] and take up his cross, and [joining Me as a disciple and siding with My party] follow with Me [continually, cleaving steadfastly to Me].*
>
> —Mark 8:34, AMPC

When we interact with a loved one who is embracing a homosexual lifestyle, we need to understand that often they are focusing on their self and their fleshly desires. They may also be focusing on their deep-seated desire to belong or feel loved and accepted. This is a tug-of-war situation.

But Jesus never forced anyone to follow Him, and neither should we. We must keep His example close to our hearts. We can never force a person to want Christ in their lives. We can't make them believe, and we cannot make them want to open their hearts more deeply to Him.

In a sermon I once heard by Andy Stanley, a pastor and motivational speaker who encourages youth to chase after purity, challenged two thousand young people to give God one year of their lives. He was encouraging them to lay down their fleshly desires, making God a central priority and part of their everyday lives for at least a whole year. Stanley assured them that their lives would never be the same, but he couldn't force them to take him up on his challenge. It was an invitation.

When we're building relationships with persons within the LGBTQ community, our role is to represent Jesus well and leave the rest up to Him. Our role is to pray, and to be salt and light.

Salt makes people thirsty when they eat it. Our approach towards any persons within the LGBTQ community must be like feeding them salt. Our lives must be lived in such a way that it makes them thirsty for God. Our lives must become an invitation for them to live the same, without forcing them into that choice. When we live like this and have friendships with persons within the LGBTQ community, they will desire to get to know Jesus.

This is one of the key building blocks when we're trying to build bridges. Always remember that when we're building relationships, we are actually working on being reconciled to Christ. We are in *"the ministry of reconciliation [that by word and deed we might aim to bring others into harmony with Him]"* (2 Corinthians 5:18, AMPC).

Example 12: Jesus Warns About Eternal Consequences

After Jesus invited the throngs and His disciples to follow Him wholeheartedly, He was very clear about the consequences of following after the flesh instead of following God. He had the audacity to tell them to lay down their fleshly desires, warning them that if they didn't they may lose their souls, that they may not get to heaven one day:

> *For whoever wants to save his [higher, spiritual, eternal] life, will lose it [the lower, natural, temporal life which is lived only on earth]; and whoever gives up his life [which is lived only on earth] for My sake and the Gospel's will save it [his higher, spiritual life in the eternal kingdom of God].*
> —Mark 8:35, AMPC

This can be a very challenging task, and many people are afraid to give warnings. But people must be warned not only of the physical consequences of living and practicing a homosexual lifestyle, but more importantly of the consequences of choosing to walk away from God while practicing that lifestyle.

One common experience, repeated by most people who have chosen to walk away from a homosexual lifestyle to pursue a life of virtue and holiness, is that they claim they didn't feel close to God while they were living that way. So it's only fair to warn of those consequences. It is our duty. Jesus goes on to say, *"For what does it profit a man to gain the whole world, and forfeit his life [in the eternal kingdom of God]?"* (Mark 8:36, AMPC)

Example 13: Jesus Is Not Ashamed to Share the Truth

And then we come to the conclusion of the chapter, where Jesus clearly explains to the throng and His disciples that they should not be ashamed of Him here on earth. He urges them,

> *For whoever is ashamed [here and now] of Me and My words in this adulterous (unfaithful) and [preeminently] sinful generation, of him will the Son of Man also be ashamed when He comes in the glory (splendor and majesty) of His Father with the holy angels.*
>
> —Mark 8:38, AMPC

When Jesus addressed the throngs in Mark 8:34, we can assume that many of them weren't His followers yet, though the invitation was presented to them. They were open to hearing His message. It's not hitting someone over the head with the Bible if they are seeking your counsel.

The throngs in this chapter were seeking truth. They had heard about Him and were hungry to hear His message. This tells us that we shouldn't be ashamed to share the gospel with anyone, including persons within the LGBTQ community. In being unashamed, we will be bold enough to both share the truth and give warnings. All of this needs to be done prayerfully, respectfully, and with dignity.[71]

Example 14: Jesus Spent Time with Sinners (Without Compromising His Holiness)

These last two examples are made evident by summarizing the entire chapter: Jesus was willing to spend time with the people, but He wasn't willing to approve of their sin or accept that they'd rather please men than be obedient to God.

Throughout the story in Mark 8, Jesus spent time with thousands of people, all of them sinners. And the way Jesus responded to them—the Pharisees, the blind man, and His own disciples—sets an impeccable example. He was man, and at the same time He was God. He had human feelings. He responded in ways we can only dream of. He accepted those around Him, was willing to hang out with them, stopped to pay attention to them, and really heard them, yet His responses contained His unwillingness to compromise the truth. This is in opposition to the liberal approach, whereby the church compromises the truth by caving in to the pressure of the world.

We must always be willing to hang out with persons who experience same-sex attractions or who are within the LGBTQ community. We need to build relationships with them, invite them into our homes, and get to know them more deeply. The fact that they experience same-sex attractions is just a

---

[71] I will explain later in this chapter how we are called by God to be watchmen on the walls, warning and speaking the truth regardless of our hesitations.

small piece of who they are. This doesn't take away from the gift, or the importance, of sexuality. It merely draws attention to the fullness of the person.

My friend Michael once said to me,

> Self-identifying according to our experiences is something the world rejects in many contexts, but it seems to not reject it in the context of sexuality and sexual identity. If you think about it, we are first and foremost chosen by God to be created as His beloved children, before our very first touch of human experience! And even after we die, we are still His beloved. To merely self-identify and define ourselves according to the fleeting human experience, is to anchor our identity on something that can NEVER put us on stable ground. Furthermore, it is a matter of pursuing *deeper self-honesty* about who we are as persons, to embrace the greater truth of being first and foremost His beloved children. *That* identity spans our existence from the *very beginning* to the *very end*; from the moment of conception to even after death!

As I've stated before, those who experience same-sex attractions are not enemies nor should they be seen as threats to the church. They are real people, with real hearts like you and me. When we interact with them, we must strive to live an impeccable example of humility—and our conversation cannot compromise the truth. Liberal Christians, tending to be open-minded, make compromises. That's not the way Jesus would do it.

Example 15: Jesus Accepts and Loves All People (Without Approving of Sin)

Acceptance of one's reality does not imply approval of their lifestyle choices. In the story of Mark 8, when the Pharisees attacked Jesus with their arguments and questions, maliciously testing Him, Jesus engaged in conversation. He accepted them and their presence, but in a loving way He stood up to them by sharing that He disapproved of their ideas.

He did the same with Peter when Peter rebuked Him. Jesus's response toward Peter was not one of hate, but rather He pointed out clearly that Peter was trying to please man instead of God. Jesus didn't approve of Peter's wrong actions and selfish desires. He accepted and loved Peter, but He didn't approve of his sin.

In one of Dr. Michael Brown's YouTube videos, he draws a distinction between *affirmational inclusion* and *transformational inclusion*, pointing out that Jesus only engaged in the second one. Did He reach out to people who sinned and tell them, "Go for it"? Dr. Brown argues that He did no such thing. He didn't encourage people to sin. Instead He met them where they were at in order to help them change.[72]

---

72 Dr. Michael Brown holds a PhD from New York University in Near Eastern Language and Literature. He has served as a professor at numerous seminaries, authored more than 25 books, and preached around the world. He hosts the nationally syndicated talk radio show *The Line of Fire* and the television show *Answering Your Toughest Questions*.

The Jesus Approach (a.k.a. Wearing Jesus Glasses)

This is one of the biggest struggles for friends and family members of those who identify as gay. They find it difficult to distinguish between acceptance of the individual and approval of the lifestyle. I often hear firsthand stories from parents and those who attend my support group of their struggles with acceptance and approval. This creates more tension.

Persons within the LGBTQ community today will loudly complain about the fact that when we don't approve of their lifestyle, we hate them, and sometimes they even bully those who disagree. Many people, including myself, are persecuted by the LGBTQ community when we don't approve. The fact that there was a protest in Saskatoon by members of the LGBTQ community when I spoke about making this distinction is proof of their strong beliefs. If we don't agree with them, we are called haters and homophobic.

Please understand that this fifteenth example can cause tension and offense. This is reality. Many were offended by what Jesus had to say as well, though He only brought truth. We need to remember this so we aren't scared to stand up for the truths upheld by the Christian faith.

Summarizing the Examples

Wearing our Jesus glasses will firstly give us tremendous compassion when gay comes home. Secondly, looking at them through these lenses will bring more clarity and clear up the confusion. When we look at others through our own eyes, we not only tend to criticize and judge what we see, but we respond with those attitudes as well. Criticism and judgment will break down a bridge rather than serving to build it up.

Jesus glasses bring light and solutions for how to love well. Through His lenses, and by practicing all these examples, we can learn to build bridges instead of walls. It will help to make us aware of what persons within the LGBTQ community go through. It will also

> *When we look at others through our own eyes, we not only tend to criticize and judge what we see, but we respond with those attitudes as well.*

help us to understand that just as we are on a journey, so is everyone else. And we must be patient, tolerant, and ready to offer grace. Jesus, in His love for each one of us, has shown grace. We need to do the same as His representatives.

Building authentic relationships is key, especially when approaching those who aren't believers yet. True and honest friendships with them will pave the road, which leads to the bridge—the bridge that leads to reconciliation with Jesus. We can never force anyone. Jesus Himself was gentle yet firm, while always being relational. He always invited but never forced anyone to follow Him. The choice to follow is an individual one.

When we have friendships with persons within the LGBTQ community, there may come a day when it is appropriate to invite them to attend a home group or even a church service. This is a great start, but we need to remember whose job it is to do the heart work. It is the work of the Holy Spirit.

As we lovingly accept others, and welcome them back into our churches, we must be patient while they sit under the teaching of the truth, and the truth will set them free (John 8:32). God does the heart work. And may we all have the courage and boldness to do our part—to love well, speaking the truth in love (Ephesians 4:15) in the right season. This includes telling them at the right time, in a respectful tone, and mostly with our lived example about how much Jesus loves and cares about them.

When we build trust, how much we care about them will become evident and they will trust us enough to allow us to come alongside them on their journey with Jesus. We must assure them that we will always be there for them. When they fall, we will be right there, as accountability partners, to support them to get back on the right path, and when they're on the mountaintop, we will be there to celebrate with them. Offering our acceptance, love, and support and having open, honest, heartfelt communication are all building blocks for the bridge which leads people to ultimately accept Jesus as their Lord and Savior, reconciling them with God the Father.

I understand that numerous persons within the LGBTQ community will argue with me on this point. They will try to convince me that they *do* have an intimate relationship with Jesus while being married to their same-sex partner. But if people are living unchastely, they are closed to the fullness of God's love and what God could give to them. When I lived a homosexual lifestyle, I believed a lie and wanted it to be true, yet God's presence went away the moment I entered into a homosexual relationship. Any time we're unwilling to submit any area of our lives, there will be a wall. This unwillingness won't build bridges.

This is so clear throughout Scripture. Jesus says, *"I am the Way and the Truth and the Life; no one comes to the Father except by (through) me"* (John 14:6, AMPC). We need to be there for persons who experience same-sex attractions just as we would be there for anyone else, since each person's eternity rests in their relationship with God. We ought to assure each individual that we are willing to help them on this exciting journey, as they discover how to have an intimate and personal relationship with Jesus.

This is God's heart, and it should be our heart, too.

The fruit of the [uncompromisingly] righteous is a tree of life, and he who is wise captures human lives [for God, as a fisher of men—he gathers and receives them for eternity].
—Proverbs 11:30, AMPC

For this process to happen, we sometimes must do difficult things. Jesus, in His interactions with people caught in their sin, did not judge or criticize, yet He brought about a transformation of many hearts. He never forced them. It was always they who accepted or rejected *Him*. That is always our choice.

We must not be afraid to be the voice for truth. This will take courage and may require us to undertake the challenging task which is described in Ezekiel: to blow a trumpet and warn at certain times when the enemy is creeping in.

We all need to have the courage to share the truth from God's Word. God calls us to be watchmen on the walls. It is our *responsibility* to be watchmen. The watchman, when he sees the enemy coming, blows the trumpet to warn the people. The sound of the trumpet is like the warning we ought to give others to indicate that their continued sin will bring consequences, eternal or otherwise:

> *And the word of the Lord came to me, saying, Son of man, speak to your people [the Israelite captives in Babylon] and say to them, When I bring the sword upon a land and the people of the land take a man from among them and make him their watchman, if when he sees the sword coming upon the land, he blows the trumpet and warns the people, then whoever hears the sound of the trumpet and does not take warning, and the sword comes and takes him away, his blood shall be upon his own head. He heard the sound of the trumpet and did not take warning; his blood shall be upon himself. But he who takes warning shall save his life. But if the watchman sees the sword coming and does not blow the trumpet and the people are not warned, and the sword comes and takes any one of them, he is taken away in and for his perversity and iniquity, but his blood will I require at the watchman's hand. So you, son of man, I have made you a watchman for the house of Israel; therefore hear the word at My mouth and give them warning from Me.*
>
> —Ezekiel 33:1–7, AMPC

It is our duty to warn, as Ezekiel 33 teaches us, that the sword (the enemy) is coming. We have a responsibility to warn people if danger is coming, because we don't want to see people die, spiritually or physically. God is going to require from us the blood of those we didn't warn. For those we warn, it remains their choice to listen:

> *I call heaven and earth to witness this day against you that I have set before you life and death, the blessings and the curses; therefore choose life, that you and your descendants may live…*
>
> —Deuteronomy 30:19, AMPC

Jesus had audacity. In His own way He was still firm, loving, and merciful. We need not be afraid. We must know that what we say might offend people. As Jesus spoke truth, He offended many people. It's not only what we say, but how we speak truth that matters. Our tone is vital.

Let me extend a caution: we don't have to repeat our warning every day. Being aware of the elephant in the room can tempt us to bring it up or challenge it every day, but we must be sensitive. When we blow the trumpet, we don't have to beat them over the head with it. It's up to them to choose to listen. The fact remains, according to 2 Timothy 3:16–17, that all Scripture is profitable for correction. If it's profitable, then we need to use it and not shy away from our responsibilities to be the watchmen on the wall:

> *Every Scripture is God-breathed (given by His inspiration) and profitable for instruction, for reproof and conviction of sin, for correction of error and discipline in obedience, [and] for training in righteousness (in holy living, in conformity to God's will in thought, purpose, and action), so that the man of God may be complete and proficient, well fitted and thoroughly equipped for every good work. (AMPC)*

We must have knowledge and understanding of Scripture and be prepared to give an answer, and even a reproach, when people are prepared to listen. We must never use the Bible to degrade anyone or in any way destroy his or her dignity. Our intent must be to warn about habitual sin and its earthly and eternal consequences.

Blowing the trumpet doesn't mean blasting it in someone's ear. Rather, it's means appropriately warning the individual of what will carry him or her further from an intimate relationship with Christ.

Where to Draw the Line

Too many people draw the line too soon with regard to the Jesus approach. Jesus isn't okay with any of us continuing in unbiblical behavior. He doesn't approve of habitual sin, or sin in any form (Psalm 5). We are to show tolerance for people, not wrong behavior. Just because Jesus is tender and loving does not mean He isn't righteous.

The pendulum is swinging too far to the other side. Where Christians were once unkind and hurtful, many are now erring on the side of failing to speak the truth in love. Often we accompany people into sin, even with the best intentions. This is false charity. If we truly love, we will call people to the biblical standard of walking in accordance with God's ways. We are to stand firm in representing all of who Jesus is.

Many Christians are challenging my stance on how Jesus would approach people who are living a homosexual lifestyle. Well, yes, Jesus did hang out with sinners, prostitutes, and dishonest tax collectors. But He didn't indulge with them, nor did He encourage them to indulge.

> *The Son of Man came eating and drinking [with others], and they say, Behold, a glutton and a wine drinker, a friend of tax collectors and [especially wicked] sinners*
> —Matthew 11:19, AMPC

And yes, He never condemned them. He always met them where they were at! He accepted them and loved them unconditionally. And He still does today. I am so thankful that He met me once where I was at.

The Jesus Approach (a.k.a. Wearing Jesus Glasses)

But this is where many people draw the line. The Jesus approach doesn't end there. Jesus *always* expected a change of heart and repentance. And when people didn't do it, He got worked up. Here's what He said:

Then He began to censure and reproach the cities in which most of His mighty works had been performed, because they did not repent [and their hearts were not changed]. Woe to you, Chorazin! Woe to you, Bethsaida! For if the mighty works done in you had been done in Tyre and Sidon, they would long ago have repented in sackcloth and ashes [and their hearts would have been changed]. I tell you [further], it shall be more endurable for Tyre and Sidon on the day of judgment than for you. And you, Capernaum, are you to be lifted up to heaven? You shall be brought down to Hades [the region of the dead]! For if the mighty works done in you had been done in Sodom, it would have continued until today. But I tell you, it shall be more endurable for the land of Sodom on the day of judgment than for you.

—Matthew 11:20–24, AMPC

There's another classic example. When Jesus met the woman caught in adultery, He drew a line in the sand and said this: *"I do not condemn you either. Go on your way and from now on sin no more"* (John 8:11, AMPC).

And there's the story of the time when He met Zacchaeus, a dishonest tax collector. The Bible doesn't mention the details of their conversation, but it does mention Zacchaeus's change of heart. When he was in the presence of Jesus, his heart changed and he repented, saying, *"I will give half of my money to the poor. If I have cheated anyone, I will pay them back four times more!"* (Luke 19:8, ICB)

Jesus accepts and loves us all. But He doesn't approve when our hearts remain in an unchanged and unrepentant state. But He will always welcome us back, because He loves us so much and He doesn't want to leave us where we're at. As we repent and walk away from the things which displease Him, *this* He will approve.

This is the Jesus approach.

Don't draw the line too soon. Keep in mind that when we blow the trumpet, some people may make the decision not to heed the warning, which is a choice to continue to live in habitual sin. Blowing the trumpet in a way a person is unwilling to hear may cause them to be seriously offended. They might close off. We shouldn't be afraid of that, but we also ought to keep in mind that we have to *love* people into a relationship with Christ. This is why having a deeply connected personal relationship with them is so important; within a relationship, a person might be more open to what you have to say.

Mark 6:1–12 contains a classic example of how Jesus offended His listeners in the synagogue, and how their being offended *"hindered them from acknowledging His authority] and they were caused to stumble and fall"* (Mark 6:3, AMPC). Being offended can become a stumbling block to hearing God's will, plans, and purposes for our lives. It prevents us from accepting God's truth and the authority of His Word.

Getting offended is part of Satan's plans for us. It's part of his bait.[73] Too many of us take the bait and eat it. We are lured into thinking we deserve to feel this way, which creates distance and separation from God.

In Mark 6:6, Mark goes on to talk about how Jesus *"marveled because of their unbelief (their lack of faith in Him)"* (AMPC). He was surprised they didn't respond the way He had hoped. We, too, are surprised when people don't respond well when we try to help them move forward with Jesus, or when those who have chosen to practice a homosexual lifestyle choose to remain in their habitual sin. When any of us are offended, we are hindered from hearing God's voice, and this can bring us to a place where we stumble and fall.

But this should not discourage us from doing what we need to do. We must accept the fact that some people may not respond the way we want them to. Then we need to move on, we can't stay in the same place. Jesus moved on and told His disciples to do the same, to *"shake off the dust that is on your feet"* (Mark 6:11, AMPC).

I believe that moving on doesn't mean that we reject the person. It means we move on, trusting the Lord with the outcome of the seeds we have sown. When Jesus was surprised at His listeners' unbelief or lack of response to what He was teaching them, He moved on to the surrounding villages where He continued His teachings. He didn't give up speaking the truth to those who needed to hear it. He did what He could, and when people didn't respond, He moved on. He didn't yell at them, He didn't try to control or manipulate them, and He did not reject them. He simply accepted the fact that some people won't have a positive response.

So when a person doesn't respond well, it shouldn't discourage us from continuing to blow the trumpet—from moving forward to another person who needs to hear the message of truth, and from faithfully delivering it in a godly and timely manner.

We need to continue to trust the Holy Spirit to do the heart work. Our responsibility as true disciples of the gospel message remains our willingness to teach *"that men should repent [that they should change their minds for the better and heartily amend their ways, with abhorrence of their past sins]"* (Mark 6:12, AMPC).

We need to listen to the guidance and direction of the Holy Spirit as we speak with and listen to others. Applying all fifteen of Jesus' examples will require us to have a willing and humble heart. We must be aware that timing and tone are vital.

We also need to meet people where they're at. Remember a time when Jesus met you where you were at. Listen carefully to others and be aware of whether they are Christians or not; if they are, discover what level of discipleship they have experienced.

And finally, let us remember to extend the same love and grace we received from Jesus to persons within the LGBTQ community.

---

73 In his book *The Bait of Satan*, John Bevere (Nashville, TN: Thomas Nelson, 1994) says that if we get offended, it is a deadly trap strategically placed by Satan. He refers to the trap as bait.

The Jesus Approach
(Wearing Jesus Glasses)

1: Jesus Shows Compassion	See Mark 8:2
2: Jesus Is Concerned for Our Well-Being	See Mark 8:3
3: Jesus Is Willing to Engage in Tough Conversations	See Mark 8:11
4: Jesus Is Careful Before He Speaks	See Mark 8:12
5: Jesus Responds Respectfully and Assertively	See Mark 8:12
6: Jesus Goes to a Place of Solitude	See Mark 8:13
7: Jesus Doesn't Get Involved in Politics	See Mark 8:13
8: Jesus Warns in a Gentle, Encouraging Way	See Mark 8:15
9: Jesus Meets Us Where We're At	See Mark 8:22-23
10: Jesus Deals with the Real Enemy	See Mark 8:33
11: Jesus Invites People to Follow Him	See Mark 8:35
12: Jesus Warns About Eternal Consequences	See Mark 8:35-36
13: Jesus Is Not Ashamed to Share the Truth	See Mark 8:38
14: Jesus Spent Time with Sinners (Without Compromising His Holiness)	See Mark 8
15: Jesus Accepts and Loves All People (Without Approving of Sin)	See Mark 8

CHAPTER FOURTEEN

The Temptations of the Flesh

There is a continual media push in today's society to insist that living a homosexual lifestyle is acceptable and of equal value to being engaged in a heterosexual relationship. Consider the sitcom *Two and a Half Men*, in which the male main characters were in relationships with multiple women. In an episode near the end of its run, they agreed to marry one another in order to present themselves as an acceptable couple for adoption. The implication is given that a homosexual marriage is just as ideal as a marriage between heterosexual partners. Today, acceptance and approval of living a homosexual lifestyle has become the norm. In contrast, by biblical standards accepting an individual isn't the same as approving their behavior. However, I'm not trying to dismiss the dilemma we all face: the battle between our flesh and our spirit.

What is the flesh? According to the Amplified Bible, it's the entire human nature without God. We need to be aware that a battle is constantly being waged between our spirit and our flesh. Here's an essential question to ask on a daily basis: who is going to win the battle?

Consider this scenario. Two pit bulls are set against each other in a fight to the death. They're kept in separate cages, but each day they attack one another when they're let out. Eventually one will die. Which dog will win? Is it the one who is stronger? Faster? Bigger? Smarter? Perhaps the one that you like the most?

It is the one that you *feed*.

The Temptations of the Flesh

How do we feed our spirit daily? Here are just a few suggestions, and I'm sure you can add many more.

- Make sure to spend quality time with God.
- Be aware of your thoughts, and redirect those thoughts if they lead to bad places.
- Read God's Word daily.
- Listen and or watch Spirit-filled sermons containing the full gospel, and avoid worldly and fleshly contamination of any kind. This can include the books we read, the music we listen to, the programs or movies we watch, etc.

Choosing life instead of death, according to Deuteronomy 30:19, is an intentional process. We are cautioned in Galatians 5:17,

The sinful nature wants to do evil, which is just the opposite of what the Spirit wants. And the Spirit gives us desires that are the opposite of what the sinful nature desires. These two forces are constantly fighting each other, so you are not free to carry out your good intentions. (NLT)

Remember, Paul said, "*I decide to do good, but I don't really do it; I decide not to do bad, but then I do it anyway*" (Romans 7:18, MSG). There is a struggle between what the Bible says and what the flesh wants. The following chart helps to illustrate the tug-of-war between the two.

Jesus's ways vs fleshly ways

What the Bible says	What our flesh wants
Sex is only permitted in marriage (between one naturally born male and one naturally born female)	I want to sleep with my partner, regardless
By "looking" and lusting, we sin	Watching porn is harmless
Acting on same-sex attraction is sin	I can love who I want
Your body is a temple of the Holy Spirit	I find pleasure in unholy sexual practices
Live according to Biblical principles	Do what makes you happy
Guard and guide your heart	Follow your heart

When I lived a homosexual life, I wanted to gratify my earthly desires. I am no different than any other person; I have the same desires to be loved and to belong. I found homosexual relationships to be very physically orientated, and believe me, when I was in the midst of such relationships, I tried to justify them. These relationships made my flesh feel good. But we are not called to gratify the desires of the flesh; rather, we are called *"to abstain from the sensual urges (the evil desires, the passions of the flesh, your lower nature) that wage war against the soul"* (1 Peter 2:11, AMPC). 1 Thessalonians 4:7–8 reminds us:

> *God has called us to live holy lives, not impure lives. Therefore, anyone who refuses to live by these rules is not disobeying human teaching but is rejecting God, who gives his Holy Spirit to you.* (NLT)

I'm so thankful that regardless of my decision to feed my fleshly desires, God was still willing to take me in. He met me where I was at and accepted me unconditionally. However, His standards remained the same with regards to not approving the practice of homosexual behavior. Here is what the Bible says about the fruit of the flesh:

> *When you follow the desires of your sinful nature, the results are very clear: sexual immorality, impurity, lustful pleasures, idolatry, sorcery, hostility, quarreling, jealousy, outbursts of anger, selfish ambition, dissension, division, envy, drunkenness, wild parties, and other sins like these. Let me tell you again, as I have before, that anyone living that sort of life will not inherit the Kingdom of God.*
> —Galatians 5:19–21, NLT

Keep in mind that fleshly desires aren't limited to unholy (unvirtuous) sexual desires and practices. Romans 8:7–8 elaborates and explains,

> [That is] because the mind of the flesh [with its carnal thoughts and purposes] is hostile to God, for it does not submit itself to God's Law; indeed it cannot. So then those who are living the life of the flesh [catering to the appetites and impulses of their carnal nature] cannot please or satisfy God, or be acceptable to Him. (AMPC)

Here I want to emphasize the importance of bringing our mind under the submission of Christ. The Bible teaches us to have the mind of Christ: "Now may the God who gives perseverance and encouragement grant you to be of the same mind with one another according to Christ Jesus" (Romans 15:5, NASB). And furthermore,

> …since Christ suffered in the flesh for us, for you, arm yourselves with the same thought and purpose [patiently to suffer rather than fail to please God]. For whoever has suffered in the flesh [having the mind of Christ] is done with [intentional] sin [has stopped pleasing himself and the world, and pleases God]…
>
> —1 Peter 4:1, AMPC

When I was living a homosexual lifestyle, I was certainly feeding my flesh. I was doing what society says we should do, which is whatever makes us happy because we only live once. The world is unwilling to submit to God. We prefer to serve ourselves, and we believe we have the right to do so.

In having the right to do so, it's no surprise that people will protest an event without sufficient understanding of the intent behind it. Yes, the LGBTQ community slammed me to the ground when they heard I was doing a lunch presentation one day. Even before they knew the content of my presentation, they called me a hater and labelled me homophobic. These are the declarations they made on a Facebook page created to address the event before they participated in the protest. I also received hateful comments and threats on my personal Facebook page. The LGBTQ community certainly didn't like the idea of my promoting celibacy.[74]

> *Though God created sexuality as good, the problem is when we fixate on the desires of the flesh.*

Though God created sexuality as good, the problem is when we fixate on the desires of the flesh. When we cave in, we pursue it blindly and can potentially make uninformed choices. Protesting an event without full knowledge doesn't make sense to me. Yet, when I lived the homosexual lifestyle I probably

---

74 They must have read about my choosing celibacy prior to the event, so many assumed I would speak out of hate or judgment.

would have wanted to participate in the protest too. When I desired gratification of the flesh above pursuing holiness, I wanted to pursue those desires and justify my decisions along that path.

> *And particularly those* who walk after the flesh *and indulge in the lust of polluting passion and scorn and despise authority. Presumptuous [and] daring [self-willed and self-loving creatures]!* They scoff at and revile dignitaries… without trembling…
>
> 2 Peter 2:10, AMPC (emphasis added)

This could have been me fourteen years ago.

The LGBTQ community certainly was very brave to protest the event. When the organizers and I started to pray, we felt the Holy Spirit prompt us not to cancel. I will admit that when I heard there was going to be a protest, I was ready to jump on a plane and just fly away. God revealed to us that I was like Daniel in the lion's den, but He promised to not only shut the mouths of the lions, but to personally feed them the bread of life and quench their thirst.

Hundreds of people around the globe prayed for the event. Volunteers came. We fed the protestors a meal and invited them into the building to listen. God truly showed up. Not only was it a "silent" protest, but lives were changed. People outside the building said that the protestors who chose to remain outside were quiet and didn't say anything.

These are the words of a person in the LGBTQ community who was quoted in the newspaper the next day: "What started as a protest…ended as a community building event."[75]

Another protester personally said to me, "Thank you, Wilna. Your talk taught me that I, too, can live holy before the Lord." Some even received Christ into their hearts; they were fed the bread of life and their thirst was quenched.

According to Isaiah 55:1–2,

> *If we can be addicted to lust and allergic to God, can we reverse this unfortunate reality and become allergic to lust and addicted to God?*

> *Wait and listen, everyone who is thirsty! Come to the waters; and he who has no money, come, buy and eat! Yes, come, buy [priceless, spiritual] wine and milk without money and without price [simply for the self-surrender that accepts the blessing]. Why do you spend your money for that which is*

---

[75] Hannah Spray and Phil Tank, "Celibacy for Gays Seminar Protested," *Saskatoon StarPhoenix*. September 25, 2013, A3. In addition, here are a few blogs and articles about the protest which were written after the event: Timothy Fraser Hampton, "The Rock of Ages Lutheran Brethren Church Tries to Pray Away the Gay," *The Media Co-op*. September 26, 2013 (http://www.mediacoop.ca/story/rock-ages-lutheran-brethren-church-tries-pray-away/19014); and Integrity/Saskatoon, "Shameful Ex-Gay Event at Local Church." September 24, 2013 (http://integritysaskatoon.blogspot.ca/2013/09/shameful-ex-gay-event-at-local-church.html).

not bread, and your earnings for what does not satisfy? Hearken diligently to Me, and eat what is good, and let your soul delight itself in fatness [the profuseness of spiritual joy]. (AMPC)

It certainly was not Satan's plan that individuals should come to desire Christ in their hearts. I felt resistance from the flesh (those who protested for their rights), Satan (the constant spiritual battle), and even the media, which reflected a more negative stance and chose to focus on the protest's point of view rather than a balanced presentation of the facts.

Will you agree that we live in a perilous day and age, as per the Bible's warnings? People have become allergic to God:

Don't be naive. There are difficult times ahead. As the end approaches, people are going to be self-absorbed, money-hungry, self-promoting, stuck-up, profane, contemptuous of parents, crude, coarse, dog-eat-dog, unbending, slanderers, impulsively wild, savage, cynical, treacherous, ruthless, bloated windbags, addicted to lust, and allergic to God. *They'll make a show of religion, but behind the scenes they're animals. Stay clear of these people... You're going to find that there will be times when people will have no stomach for solid teaching, but will fill up on spiritual junk food—catchy opinions that tickle their fancy. They'll turn their backs on truth and chase mirages. But you—keep your eye on what you're doing; accept the hard times along with the good; keep the Message alive; do a thorough job as God's servant.*

2 Timothy 3:1–5, 4:3–5, MSG (emphasis added)

Once at a seminar, a woman named Dawn questioned whether, if we can be addicted to lust and allergic to God, we could also reverse this unfortunate reality and become allergic to lust and addicted to God. Quite the statement, I'd say. This is the challenge many people face when we talk to people living a homosexual lifestyle. They don't want to hear that what they are doing is a manifestation of the flesh.

Sin is an issue for all of us. This is why we *all* need Jesus.

CHAPTER FIFTEEN

Unchosen Attractions vs. Chosen Identity

I know many people who still experience same-sex attractions but have chosen Christ above everything else. They choose to live a chaste life, and those who are not in a holy opposite-sex marriage live celibately. They are living for Jesus.

Living for Jesus has given me much freedom. I personally don't experience same-sex attractions any longer, but I have come to realize that a person can make Christ the center of his or her heart and still experience those attractions—the choice has to continually be made to not act on them.

We need to understand the difference between experiencing same-sex attractions, physically practicing and living a homosexual lifestyle, and choosing to put Jesus at the center of our hearts, thus choosing not to practice a homosexual lifestyle.

You may find that the following illustration brings some clarity to the topic.

Unchosen Attractions vs. Chosen Identity

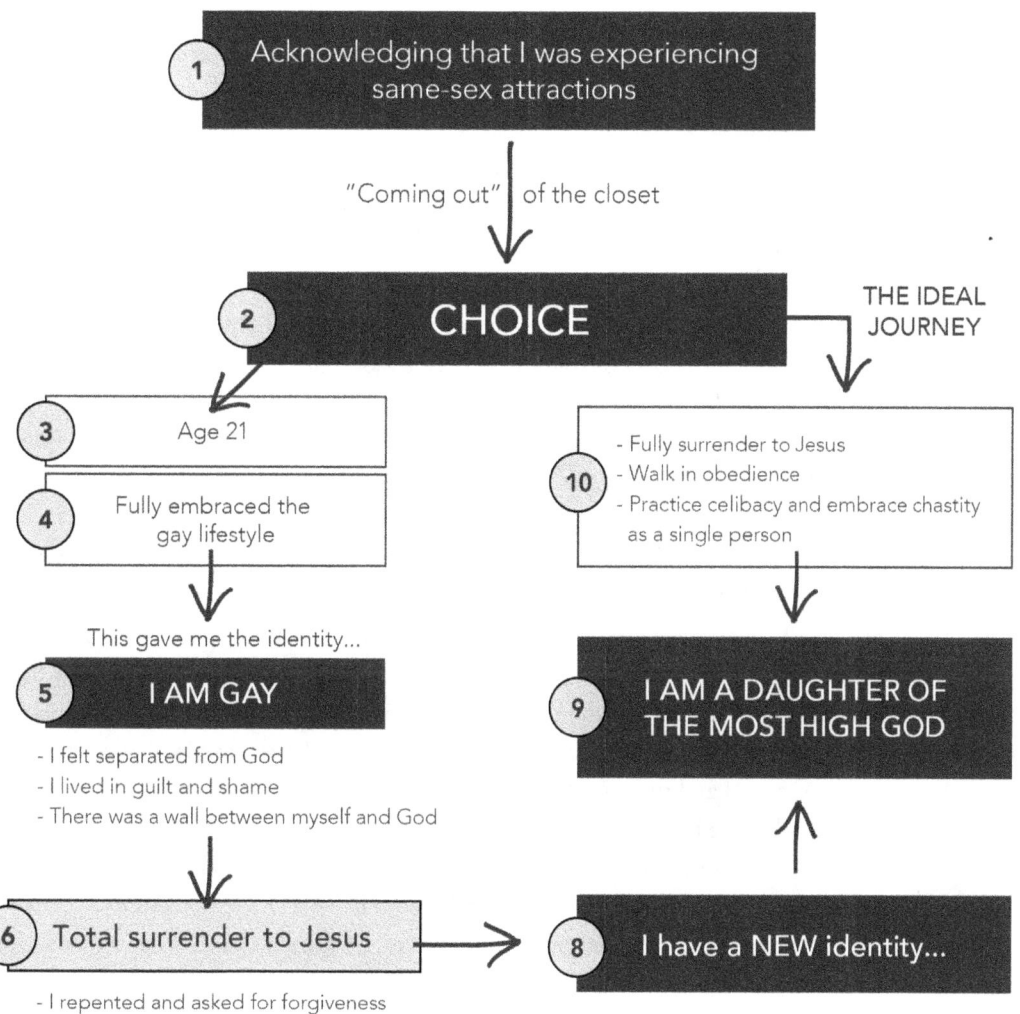

I will explain the diagram using my own life as an example. The first box (1) represents the time when I realized that I experienced same-sex attractions. Though I never came out of the closet or announced it, I did get to a place where I needed to choose what I was going to do with the attractions (2).

Let's start on the left side of the diagram. When I was twenty-one (3), I entered into my first homosexual relationship and fully embraced a homosexual lifestyle (4). This gave me the identity "I am gay" (5). As I explained earlier, the moment I entered into living and practicing a homosexual lifestyle, I became separated from God. The only way this wall and separation went away was when I surrendered fully to Jesus and made Him the hub of my life (6). I then repented and received His forgiveness, choosing to walk away from the homosexual lifestyle and be celibate. This gave me a new identity (8) as a daughter of the Most High God (9). Today, I no longer self-identify as gay.

Before I go further, I want to talk about the box at the bottom of the diagram (7). Barbara Johnson calls this stage of life "The Division of Labor." At a conference, she said, "I realized there is a division of labor with God… it is God's job to fix [transform the heart of] my son, and it is my job to love him."[76]

Remember that your love, support, and prayer can help a person move from the left side of the diagram to the right. Never underestimate the role you play. If it wasn't for people praying for me, I wouldn't be where I am today.

And then we must never forget who else plays a major role in a person moving from the left side to the right side: the Holy Spirit. We do our part and the Holy Spirit will do His part. It is our job to love the person and it is God's job to transform them.

Now, let's go back to the start of the diagram and look at the ideal journey. I don't believe everyone has to walk the same path I did. This is part of my dream, that when every Bible-believing church is equipped, educated, and enlightened about this topic, they will be ready to come alongside those who acknowledge their same-sex attractions and who ask for help and support. The person must be willing to adhere to the help, of course, and be willing to submit. They must be willing to have accountability partners to come alongside them. But if they do, this journey could be so simple. Really, it's only three steps. It moves from (1) to (2) and then jumps to (10).

I believe my life could have been much simpler if I'd had some much-needed help and support from my parents, the church, and those who loved me. I had enough truth in me to have chosen the path I'm on now, if only the topic of homosexuality hadn't been so hidden.

In talking with young people, I challenge them today to give God a chance and to please not even try to live a homosexual lifestyle. I know what it did to me and I want to spare them the consequences and despair. That's one of the goals of writing this book, that you and I can come alongside those who acknowledge their same-sex attractions. We need to support them, love them, pray for them, be their accountability partners, and also help them get up when they fall. We need to journey with them, not against them. Again, never underestimate your role.

---

76   Barbara Johnson, "David—Gay Son & Family Restoration." March 13, 2008 (http://www.youtube.com/watch?v=x-l62XmuyBsk).

We need to understand that sexuality is only one facet of who we are, and it shouldn't define our identity. It's simply not enough. We are far more intricate and beautiful than what those types of identity labels could ever reflect. Plus, any way of identifying ourselves that places ourselves above our loving God—that's idolatry. And out of my love for Jesus, I don't want to place anything above Him anymore, especially myself. God calls us to continually die to self; that's how we further unify ourselves to Christ's death on the cross.

I find that so few are willing to die to the LGTBQ identity—even those who self-identify as gay Christians. One friend who did move away from that identity told me that his prior choice to hold onto his LGTBQ identity had been based in his deep desire to belong. He also said that it reflected his lack of trust in God at the time, that God could have something better in mind for him. He clung onto that identity for the longest time before he realized that he desired to experience further unification to Christ on the cross. In his heart, he knew that he needed to die to himself and his attachment to his former LGBTQ identity. He didn't know what lay ahead, but he's grateful now that he made that leap of faith.

This was similar to my own experience. He and I both realized that we were worshipping the creature instead of the Creator. It reminds me of the following passage: *"For they exchanged the truth of God for a lie, and worshiped and served the creature rather than the Creator…"* (Romans 1:25, NASB). This is a lifelong process connected to our willingness to die to self. As Joyce Meyer often says, "I am not where I want to be, but I am not where I used to be." Though I'm not perfect, I have renewed hope as I walk with the Lord.

In embracing this new identity, anchored first and foremost in Christ, I made Jesus the hub of my life, surrendering my will to Him regarding my sexuality and in every other area, which has brought about transformation and change. Experiencing restoration from any kind of brokenness starts by choosing Jesus Christ above everything else, and by allowing Him access to every room of our houses. It's all about whom or what we choose to serve.

Remember my earlier explanation about the flesh versus the spirit? Choosing Jesus means that I choose to serve and obey Him. It cost me something—I had to die to self! I want to please Him and become His servant, not a slave of my flesh any longer. Romans 6:16 challenges us,

> *Do you not know that if you continually surrender yourselves to anyone to do his will, you are the slaves of him whom you obey, whether that be to sin, which leads to death, or to obedience which leads to righteousness (right doing and right standing with God)?* (AMPC)

The Message Bible reveals the true freedom we find when we come to Christ and make Him our Master. What is true freedom?

But offer yourselves to the ways of God and the freedom never quits. All your lives you've let sin tell you what to do. But thank God you've started listening to a new master, one whose commands set you free to live openly in his freedom!

—Romans 6:17–18, MSG

While speaking to groups, I'll often use my dogs as illustrations. First I'll make them sit on the stage. Then I walk away and ask the audience to start talking to each other. Next, I remove my mic and call the dogs by name. They hear my voice and respond immediately! Afterward I take them back onstage and do it all over again. But this time I'll ask a member of the audience to call my dogs. The dogs don't respond—because they only know and trust their master's voice!

The spiritual world is no different. When we accept Jesus into our hearts, He becomes our Master—if we let Him. Ideally, we daily learn to hear His voice and respond to it. He says, *"My sheep hear My voice"* (John 10:27, NKJV), so we start listening to Him. And if we want to obey and please Him, because we love Him, we learn that there is a reward now and for eternity. As Jesus says, *"I have come so that they may have life and have it in abundance"* (John 10:10, HCSB). This means abundant life here and now, and also for eternity. When He becomes our Master, we *want* to listen to His voice, and not the voice of Satan, the voice of our flesh, or the voice of the world around us.

And of course we would do well to seek the counsel of others, otherwise we might fall to our own desires, thinking they are of God. Only in fully surrendering to your Master, Jesus, will you become victorious—and remain victorious—in not living or practicing a homosexual lifestyle, despite experiencing same-sex attractions. Romans 6:22–23 celebrates such surrender:

But now that you've found you don't have to listen to sin tell you what to do, and have discovered the delight of listening to God telling you, what a surprise! A whole, healed, put-together life right now, with more and more of life on the way! Work hard for sin your whole life and your pension is death. But God's gift is real *life,* eternal *life, delivered by* Jesus, our Master. (MSG, emphasis added)

We can't serve two masters. That's what it boils down to in practicing a homosexual lifestyle. Who are you going to serve?

But I have this [one charge to make] against you: that you have left (abandoned) the love that you had at first [you have deserted Me, your first love].

—Revelation 2:4, AMPC

Luke 16:13 clarifies,

No servant can serve two masters; for either he will hate the one and love the other, or he will stand devotedly by the one and despise the other. You cannot serve both God and mammon [that is, your earthly possessions or anything else you trust in and rely on instead of God]. (AMP, emphasis added)

In living a homosexual lifestyle, my master was my flesh. I surrendered to my fleshly desires, wanting to feel good, and therefore I became a slave of my flesh. I started to obey my fleshly desires rather than God's will for my life, which was to live holy before Him. I was feeding my flesh and not my spirit. My flesh became stronger, ruling over my spirit.

Remember the two pit bulls?

Ironically, my decision to live a homosexual lifestyle didn't make me gay, according to the historical sense of the word. The word gay means: "having or showing a merry, lively mood."[77] In fact, I felt the opposite most of the time. Even before anyone told me that practicing a homosexual lifestyle was unacceptable, I felt ashamed, depressed, and guilty.

I felt such a leanness in my soul. I was *not* happy. I had no joy, and this wasn't mere Christian guilt. Rather, I could see the truth of my femaleness written into my own body. I knew that if I was to be with someone, it would be a naturally born male, someone complementary to how God made me as female.

We all need to face the reality that we are mortal beings and we're all going to die one day. And then what? We don't want to get to that day, stand before God, and have Him look at us and say, "Go away from me. I don't know you! You served another master than me."

> *Therefore, you will [a]fully know them by their fruits. Not everyone who says to Me, Lord, Lord, will enter the kingdom of heaven, but he who does the will of My Father Who is in heaven. Many will say to Me on that day, Lord, Lord, have we not prophesied in Your name and driven out demons in Your name and done many mighty works in Your name? And then I will say to them openly (publicly), I never knew you; depart from Me, you who act wickedly [disregarding My commands].*
> —Matthew 7:20–23, AMPC

When I lived a homosexual lifestyle, I felt separated from God. I had many thoughts about what would happen to me when I died. Charlene Cothran, a former gay activist and former publisher of *Venus Magazine*, has said this about her own mortality:

> When you look at your own mortality, it really forces you to think about what is behind the grave… where are you really going to spend eternity? Just getting buried in the ground is not it. What is going to happen after that… may come sooner than you think… People are not paying attention to the ever after! Facing my own mortality… forced me to begin to think about things that are spiritual.[78]

---

77 Dictionary.com, "Gay." Date of access: September 13, 2017 (http://www.dictionary.com/browse/gay).

78 Charlene Cothran, "Gay Activist Finds Christ," *YouTube*. March 5, 2011 (https://www.youtube.com/watch?v=uQ-GA-n4JyOY).

The fact is that one day God is going to ask us, "What did you do with My Son, Jesus? Was He your Master, or did you have another master?"

Charlene Cothran goes on to say in the same video:

> *When you choose to love God the way He is and simply follow His order and His Word… He will come in… and will change you… and put in you a joy and a peace.*[79]

Just like Cothran, I too have come to know this peace, and I didn't have peace before I made Jesus, my Master.

God defines our life and identity beyond our temporal time here on earth. We aren't defined throughout eternity by our sexuality or marital status. Our time on earth is brief. Many people live for the present on earth and forget about eternity. Who are you going after daily? Who are you a slave to? The one you obey will define who you are and also what your identity is. The bottom line is that our lives are all about seeking His kingdom first:

> *But seek (aim at and strive after) first of all His kingdom and His righteousness (His way of doing and being right), and then all these things taken together will be given you besides.*
>
> —Matthew 6:33, AMPC

This brings us to the next and very sensitive, challenging question: can you be gay and be a Christian? Let me rephrase it this way: can you be a practicing homosexual and be a true follower of Christ?

Before I answer, I think it's important to clarify the word "Christian." What does it mean to be a Christian? I quote Kyle Idleman from his book, *Not a Fan*. In the beginning of the book, he talks about the act of defining a relationship: "This is the official talk that takes place at some point in a romantic relationship to determine the level of commitment."[80] Then he differentiates between being merely a fan of Jesus and being a true follower. A fan, according to Idleman, is "an enthusiastic admirer."[81] They:

> *God defines our life and identity beyond our temporal time here on earth. We aren't defined throughout eternity by our sexuality or marital status.*

…cheer for him when things are going well, but… walk away when it's a difficult season.[82]

---

79 Ibid.
80 Kyle Idleman, *Not a Fan: Becoming a Completely Committed Follower of Jesus* (Grand Rapids, MI: Zondervan, 2011), 22.
81 Ibid., 24.
82 Ibid., 25

...know all about Him, but they don't *know* Him.[83]
...want to be close enough to Jesus to get all the benefits, but not so close that it requires anything from them.[84]
...often confuse their admiration for devotion. They mistake their knowledge of Jesus for intimacy with Jesus.[85]
...don't mind doing a little touch-up work, but Jesus wants complete renovation.[86]
...have made a decision to believe in Jesus without making a commitment to follow Jesus.[87]

With regard to true followers of Jesus, Idleman says that:

...becoming a follower [comes] with a high price tag... Following Jesus always costs you something.[88]
...[f]ollowing Jesus isn't something you can do at night where no one notices. It's a twenty-four-hour-a-day commitment that will interfere with your life.[89]
I began to see what he wanted from me as a follower. Instead of identifying myself as a follower because I know about Jesus, I understand that I am a follower because I *know* Jesus.[90]
...[f]ollowing him requires your whole heart.[91]

Idleman then defines what it means to be a Christian: "There is no forgiveness without repentance. There is no salvation without surrender. There is no life without death. There is no believing without committing!"[92] In my own words, this means that becoming a true follower of Jesus requires me to choose to make Him my Master, follow Him wholeheartedly, surrender to His Lordship, obey Him, and be willing to die to self, which means that I don't go after my fleshly desires; I want to please Him in everything I do.

Now, let's get back to the question: can you be gay and be a Christian? I think it's important to evaluate whether you are merely a fan of Jesus or a true follower.

It's also important to determine if a person is actively practicing a homosexual lifestyle or if they are merely experiencing same-sex attractions. As I've explained earlier, you aren't doing anything wrong per

---

83   Ibid.
84   Ibid.
85   Ibid., 27.
86   Ibid., 31.
87   Ibid., 32.
88   Ibid., 29–30.
89   Ibid., 34
90   Ibid., 48.
91   Ibid., 59.
92   Ibid., 35.

se by merely acknowledging that you experience same-sex attractions. It becomes wrong when you engage in unchaste pursuits. Why? Because it closes the door to virtue and disregards the reality of how we were created. Therefore, my answer is this: you can't be a true follower of Jesus and practice a homosexual lifestyle at the same time. If you actively live in a way that is closed to fullness of virtue, homosexually or heterosexually, you must know that any habitual sin will eventually separate you from God and in the long run cause you to stumble and fall away.

But God alone is the judge of the individual and how he or she responds to Him.

When His presence went away from me, my response was to turn back to Him and walk away from living and practicing a homosexual lifestyle. In that moment, our relationship was restored. Could I live and practice a homosexual lifestyle and be a true follower of Christ? No. A fan, on the other hand, could possibly live in disobedience.

I've defined a Christian as someone who chooses to put Christ at the center of their hearts. Christians who experience same-sex attractions will choose to die to their LGBTQ identity and wholeheartedly identify themselves first and foremost as sons or daughters of God. The same can be true of straight Christians who live out their identity with a heart open to growing in the fullness of virtue.

Christians can do this while acknowledging the attractions they experience. If they truly put Christ above themselves, as we are all called to do, they will not self-identify as either gay or straight. They will move beyond these identities which are enshrined in contemporary gender ideology. Christians who are open to growing in the fullness of virtue will choose to live holy before the Lord.

We must give Him our whole hearts and make Him our Master, following Him regardless of what it costs us. This will not only transform our identity and how we see ourselves overall, but it will transform the way we live.

> *You can't be a true follower of Jesus and practice a homosexual lifestyle at the same time.*

This will occur with everyone who opens their heart fully to God's transformative power. Just know this: it is so worth it. It will bring peace above and beyond your understanding, and beyond what you have ever experienced.

So, do you identify merely as a fan of Jesus, or do you identify as a true follower? Even if you identify as a true follower, do you live according to His example of dying to self and earthly attachments? Or do you cling to the LGBTQ label (or any unbiblical behavior which separates you from God) as though it still defines your identity as a person? Has Jesus Christ truly become your master? Are you ready to trust Him by opening your heart to fully let go of this world? If He is your master, this is true freedom. It will be evidenced by the joy of pursuing a virtuous life. If you're not willing to do that, He may not be your Master, regardless of how much you think He is.

What is true freedom?

Unchosen Attractions vs. Chosen Identity

So, since we're out from under the old tyranny, does that mean we can live any old way we want? Since we're free in the freedom of God, can we do anything that comes to mind? Hardly. You know well enough from your own experience that there are some acts of so-called freedom that destroy freedom. Offer yourselves to sin, for instance, and it's your last free act. But offer yourselves to the ways of God and the freedom never quits. All your lives you've let sin tell you what to do. But thank God you've started listening to a new master, one whose commands set you free to live openly in his freedom!

—Romans 6:15–18, MSG

CHAPTER SIXTEEN
Holy Sexuality

GOD CREATED US TO BE HIS BELOVED (AND ADOPTED) CHILDREN, AND HE LOVES US VERY MUCH. He indeed wants us to love and to be loved. However, our Christian faith, and in fact most other religions out there, calls and invites us to be open to growing in the fullness of virtue. This includes the virtue of chastity, whether we are married or single. Married and practicing chastity? Yes, this invitation is open to all of us, and it's in our power to choose love that is free from lust.

Outside of biblical marriage, we are not free to engage in sexual or emotional gratification or fulfillment that doesn't honor God, even

Chaste love strives for holiness above all else.

if it may be consensual. Chaste love strives for holiness above all else. How we respond to the call to grow in the virtue of chastity is between us and God, but know that it's a call to all people in all states of life, regardless of the attractions they experience.

I quote Christopher Yuan from his book, *Out of a Far Country*:

God says, "Be holy for I am holy." I had always thought that the opposite of homosexuality was heterosexuality. But actually the opposite of homosexuality is holiness. God never said, "Be heterosexual, for I am heterosexual." He said, "Be holy for I am holy."

For the longest time, I could never see myself becoming straight. It was a burden, because I felt I had to somehow become straight to please God. So when I realized that heterosexuality should not be my goal, it was so freeing. The thing was, if I did become straight, I would still deal with lust. Therefore, I knew that I shouldn't focus on homosexuality or heterosexuality, but on the one thing that God calls everyone to: holy sexuality. Holy sexuality

Holy Sexuality

is not focused on orientation change—becoming straight—but on obedience. And I realized that obedience means, no matter what my situation, no matter what my feelings—gay or straight—I must obey and be faithful to God...

Holy sexuality means one of two scenarios. The first scenario is marriage. If a man is married, he must devote himself to complete faithfulness to his wife. And if a woman is married, she must devote herself to complete faithfulness to her husband. The idea that I might marry a woman had seemed like an impossibility—though God could do the impossible. But the truth was, I did not need to be attracted to women in general to get married; I needed to be attracted to only one woman. Heterosexuality is a broad term that focuses on sexual feelings and behaviors toward the opposite gender. It includes lust, adultery, and sex before marriage—all sins according to the Bible. God calls married people to something more specific—holy sexuality. Holy sexuality means focusing all our sexual feelings and behaviors exclusively toward *one* person, our spouse. The second scenario of holy sexuality is singleness. Single people must devote themselves to complete faithfulness to the Lord through celibacy. This is clearly taught throughout Scripture, and abstinence is not something unfair or unreasonable for God to ask of His people. Singleness is not a curse. Singleness is not a burden. As heirs of the new covenant, we know the emphasis is not on procreation but regeneration. But singleness needs not be permanent. It merely means being content in our present situation while being open to marriage—and yet not consumed by the pursuit of marriage.[93]

I would add that we are to be rooted in Christ, with all our actions and decisions directed towards His glory. God created us with strong desires, such as to get married, to have children, and to love them. Even our sexual desires are created by God. Yet we must learn how to use these desires to bring Him glory.

Satan and the world have distorted these God-created desires into lust, thus making us desire to fulfill and please the desires of our flesh. We must learn not to lust after the flesh but to deeply desire God, meaning that we should desire to do things His way by doing what is right in His sight. Only this brings full satisfaction. In her book *Hinds' Feet on High Places*, author Hannah Hurnard explains,

> The Song of Songs expresses the desire implanted in every human heart, to be reunited with God himself, and to know perfect and unbroken union with him. He has made us for himself, and our hearts can never know rest and perfect satisfaction until we find it in him. It is God's will that some of his children should learn this deep union with himself through the perfect flowering of natural human love in marriage. For others, it is equally his will that the same perfect union should be learned through the experience of learning to lay down completely this natural and instinctive desire for marriage and parenthood and accept the

---

93 Christopher Yuan, *Out of a Far Country*, 187–188.

circumstances of life which deny them this experience. This instinct for love, so firmly implanted in the human heart, is the supreme way by which we learn to desire and love God himself above all else.[94]

For those experiencing same-sex attractions who dread the idea of living single and celibately, not only will this help you to accept and be content with the reality of your attractions, it can also become:

an altar of sacrifice, and every such surrender and abandonment of ourselves to his will is a means of furthering us on the way to the High Places to which He desires to bring every child of his while they are still living on earth.[95]

By being single and celibate, we devote all our focus on Him, laying down our own will and fleshly desires. In the process, we experience unbroken union with Him. This is perfect satisfaction, and it's how I personally describe holy sexuality.

Here is another description of holy sexuality, as shared by my friend Michael:

Holy sexuality is sexuality that is open to growing in the fullness of virtue. One of those virtues is the virtue of chastity. Chastity however, is not the same as abstinence or celibacy. In short, celibacy is a Yes to God *because of* a chaste heart. If we truly love Christ, we will be open to growing in the virtue of chastity.

In understanding the concept of holy sexuality, we must understand God's will. We are to live to please God and honor Him in all we do. We may just be surprised at the results of focusing on Him instead of on ourselves:

God's will is for you to be holy, so stay away from all sexual sin. Then each of you will control his own body and live in holiness and honor—not in lustful passion like the pagans who do not know God and his ways. Never harm or cheat a fellow believer in this matter by violating his wife, for the Lord avenges all such sins, as we have solemnly warned you before.

—1 Thessalonians 4:3–6, NLT

When I practiced a homosexual lifestyle, I felt distant from God. I was convicted by Him. What I was doing didn't please Him. I hadn't been called to live like that. I had been called for something more:

---

94   Hannah Hurnard, *Hinds' Feet on High Places* (Carol Stream, IL: Tyndale House, 1987), 10.
95   Ibid.

God has called us to live holy lives, not impure lives. Therefore, anyone who refuses to live by these rules is not disobeying human teaching but is rejecting God, who gives his Holy Spirit to you.
—1 Thessalonians 4:7–8, NLT

I can't emphasize enough what the Bible says about holiness, righteousness, and virtue. Here's another scripture, which speaks of Jesus:

You have loved righteousness [You have delighted in integrity, virtue, and uprightness in purpose, thought, and action] and You have hated lawlessness (injustice and iniquity).
—Hebrews 1:9, AMPC

As imitators of God, we need to copy and follow His example just as well beloved children imitate their father (Ephesians 5:1).

In the following diagram, I'll use my own life as an example of living holy before the Lord.

Embracing Holy Sexuality

Acknowledging the experience of same-sex attractions

↓

God can do impossible things!

↙ ↘

Persons who experience opposite-sex attractions
(can be single)

↓

TOTAL SURRENDER TO JESUS

- Can choose to marry
- Refrain from pre-marital sex
- Marriage must be between one naturally-born male and one naturally-born female

- Abide in Jesus, daily
- Jesus is at the centre of their hearts
- Jesus is the rock of their relationship
- Abstain from sexual relations at times to focus on God
- Do not withhold from each other
- Do not use each other's bodies for lustful pleasures
- Live in obedience to God

↓

Heterosexual - single or married - celebrating life!

Wilna's Journey:
SINGLENESS

2003

I acknowledged that:
- I am powerless over my attractions
- Efforts to change myself are unsuccessful
- There is power greater than myself (Jesus!)
- The choices I make still influence my future

↓

TOTAL SURRENDER TO JESUS

- I gave my same-sex attractions to Jesus
- I abide in Jesus, daily
- Jesus is at the centre of my heart
- I am obedient to what Jesus asks of me
- I choose celibacy and refrain from all sexual acts
- I live to please God in all that I do
- I am honest about my former same-sex attractions

↓

I am still single, celibate, and celebrating life!

← *Holy Sexuality* →

The box at the top of the diagram represents the time when I first acknowledged and accepted the reality that I experienced same-sex attractions. Without realizing it, through the conviction of the Holy Spirit I began practicing the guidelines of a twelve-step program.

As they teach you in a twelve-step program, in the first step you acknowledge the things you are powerless over. I finally realized that all my own efforts were in vain, and would continue to be in vain. You also acknowledge that all your attempts to manage your own life have resulted in chaos.

I needed to move on to step two, where I could acknowledge a power greater than myself, a power that can help me. I knew who this was: Jesus. This is also the second step in the diagram. I realized that God was the only one who could help me. I also believed that He could do impossible things. Then I gave the desire to change over to Him and asked Him to help me. If you remember, I did this in 2003, coming to the place of total surrender. I cried out to God to change me, as I didn't want to live without His presence in my life any longer.

Complete surrender is key. I invited God into the closet of my heart and made Him the hub of my life. This was the starting point of restoration, redemption, and healing. I wasn't instantly changed from a homosexual person into a heterosexual person, as I had hoped, but I was changed in that I had a renewed thirst for holiness and desired God more than anything.

> *Complete surrender is key.*

In my case, I now practice celibacy and also *celebrate* life as a single person. I am content to be single and celibate. I enjoy the fact that I can put all my focus on God and not be distracted by other things. I see singleness as a blessing, not a curse. Unchaste sexual thoughts and desires are hardly existent in my life, as I redirect my focus towards God the moment they occur. I acknowledge sexuality as a beautiful gift, but I have found that true joy is found in *giving* a gift, especially an important gift like sexuality! For that reason, I find joy in giving my sexuality back to God, who prepares my heart and soul for what might come next in His plan.

On the right side of the diagram, under "Wilna's Journey," you will see the word "Singleness." I believe that part of my calling is to declare that singleness isn't a bad thing. Rather, it can be celebrated. And as a single person, I embrace the teachings from God's Word and what He requires from me. I abstain from all forms of sex and I choose chastity. I live to please Him.

I am also honest about the same-sex attractions I used to experience. I testify to how they have diminished as I give God all the glory. The transformation hasn't been due to my own efforts, but rather His redemptive work. I also realize that my daily choices influence my virtue.

Even when you are immediately convicted by God's love and truth, transformation of a lifestyle pattern is a lifelong process. I respect and am sensitive to those who have a similar journey and who may not have the same outcome. The fact remains that our same-sex attractions may never fully go away as long as we walk the earth. Yet God can do impossible things! He also gives us the strength to turn to

Him if we choose to, regardless of the attractions we experience. The Bible says that He chooses us, but it is up to us to choose Him back!

Let's continue now to the left side of the diagram, to the section devoted to persons who experience opposite-sex attractions. Because God can do impossible things, He could have wiped out the same-sex attractions I experienced. As of this point, I am single and open to a heterosexual relationship, yet I will embrace my singleness until God further reveals His plans.

People who experience opposite-sex attractions are also called to a high standard with regards to their sexuality. They, too, must obey God's teachings and practice holy sexuality, even inside marriage. And just to clarify, not everyone who experiences opposite-sex attractions will marry. For them, the same standard of holy sexuality applies.

Holy sexuality for an opposite-sex couple looks like this. They will choose to marry and not have sex before marriage. Marriage is between one naturally born male and one naturally born female, who are complementary to one another according to how God physiologically created us. They are to make Jesus the center of their hearts and relationship with each other, meaning that He is the Rock upon which the marriage is built. Married couples must pray together, because couples who pray together stay together. They must live to please the Lord in all they do. This includes dying to self and one's attachments to this world. Chastity must be practiced in marriage, too. Chastity in marriage means that neither will use the other's body for their own lustful pleasure. They choose to respect each other. They see sexuality as a God-given gift and choose to abstain from sex at certain times—not to punish themselves or each other, but to spend time with the Lord and focus on Him, as He must be the most important person in their lives.

> *Marriage is between one naturally born male and one naturally born female, who are complementary to one another according to how God physiologically created us.*

The following points summarize the way I see holy sexuality.

1. Because I love God, I want to please Him in everything I do, and I daily choose to do what is acceptable to Him.

> *And try to learn [in your experience] what is pleasing to the Lord [let your lives be constant proofs of what is most acceptable to Him]. Take no part in and have no fellowship with the fruitless deeds and enterprises of darkness, but instead [let your lives be so in contrast as to] expose and reprove and convict them.*
>
> —Ephesians 5:10–11, AMPC

As Christians, we are to live a testimony that convicts others to live for Christ. Therefore, living lives of integrity and following Jesus wholeheartedly should draw others to Christ. Our love for Him should be what drives us to continue to follow the narrow road which is not always the easiest, according to our flesh.

2. I conform to God's will in thought, purpose, and action.

And so, dear brothers and sisters, I plead with you to give your bodies to God because of all he has done for you. Let them be a living and holy sacrifice—the kind he will find acceptable. This is truly the way to worship him. Don't copy the behavior and customs of this world, but let God transform you into a new person by changing the way you think. Then you will learn to know God's will for you, which is good and pleasing and perfect.

—Romans 12:1–2, NLT

Have I arrived yet? No, but in my lifelong journey towards holiness, I'm constantly growing and open to correction. God works in our lives according to our willingness and with the wisdom to know what we can handle.

3. I surrender daily and abide in Jesus, as He is my power source through whom I can do all things. Jesus says,

I am the Vine; you are the branches. Whoever lives in Me and I in him bears much (abundant) fruit. However, apart from Me [cut off from vital union with Me] you can do nothing.

—John 15:5, AMPC

We must surrender daily to the Lord's will in our lives. Striving in our own strength is exhausting and unproductive. We cannot live victorious lives in our own strength. We will have zero power to live victorious lives unless we daily abide in Jesus.

4. I choose to feed my spirit with His Word on a daily basis. I pray and also make time for Him to speak to me. We are commanded,

Study this Book of Instruction continually. Meditate on it day and night so you will be sure to obey everything written in it. Only then will you prosper and succeed in all you do.

—Joshua 1:8, NLT

5. My body is a temple to the Holy Spirit and I want to honor and bring glory to God in and through my body. Therefore, as a single person, I choose to abstain from any form of sex and even guard and protect my mind and heart against any thoughts in regards to this. Paul cautions,

Don't you realize that your body is the temple of the Holy Spirit, who lives in you and was given to you by God? You do not belong to yourself, for God bought you with a high price. So you must honor God with your body.

—1 Corinthians 6: 19–20, NLT

I don't see being single as a curse. Rather, it is an opportunity to live a chaste life. In living according to His standards and caring for my body as God requires, I know God is pleased.

6. I guard my heart because Scripture says,

The heart is deceitful above all things, and it is exceedingly perverse and corrupt and severely, mortally sick! Who can know it [perceive, understand, be acquainted with his own heart and mind]?

—Jeremiah 17:9, AMP

All of us have gone astray. All of us have at some point lost our true direction. In Genesis 6, God even regretted making humankind.

The Lord saw that the wickedness of man was great in the earth, and that every imagination and intention of all human thinking was only evil continually. And the Lord regretted that He had made man on the earth, and He was grieved at heart... And God looked upon the world and saw how degenerate, debased, and vicious it was, for all humanity had corrupted their way upon the earth and lost their true direction.

—Genesis 6:5–6, 12, AMPC

7. I choose to walk in obedience to God, because a disobedient person is a person who is obstinately opposed to the divine will of God.

So kill (deaden, deprive of power) the evil desire lurking in your members [those animal impulses and all that is earthly in you that is employed in sin]: sexual vice, impurity, sensual appetites, unholy desires, and all greed and covetousness, for that is idolatry (the deifying of self and other created things instead of God). It is on account of these [very sins] that the [holy] anger of God is ever coming upon the sons of disobedience (those who are obstinately opposed to the divine will)...

—Colossians 3: 5–6, AMP

Holy Sexuality

We need to walk in obedience to God.

When I initially chose to live celibate and embrace holy sexuality, it seemed to be a difficult, maybe even impossible, choice. But after fourteen years of joyfully living and practicing chastity, which includes living celibately, I experience so much peace, contentment, and joy. When I daily focus on the Lord, He gives me the strength I need for my spirit to conquer my flesh.

Don't get me wrong: even though I did what I needed to do, God did all the heart work. But it takes courage. It takes laying down my own fleshly desires. It means choosing Christ above everything else.

When I fell in love with the first woman I met in my new job after choosing celibacy in 2003, it took almost everything not to cave in to those desires. But when I kept God as my focus, He helped me to overcome. In the process of surrendering my all-and-all daily, and by abiding in Him, God stepped in and brought about transformation, redemption, restoration, and healing. This I never would have been able to do on my own.

> *Practicing unchaste sexual behavior isn't holy sexuality. It's a sin in God's eyes.*

I once heard a sermon by Andy Stanley during which he addressed thousands of youth: "Get out of debt, stay out of bed, and clean up your closet."[96] This resonated with what I had been doing for the past fourteen years and it paid off.

I want to challenge you as the reader to do the same. Start with giving God one year of your life. Devote it all to Him and you, too, will be astounded at what He will do.

Remember: the reality remains that some people experience same-sex attractions. But they can choose to not practice homosexual behavior. Practicing unchaste sexual behavior isn't holy sexuality. It's a sin in God's eyes. We all try to overcome our sin in our own strength, but it's the power of the Holy Spirit in our lives that will make the daily difference as we invite Him in.

It's always important to focus on the state of the heart while asking if we are open to growing in the fullness of virtue.

---

96 Andy Stanley, "You'll Be Glad You Did, Part Two," *YouTube*. April 26, 2014 (https://www.youtube.com/watch?v=Enpt-JXMe3rI).

CHAPTER SEVENTEEN

What Is the Role of the Holy Spirit?

God is in the business of the heart. In fact, He does all the work of the heart.

However, we play a role, too. Remember the division of labor box? Our love, support, and prayers play a huge role in the process of bringing our homosexual loved ones to discover God's love. As we act as ambassadors for Jesus, we are signposts pointing others to Christ. So never underestimate your role. Praying for a person experiencing same-sex attractions will have a powerful impact.

Paul sums this up by talking about himself and Apollos:

Who do you think Paul is, anyway? Or Apollos, for that matter? Servants, both of us—servants who waited on you as you gradually learned to entrust your lives to our mutual Master. We each carried out our servant assignment. I planted the seed, Apollos watered the plants, but God made you grow. It's not the one who plants or the one who waters who is at the center of this process but God, who makes things grow. Planting and watering are menial servant jobs at minimum wages. What makes them worth doing is the God we are serving. You happen to be God's field in which we are working.

—1 Corinthians 3:5–9, MSG (emphasis added)

The truth of the matter is that God grows us, transforming us from the inside-out. In Ephesians 2:8–9, we are specifically told,

Saving is all his idea, and all his work. All we do is trust him enough to let him do it. It's God's gift from start to finish! We don't play the major role. If we did, we'd probably go around bragging that we'd done the whole thing! No, we neither make nor save ourselves. God does both the making and saving. (MSG)

Once a person has an intimate relationship with God, He will do the work in their personal life. Each individual must surrender to Him.

Remember, I speak from personal experience. No psychiatrist could do for me what the Holy Spirit has done. He does not "fix" a person, but when we allow Jesus to come into the basements of our houses, when we surrender to His Lordship, He transforms our lives and our hearts. He does all the work!

All we need to do is cooperate. Surrendering, making Him our Master, and obeying Him is key.

CHAPTER EIGHTEEN

The Stages of Grief

Along our journey with others, we may experience heart-wrenching emotions. It's normal to feel grief, and we must respect the hearts of those who are grieving—whoever they are.

There are several stages of grief that we would do well to learn about. When a loved one tells you he or she is gay, we may experience these stages in various ways, and not necessarily in a specific order. As well, a person might cycle in and out of various stages.

For those parents and loved ones who are initially discouraged, shocked, or angry at the acknowledgement of same-sex attractions, please realize that this is a necessary first step to bring something to the light that was hidden and a burden. This takes courage for individuals to address and acknowledge. Instead of seeing this as an obstacle in your relationship, please see it as an opportunity to offer greater support. In entering into this dialogue, you have been invited into a deeper relationship with your loved one. Embrace the opportunity to come alongside them in their journey towards a deeper relationship with the Lord. Please remember that this conversation isn't about your discomfort but rather maintaining the other person's dignity and value.

I get many emails from desperate parents after they either receive a letter, or in some cases a text, from children who announce that they're gay. Here's one real-life example:

Hi my name is Suzie.[97] I'm still in somewhat of a fog, as my… daughter revealed to us on Saturday night, that she is "not straight." I'm not even sure what to write, not being able to clearly think through what has just occurred. My friend heard you speak, and recommended that I look you up. As a Christian, I know how I think I should respond but I'm not sure how to do that. I'm having a lot of trouble sleeping, trouble functioning at work and there is an inability to think about anything else. Some questions: What happened? Where did I go wrong? Why didn't I notice something quicker? She is a Christian but is being led down a path that I just

---

97 The name has been changed to protect the individual.

don't think is in line with what God wants for our lives. A prayer support group would be a help. Suzie.

I know my own parents were devastated when it became obvious that I was in a homosexual relationship at the age of twenty-one, yet I never had a conversation with my family members to address my same-sex attractions. I was too ashamed, confused, and scared. We had conflict, yes, but not conversation. My mom tried to address it, but I was unwilling to acknowledge it. At the time, the topic of homosexuality was rarely addressed in general, and certainly not in a constructive manner. My mom sent me to psychiatrists, but she and I never talked directly about homosexuality. I never had a safe place, even in the psychiatrists' offices, to address my attractions. I really hadn't known I was attracted to women until I was twenty-one. I didn't understand what I was experiencing and I didn't have the opportunity or ability to voice it.

The earlier that a person can have open, constructive, healthy, godly conversations about their same-sex attractions, the better. Having open conversations could have saved me twenty years of exploring a lifestyle and identity which brought me shame. I knew I was countering God's divine order.

I'm not blaming my parents for my choices. I'm advocating on behalf of those who experience same-sex attractions in the hope that their experiences can be better received through respectful conversation. Getting the right help at the right time could possibly guide a person to follow the narrow path rather than give in to the flesh.

This is why it's vital for family members, friends, and the church to be a safe place. That way, they can come alongside persons in a constructive manner the moment they acknowledge that they experience same-sex attractions. Note also how different this world would be if people knew that not all attractions are sexual or romantic in nature. Creating a space where open and honest conversations can happen is part of our healing process.

I didn't tell anyone I had lived a homosexual lifestyle until I was forty-four. At that time, I wrote my family a letter sharing about how I had lived a homosexual lifestyle and was now willing to acknowledge it. My letter clarified that I had chosen since 2003 (five years earlier) to live celibate and embrace holy sexuality. My older sister was the only one, at the time, who was willing to have a conversation.

My mom was in the final stages of Alzheimer's and I understood why I didn't get a response from her. I know she would have responded if she could. I imagine my mom would have found it valuable to know that I have come to terms with who I am and to understand that I have found peace in choosing Christ above all.

Most parents desire to have restored relationships with their children. This is a possibility through honest, open communication, whether a parent agrees with what their children are doing or not. It is important to tell our children that we love them and care about them. It's also important for us to stand for *something* instead of *nothing*. That means we can express, in a very careful and loving way—and hopefully within the context of a growing relationship—our openness to listen and to hear their hearts. This is far more beneficial than being in a constant cycle of conflict.

At the same time, we must be sure to guard ourselves against emotional manipulation. This is true for all people involved. Overall, we could all grow in our ability to have difficult conversations, even if it may be uncomfortable to talk and listen to one another. While doing so, we should never lose sight of our goal to draw our loved ones towards heaven. This is part of the incentive of putting together a parent support group—parents need tools to be more receptive to their children.

Taking the above into account, I host a support group once a month. Through my journey with these parents, I am continuing to learn a lot about the devastation parents go through. Dreams are shattered. Parents consider the pain and loneliness their child may experience, the ridicule and judgment they may be subjected to, the consequences of a homosexual lifestyle, and the conflict they face in disagreeing about what to do about it. Parents deal with guilt and shame, too. Some worry about their children's eternal destination, as many of them renounce their faith in God.

Through my support group and reading emails from parents, it is painful to hear how many parents blame themselves while they try to figure things out.

I know today that my mom did what she thought was best, because she loved me and she really didn't know better. Thankfully, my mother and I reconciled a long time ago.

Family members and friends go through many different stages of grief when they realize their loved one experiences same-sex attractions. Joe Dallas, who personally journeyed with same-sex attractions, mentions these stages of grief in his book *When Homosexuality Hits Home*, and many of my comments on the stages are due to his input on this topic.

Please understand, as family members and loved ones you will experience many, if not all, of these stages of grief in varying ways. It is important to recognize where you're at, to give yourself some time and not rush the grieving process. The process could take months, or it could last a lifetime! You may also go through the same stages over and over, or switch back and forth.

Regardless of how long the process takes, we must go through them.

In her book *Codependent No More*, author Melody Beattie quotes Elisabeth Kübler-Ross, who in 1969 famously developed a five-stage approach to understanding grief: "It is not only a normal process, it is a necessary process and each stage is necessary."[98] Beattie goes on to also quote Fritz Perls, a well-known psychiatrist who pioneered the practice of psychotherapy: "The only way out is through."[99] (Kindle version location 2095)

Grieving for a loved one who has come out can bring up a lot of emotions, and they aren't limited to guilt and shame. An even more extreme reaction might be, "I wish my child was never born." We will deal with these feelings—guilt, shame, inadequacy, wishing a child hadn't been born—before talking about the stages of grief.

Because most parents have dreams for their children, many try so hard to figure out what went wrong. They often blame themselves. I think this is a natural response. It breaks my heart when a parent sits in our group, crying their hearts out and trying to figure out how they failed their child. They

---

98   Melody Beattie, *Codependent No More* (New York, NY: Simon and Schuster, 1998), Location 2095 (Kindle).
99   Ibid.

so desperately want to change the situation. In their shame, they may not want to share their present situation with anybody. I hear quite often that parents carry the knowledge of their child experiencing same-sex attractions for a long time without having the courage to talk about it, because of shame.

Addressing this guilt and shame is often a complex process. I have heard parents say, "I have a gay child"; they are struggling with their own response to what their child is going through. Or they may say "I have a *gay child*"; the issue for them is more about the child than their self, and they probably feel disappointment and frustration.

Regardless, many parents will want to try to figure out what they've done wrong. Satan would love to aid in this process. He not only wants to kill, steal, and destroy the loved one's life, but also the life of the parent. He wants the parents to feel guilty and to blame themselves.

I quote Angela Yuan, co-author of the book *Out of a Far Country*:

> Receiving news of his death would have been easier to accept than all of this! I was overwhelmed by the reality that my son was gay… and didn't want to change. Our family was broken… and my life was falling apart. Every dream I'd had for years—for my marriage, for my sons, for my future—was gone. I could see no more reason to live. I was certain that I'd have no satisfaction or happiness in this world. I saw only sadness, disappointments, and rejection. And I wanted no more of it.[100]

Stage One: Denial

In *Codependent No More*, Melody Beattie describes denial as the first stage:

> This is a state of shock, numbness, panic, and general refusal to accept or acknowledge reality. We do everything and anything to put things back in place or pretend the situation isn't happening. There is much anxiety and fear in this stage.[101]

Joe Dallas describes how denial kicks in when we're confronted with something unacceptable, something wildly contrary to our expectations and dreams. He often uses phrases like: "He can't be gay" or "Can you help my family member?" or "He's confused" or "He *thinks* he's gay."[102]

Parents who attend my support group deal with the shocking news in different ways. In many instances, I find that men in general don't want to attend these meetings. I have been told by their wives that the meetings serve to remind them of reality. They prefer not to talk about it. This, too, is denial.

---

100 Angela Yuan, *Out of a Far Country*, 14.
101 Beattie, *Codependent No More*, location 2028.
102 Joe Dallas, *When Homosexuality Hits Home: What to Do When a Loved One Says "I'm Gay"* (Eugene, OR: Harvest House, 2004). Excerpted from *Issues Etc.* (http://www.issuesetcarchive.org/issues_site/resource/archives/dallas.htm).

The fact is that the problem isn't going to disappear. Facing our giants is better than running from them.

Stage Two: Anger

Even though I have never received a phone call like this, Joe Dallas has said that he gets many calls in which parents say that their child has just come out of the closet. In extreme cases, they may say that they'll kill their child. Anger is certainly evident in these types of phone calls.

> When it sinks in that the unthinkable is true, anger is a common response… This can be the most destructive of all the grief stages, so for the sake of everyone involved, be careful how you react.[103]

If you've already reacted in an unhealthy way, you will need to apologize. There are many stories of parents who told their child, in a rage, that they'd rather see them dead than gay. So again, be careful. There's nothing wrong with anger, but a great deal of wrong comes from misusing it.

It is very important to acknowledge our feelings, yet we must always use caution in how we respond. Too often I hear parents say that they want to force their children to change, or they set up unattainable expectations. In my case, my mom gave me an ultimatum, that if I chose my partner she would write me out of her will. This was all done in anger and really didn't have great effects on either of us. We can't control people—that is a sign of codependency and it will only make our lives unmanageable.

Paul cautioned the Ephesians, "*When angry, do not sin; do not ever let your wrath (your exasperation, your fury or indignation) last until the sun goes down*" (Ephesians 4:26, AMPC). There's the challenge. As it says in 2 Timothy 2:23–26,

> *Refuse to get involved in inane discussions; they always end up in fights. God's servant must not be argumentative, but a gentle listener and a teacher who keeps cool, working firmly but patiently with those who refuse to obey. You never know how or when God might sober them up with a change of heart and a turning to the truth, enabling them to escape the Devil's trap, where they are caught and held captive, forced to run his errands.* (MSG)

God's Word will always guide us on what to do, or not to do, even when we're angry.

---

103 Ibid.

The Stages of Grief

Stage Three: Bargaining/Negotiating

After the anger subsides and we have calmed down, bargaining can follow. Melody Beattie writes, "After we have calmed down, we attempt to strike a bargain with life, ourselves, another person, or God. Fact is, we need to acknowledge this."[104]

I see this happen time and time again in my parent support group. When people come to our group for the first time, they are usually in an anger or panic mode. It subsides over time. As Paul encourages us, "*If possible, as far as it depends on you, live at peace with everyone*" (Romans 12:18 AMP). Living at peace with everyone doesn't mean that we agree with everything they do.

Too often I hear parents say to me that when they accept their child, he is going to think they approve of his lifestyle choices. Peace means that we accept one another and neither of us are trying to change the other. We merely say that we love each other and are willing to sit around a table and have normal conversation. In this process of meeting each other around the table, we can have respectful conversations in which we negotiate touchy things that need to be discussed.

Around the table is where you can tell your gay son that you love him, and that his partner is welcome in your home—but because you only believe sex is permissible in marriage between one naturally born male and one naturally born female, you will not allow the two of them to sleep together under your roof. They are welcome to attend family meetings, but if they don't agree with this policy, they are welcome to find accommodation elsewhere.

In the process of negotiating these things, we all need to ask ourselves this question: what is it going to take to be in a relationship with each other? Parents need to ask this, and so does the gay child. I believe that if we love each other enough, we will be willing to sit around a table, have conversations, and come to answers through the negotiation process.

This requires communication. Most importantly, it requires listening to a person's heart and not getting caught up in the politics of the issue. That's what makes this potentially the most constructive part of the grieving process. Getting caught up in politics can shift our focus to the elephant in the room instead of remembering that, regardless of what has happened or how it has happened, Jesus wants to restore and heal the brokenness in all of us.

Stage Four: Depression

I personally believe this is the most difficult stage of grief. Most people try to avoid thinking or talking about it, yet we need to go through it. It teaches us our tremendous need for God. The only way to get to the other side is to go and grow through it. In this stage, a person usually gets so depleted that the only thing left is to look up from the deep pit and take God's hand. And that's okay.

Melody Beattie writes this about this stage:

---

104   Beattie, *Codependent No More*, location 2063.

When we see our bargain has not worked, when we finally become exhausted from our struggle to ward off reality, and when we decide to acknowledge what life has socked to us, we become sad, sometimes terribly depressed. This is the essence of grief: mourning at its fullest.[105]

In this stage, according to Joe Dallas, you may say, "He's gay; I'm miserable."[106] You may not know how to get from one point to the next.

That's when God says, "Hop up and grab on," Your job is not to figure out how or when the situation will change. Rather, it's to draw close to Him and let Him get you where you need to be.[107]

"Hop up and grab on," to me, means abiding in the Vine, for without Him we can do nothing (John 15:5). It is vital that you remain connected to God through His Word so that He can get you from one point to the next in this complicated time. It also means tending to your own garden, making sure to water it and prevent withering.

When we fly, the flight attendant will go over the safety booklet. When she gets to the part about the oxygen mask, do you remember what she says? Put the mask on your face before trying to help another. Because if you don't, you and the person next to you may die.

Through the grieving process, and specifically in the depression stage, learn to tend to your own spiritual needs first.

Practice spiritual fitness daily. This will make you stronger and allow you to survive. Don't try to survive for both you and your gay child. You need to take care of yourself for a while.

I also believe this is the perfect time to pray the Serenity Prayer, and pray it often. It goes like this:

God, grant me the serenity to accept the things I cannot change, courage to change the things I can, and wisdom to know the difference.[108]

Stage Five: Acceptance

This stage comes at the end… and it brings peace. It's not the kind of peace that means you're happy, but that you are at peace with reality. You don't fight it anymore. You may say at this point, "Yes, my child is gay, but I love him and we can still enjoy life." We can also have fun and laugh together.

---

105 Ibid., location 2070.
106 Dallas, *When Homosexuality Hits Home: What to Do When a Loved One Says "I'm Gay"*, excerpted from *Issues Etc.* (http://www.issuesetcarchive.org/issues_site/resource/archives/dallas.htm).
107 Ibid.
108 *Wikipedia*, "Serenity Prayer." Date of access: September 13, 2017 (https://en.wikipedia.org/wiki/Serenity_Prayer). The original writer of the Serenity Prayer is said to be theologian-philosopher Reinhold Niebuhr.

The Stages of Grief

In this stage, you let go and let God. In this stage, you take time and look back. You're done fighting; you realize that all the kicking and screaming didn't really do any good, but you have learned from it. Nothing is ever wasted. You recognize and are glad that you allowed yourself to feel the pain, and then you thank God for carrying you through. You accept things for what they are. You also thank God for the lessons He taught you, for those dead branches He cut off, and for His ongoing pruning, in order for *you* to bear better fruit. You actually get to a place where you thank God for the experience with your child, even amid the suffering, as you might not have learned certain lessons otherwise.

You also become willing to share your journey with others to help and encourage them. In this stage, you realize that you can't change anybody; you can't even change yourself. You trust the Lord for the final outcome. You know He is in control and that the Holy Spirit is at work, even though you may not see anything yet.

> We need to surrender to God our expectations and our desire to persuade and intervene. If we don't, we will not cope well. This is acceptance.

We need to surrender to God our expectations and our desire to persuade and intervene. If we don't, we will not cope well. This is acceptance. And remember, acceptance doesn't mean that you approve of a particular lifestyle. But the peace you have helps you to trust the Lord so that He can intervene and do the work in your loved one's heart.

CHAPTER NINETEEN
Coping and Praying

How do we cope when gay comes home? Let's review some of the basic principles:

- We cannot change anybody—only God can.
- It takes a lot of courage to come out of the closet.
- Sin is sin and it is not our place to judge another person's heart.
- Building a relationship is far more beneficial than taking the condemning path.
- Acknowledge the grieving stages and be patient with yourself and the process.
- You must give this person to God and allow Him to do the heart work.
- Your role is two-sided: you must love the individual and show the same love and respect to his or her partner. If you don't choose love and respect, you will lose your relationship with both individuals.
- With God, everything is possible.
- Same-sex attractions aren't specifically chosen, though our choices influence our lives going forward.
- Know the Word of God, and memorize and speak out the promises of God on a daily basis. Proclaim it over the person you are praying for. Speak life and not death. Declare and trust in the promises of God and then behave accordingly.
- Don't say and do things that will nullify your prayers.
- Keep in mind Romans 12:18: *"If possible, as far as it depends on you, live at peace with everyone"* (AMP).
- Love, love, love, but be aware of false charity. Love always draws forth a deepening desire for virtue.
- When we are humble, we won't consider ourselves superior to those who are attached to certain lifestyles.

Coping and Praying

- Listen well. Listen to understand, not just to formulate a response.
- Care about the individual's heart.
- Show kindness and compassion, even though you might not fully understand.
- Pray without ceasing and get others to pray with you for the conversion of all hearts.
- Don't try to journey on your own—join with accountability partners or others who have taken a similar journey.

Chapter Twenty

Cautions in Your Prayer

When I teach people about prayer, one thing I try to get across is that it's not beneficial to tell God what You want Him to do. For example, "We pray that Wilna will meet a handsome guy who will sweep her off her feet. Wilna is confused and she must just meet Mr. Right and she will be fine." This may not be God's will for Wilna. God's will is that Wilna surrenders to Him and is in an intimate relationship with Him.

To put it a bit differently, perhaps to bring clarity, I'll use the example of praying for an alcoholic. Remember, Scripture doesn't condemn drinking, but rather getting drunk. Similarly, the Bible doesn't condemn same-sex attractions, just acting in unchaste ways.

For the alcoholic, we often pray like this: "Dear Lord, please help Wilna to stop drinking." A more appropriate prayer would be: "Dear Lord, help Wilna to surrender her heart to You. Help her to put You at the center of her heart. I know and thank You that out of a place of surrender You will convince her that getting drunk every day isn't Your will for her life. Thank You for using whatever means necessary to get her to a place of surrender in her life. Thank You that You can do seemingly impossible things. Amen."

Here are some statements about prayer to keep in mind:

1. Prayer is asking God for what we cannot do.
2. God can do everything with prayer.
3. When it is hardest to pray, we need to pray the hardest…
4. If prayer isn't driving sin out of your life, sin will drive prayer out of your life.[109]

---

109 These four points have been taken from a course called "Equipping Steps," taught by Danie de Bruyn. The course material was prepared by Little Falls Christian Centre in Little Falls, Roodepoort in South Africa.

Cautions in Your Prayer

Prayer is a two-way conversation. We need to make time and not be lazy. God wants to speak to all of us, but we usually don't make time to listen! In coming alongside and journeying with a loved one who is experiencing same-sex attractions, a life of prayer is going to get you through. When Jesus talked about prayer he said *when* you pray, not *if* you pray:

> *And when you pray, you shall not be like the hypocrites. For they love to pray standing in the synagogues and on the corners of the streets, that they may be seen by men. Assuredly, I say to you, they have their reward. But you, when you pray, go into your room, and when you have shut your door, pray to your Father who is in the secret place; and your Father who sees in secret will reward you openly.*
>
> —Matthew 6:5–6, NKJV

The word "room" above can also be translated as "closet." The Greek word in this context is *tameon*, which means "the place where treasures are stored."[110] The place where you spend time with God is the place where the real treasures are found.

A life of prayer is a powerful habit to develop, yet we must understand that how God works may look different from our expectations and desires. Praying for our gay loved ones needs to come from a place of surrendering them into the hands of God. He will do the work of the heart which He does so well.

In the process of Him transforming the heart and life of a gay loved one, our role is to thank Him. This means counting our blessings and praising Him in the midst of the storm. We need to let go of unrealistic expectations. Remember, my mother continued to hope that I would get married even in her final stages of Alzheimer's.

Even though it's not impossible for a person who experiences same-sex attractions to be transformed and marry someone of the opposite sex, expecting this to happen for every person is unrealistic.

Even though it's not impossible for a person who experiences same-sex attractions to be transformed and marry someone of the opposite sex, expecting this to happen for every person is unrealistic. The greater the expectation, the greater the disappointment. It's not about letting go of God's standards, it's about letting go of thinking we need to control or fix people.

---

110 *E4—Champions Encounter* (Little Falls, South Africa: Little Falls Christian Centre, 1998), 9. From the second edition.

CHAPTER TWENTY-ONE
A Very Simple Prayer

ASKING THE LORD TO TRANSFORM THE HEART OF A GAY LOVED ONE DOESN'T REQUIRE A complicated prayer. Scripture is clear that we don't have to use complex language for God to hear us. Matthew 6:7 says, *"And when you pray, do not heap up phrases (multiply words, repeating the same ones over and over) as the Gentiles do, for they think they will be heard for their much speaking"* (AMPC).

Another beautiful story of a simple prayer is found in Mark 10, when Jesus found a blind beggar called Bartimaeus by the roadside. All he asked (well, he actually shouted) was this: *"Jesus, Son of David, have pity and mercy on me [now]!"* (Mark 10:47, AMPC) Many rebuked him for bothering Jesus, but his simple cry stopped Jesus in His tracks. Jesus heard his simple cry for mercy!

> *And Jesus stopped and said, Call him. And they called the blind man, telling him, Take courage! Get up! He is calling you. And throwing off his outer garment, he leaped up and came to Jesus. And Jesus said to him, What do you want Me to do for you? And the blind man said to Him, Master, let me receive my sight. And Jesus said to him, Go your way; your faith has healed you. And at once he received his sight and accompanied Jesus on the road.*
>
> —Mark 10:49–52, AMPC

By this story, it is clear that we don't need too many words when we pray for our gay loved one. Here is a simple prayer:

Dear Jesus,

I bring Wilna (for example) before you, and I pray, in Jesus's name, you will draw her to you. I pray she will get to the place where she surrenders her total self and everything to you. I pray she will know she is loved by you and you accept her just the way she is. I pray, Jesus, she will put you at the center of her heart. I thank You that You will convince and convict her of what You want her to change. I thank You for what You can do and will do. I thank You for Your promises are yes and amen, and You say in Your Word that nothing is impossible for you. I praise You, amen.

Another simple prayer comes from Ephesians 3:14–20, in which you insert your loved one's name into the verses and speak it out loud so that your own ears can hear it.

In praying for others, our own heart needs to be right before God. In going through a twelve-step program for codependents in 2016, I not only learned a lot about letting go and letting God, but also how to pray for others and for myself. I found the following, which was printed on a pamphlet, very interesting:

If you don't know Christ… you can't pray, "Our Father."
If you glorify yourself… you can't pray, "Hallowed be Thy Name."
If you reject His rules… you can't pray, "Thy Kingdom come."
If you won't submit… you can't pray, "Thy will be done."
If your life is only for here and now… you can't pray, "On earth as it is in heaven."
If you are self-sufficient… you can't pray, "Give us our daily bread."
If you won't forgive… you can't pray, "Forgive us our debts."
If you seek sin… you can't pray, "Lead us not into temptation."
If you are a friend of evil… you can't pray, "Deliver us from evil."
If you build your own kingdom… you can't pray, "Thine is the kingdom."
If you want power… you can't pray, "Thine is the power."
If you always take credit… you can't pray, "Thine is the glory."

It is important for our hearts to be right before the Lord.

Boyd Hopkins has written a prayer based on the Lord's Prayer which he has titled "Praying as Jesus Taught Us to Pray." This prayer was very effective in softening the hearts of those praying at the speaking event which attracted protestors from the LGBTQ community. This prayer was powerful in setting a loving and respectful tone for our interactions with the protesters. Praying the Lord's Prayer with such careful intention helped the community of believers better grasp Jesus's perspective. Those coming to pray were able to put on their Jesus glasses. Here is the prayer, as written by Boyd Hopkins:

How are we to pray? Pull the Lord's Prayer straight out of scripture from Matthew 6:9–13. Put the person (you/family/friends), or situation, you are praying for into it and pray it.

Vs. 9… My Father in heaven, hallowed be your name. I stand in awe of your name and I glorify you! (Here I make God the focus of my situation rather than letting the situation take my focus off of God)…

—LET IT BE DONE! *(amen means "Let it be done!")*

Vs. 10... Your kingdom come (in my life/situation; my friend's life/situation; my Church's life/situation)...

—*LET IT BE DONE!*

...your will be done on earth (in my life/situation; my friend's life/situation; my Church's life/situation)... as it is in heaven.

—*LET IT BE DONE!*

Vs. 11... Give me (in my life/situation; my friend's life/situation; my Church's life/situation)... today my daily bread—every provision I need, be it monetary or otherwise.

—*LET IT BE DONE!*

Vs. 12... Forgive me my sins, as I also have forgiven those who have sinned against me or hurt me in any way (in my life/situation; my friend's life/situation; my Church's life/situation).

—*LET IT BE DONE!*

Vs. 13... And lead me not into temptation, but deliver me from the evil one and his power and work against me (in my life/situation; my friend's life/situation; my Church's life/situation).

—*LET IT BE DONE!*

Father... All glory, all honor, all power is yours, now and forever (in my life/situation; my friend's life/situation; my Church's life/situation). I glorify you. You are all powerful over my situation. I say it now in Jesus name!

—*LET IT BE DONE!*

Jesus's prayer is a proclamation of power! Jesus told the disciples, whom he was personally nurturing to be the nucleus of the Christian Church, to pray in this way. This is pretty good credentials for a prayer method! We need to understand that the Lord's prayer is not some sort of whining arm-twister. In the Greek language (the language the New Testament was originally written in) this prayer is written in the command, or imperative, mode. It is command. It is a faith declaration. *It can only be prayed by a heart that has been surrendered to God and which knows in whom it has believed.* It is repentance and yielding to the power of God. It cries out, "Father, even when I am not sure of what your will is, Let it be done!" It is approaching the throne of grace with BOLDNESS in Jesus's awesome and majestic name (Hebrews 4:16). *LET IT BE DONE!*[111]

You will cope... when you start to pray. Prayer changes things. Prayer is powerful. Get others to pray with and for you, and pray for your homosexual loved one—or, for that matter, for any person struggling with deep-rooted issues or sin in their life.

Belonging to a support group is essential so that more people can pray, and so that you can speak openly about your pain in a place where there is understanding and compassion. Don't try to walk this

---

111 Hopkins wrote this prayer in 2004. During a prayer meeting prior to my speaking event which attracted protesters, he handed it out to prayer warriors.

journey on your own. What we pray, we must practice. It's important to not only know the principles of God's Word, but also act upon them.

CHAPTER TWENTY-TWO
Five Building Blocks for When Gay Comes Home

This chapter is an elaboration of Pastor Bruce Martin's sermon "The Modern Family, Part Two," which he gave in April 2012 at Cavalry Temple in Winnipeg, Manitoba.

1. Prayer

It has been said, from a parent's perspective, that when your children are young, you talk to them about Jesus. However, when those children are grown up, you talk to Jesus about them. This means that we need to pray for our children.

Sometimes prayer is the only thing we can do. We have heard numerous stories of perseverance in prayer and how God is faithful to answer and hear us. Scripture is clear about the fact that *"from the first day that you set your mind and heart to understand and to humble yourself before your God, your words were heard, and I have come as a consequence of [and in response to] your words"* (Daniel 10:12, AMPC).

When we bring our supplications and requests to God, He hears us the first time. Pray alone, pray with your spouse, or pray with trusted friends.

> *Pray at all times (on every occasion, in every season) in the Spirit, with all [manner of] prayer and entreaty. To that end keep alert and watch with strong purpose and perseverance, interceding in behalf of all the saints (God's consecrated people).*
>
> —Ephesians 6:18, AMPC

The Message Bible says, "In the same way, prayer is essential in this ongoing warfare. Pray hard and long" (AMPC).

The Word also says, in 1 Thessalonians 5:17, *"Be unceasing in prayer [praying perseveringly]"* (AMPC). I looked up the meaning of *unceasing* and *persevere*. The first means "never ceasing, continuous,"[112] and the second means "to persist in a state, enterprise, or undertaking in spite of counterinfluences, opposition, or discouragement."[113]

In the book of Daniel, it is evident that he had a life of persistent prayer. Scripture tells us that he prayed at least three times a day—not that the number counts, but from all the scriptures I have quoted it is no secret how important fervent and unceasing prayer is.

> *[Daniel] went into his house, and his windows being open in his chamber toward Jerusalem, he got down upon his knees three times a day and prayed and gave thanks before his God, as he had done previously.*
>
> —Daniel 6:10, AMPC

Daniel kept asking. Don't stop asking and thanking the Lord. Rather,

> *Be cheerful no matter what; pray all the time; thank God no matter what happens. This is the way God wants you who belong to Christ Jesus to live.*
>
> —1 Thessalonians 5:17, MSG

Praying for someone who is struggling with habitual sin is like standing in the gap. This is a powerful principle and yet another reason that we need to continue to pray. May you be the faithful one to do this:

> *And I sought a man among them who should build up the wall and stand in the gap before Me for the land, that I should not destroy it, but I found none.*
>
> —Ezekiel 22:30, AMPC

I can't emphasize enough the importance of prayer. Effective prayer lifts our faith.

2. Humility

If you speak and act as if you have never sinned and consider yourself superior to another person, you will never win him or her for Christ. It's very common for parents to contact me after their son or daughter comes out and immediately tell me about the sin of their beloved. I hardly ever hear about their own weaknesses or wrongdoings. In pointing fingers and only highlighting the sin of our gay loved one—that

---

112 *Merriam-Webster*, "Unceasing." Date of access: September 18, 2017 (https://www.merriam-webster.com/dictionary/unceasing)

113 *Merriam-Webster*, "Persevere." Date of access: September 18, 2017 (https://www.merriam-webster.com/dictionary/persevere)

is, if they choose to live a homosexual lifestyle—we are not humble. We are pridefully reacting as if we think we are better than they are.

We must stay humble, for we have all sinned and need the Savior. This is why we all need to pray like David did in Psalm 51:10–13:

Create in me a clean heart, O God, and renew a right, persevering, and steadfast spirit within me. Cast me not away from Your presence and take not Your Holy Spirit from me. Restore to me the joy of Your salvation and uphold me with a willing spirit. Then will I teach transgressors Your ways, and sinners shall be converted and return to You. (AMPC)

We need not point out the flaws of others, but we must acknowledge our own. We must have an attitude of humility. This is the first step for God to hear us and heal our family (land), according to 2 Chronicles 7:14:

If My people, who are called by My name, shall humble themselves, pray, seek, crave, and require of necessity My face and turn from their wicked ways, then will I hear from heaven, forgive their sin, and heal their land. (AMPC)

This verse clearly indicates that humility starts with us, God's people.

3. Speech

As James 3:6 says, *"the tongue is a fire"* (AMPC); it can build or break, bless or curse, and cause pain or bring comfort.

Sometimes we need to shut our mouths. Other times we must speak, yet we need to do it in such a way that it won't create more division or tension:

Let your speech at all times be gracious (pleasant and winsome), seasoned [as it were] with salt, [so that you may never be at a loss] to know how you ought to answer anyone [who puts a question to you].
—Colossians 4:6, AMPC

Also, we need not be worried about what to say. Planning ahead usually won't work. We need to ask the Holy Spirit to help us. *If* we ask the Holy Spirit to guide and direct us, when we speak He will speak through us: *"For the Holy Spirit will teach you in that very hour and moment what [you] ought to say"* (Luke 12:12, AMPC).

As Bruce Martin has said, "Somewhere, somehow, ask the Holy Spirit to guide and lead you to convey the truth from God's Word."[114]

---

114 Bruce Martin, "The Modern Family, Part Two," Cavalry Temple, Winnipeg. April 22, 2012.

4. Love

We are to love and not condemn, to love and not judge. We must learn to discern between our role and the role of the Holy Spirit. The Holy Spirit convicts and convinces. Our job is to love: *"Above all things have intense and unfailing love for one another, for love covers a multitude of sins [forgives and disregards the offenses of others]"* (1 Peter 4:8, AMPC).

The Message Bible summarizes it this way:

Everything in the world is about to be wrapped up, so take nothing for granted. Stay wide-awake in prayer. Most of all, love each other as if your life depended on it. Love makes up for practically anything. Be quick to give a meal to the hungry, a bed to the homeless—cheerfully. Be generous with the different things God gave you, passing them around so all get in on it: if words, let it be God's words; if help, let it be God's hearty help. That way, God's bright presence will be evident in everything through Jesus, and he'll get all the credit as the One mighty in everything—encores to the end of time. Oh, yes!

—1 Peter 4:8–11, MSG

5. Show More Love

Of faith, hope, and love, the greatest is love (1 Corinthians 13:13). We must show agape love—the love of God. We must ask the Holy Spirit to work in and through us to demonstrate it. We all need this kind of love, love that is compassionate and unselfish, unconditional and sacrificial.

But the fruit of the Spirit [the result of His presence within us] is love [unselfish concern for others], joy, [inner] peace, patience [not the ability to wait, but how we act while waiting], kindness, goodness, faithfulness…

—Galatians 5:22, AMP

Agape love means love that is a result of God's presence within us. Showing this kind of love means showing more kindness. The dictionary defines kindness as a "friendly feeling; liking."[115] Kindness, to me, also means that we have much compassion in our hearts. The world will surely be a better place if we all do just that.

---

115 Dictionary.com, "Kindness." Date of access: September 18, 2017 (http://www.dictionary.com/browse/kindness).

CHAPTER TWENTY-THREE

Support Groups

As in any situation where individuals don't act the way they should, family members or friends can find it challenging to cope and love them unconditionally. For this reason, it is vital to be part of some kind of consistent support system. It could be weekly or monthly. I fully endorse the twelve-step program which was initially written for alcoholics. This program is a helpful tool in sorting out what is indeed your personal responsibility to change and what isn't. The system has been adapted in Christian circles and we must be willing to use it.

Support groups are for anyone who journeys alongside a person they love who experiences same-sex attractions. Many come to a support group hoping their loved one will change, but the reality is that God isn't finished with any of us. Thus, in this journey many come to find that God is also working in their own lives.

Here's an example of a mother who has been journeying with her transgender daughter for two years after she came out.

> *Many come to a support group hoping their loved one will change, but the reality is that God isn't finished with any of us.*

Yes. We can pray, we can love even if they [our loved one] don't see it or reciprocate it, even if we don't see them or talk to them. We can't save them, only Jesus can do that. If I've learned anything in the last two years it's that I have a choice to make as well. I have to choose to trust the Lord enough that I can hold my children with an open hand. They truly aren't mine, they are His. I can't save them, only teach them and model for them a godly life. After that, the decision is theirs. I've learned that I need to choose to either stop living and existing in a constant state of depression, shame, and anxiety for my daughter or choose to let Abba use the brokenness in my life to change me, to bring me closer to Him. I do live in freedom, joy, and peace. It truly is well with my soul, my circumstances are all subject to change but my anchor will hold through anything. Jesus is my rock. That is where I choose to live. I have so much life happening around me, I need to embrace it and keep moving forward. It's not easy, every day, sometimes every moment, I need to choose again. I am believing for a harvest of souls from the LGBTQ community, God is steadying and making ready my heart to be there for them when they come.[116]

Truly this woman reveals the peace of fully resigning her will to the will of God. She shows the power of dying to self and letting go.

The success of any support group relies on people actively seeking out support and engaging in it on a regular basis. In participating in a support group, you realize that you are not alone. Others have gone through the same struggles and survived.

This is why I felt led to start a support group for parents, friends, and family members who have a loved one who experiences same-sex attractions. As described in Chapter Eighteen, people often find it hard to cope and don't know how to respond when their loved one comes out. Attending a support group not only helps us to open up about deep pain and disappointments, but it allows others to share how they have coped and grown. We are not to journey alone. When we allow others to come alongside us, we find the strength to go on and also get help when we fall down.

However, sometimes it's best that parents *not* tell their children that they attend a support group, at least not in the beginning. Why? Because it can easily be misinterpreted to mean

> *It's not about being right or choosing sides. The desire to be right often kills conversation.*

that their love for their child is conditional. However, if you do decide to talk about it with your child, it would be prudent to clarify that the main purpose is ultimately to prayerfully grow into a deeper understanding of their situation by walking with others who are on a similar journey.

We must be *with* people and *for* God, cautious that we don't affirm habitual sin but committed to accepting and loving the individual. It's not about being right or choosing sides. The desire to be right often kills conversation. Our focus needs to be on having a right relationship with the Lord.

How can we be available to the person struggling with their attractions in a way that encourages intimacy with the Lord? The support group I began in 2013 meets once a month and stretches around Canada and across borders. Even though not all people can physically attend, we have a prayer call on Fridays and people can tune in from wherever they are. Also, we send out regular emails and many members of our group use video-calling or meet others for coffee. We make ourselves available to one another and God does the work of transformation in our lives—all of our lives, for we are all "under construction."

---

116 This woman has attended my support group. Her name has been omitted to maintain her privacy.

CHAPTER TWENTY-FOUR
What Matters Most

At a Women of Faith conference, Barbara Johnson spoke about the years of turmoil, hardship, and pain she and her husband experienced when their gay son disowned them. They didn't see him for eleven years:

> I have learned through painful mistakes, the only thing I can do to help my son was to love him with the same love Jesus gave me a long time ago! I realized there is a division of labor with God. It is God's job to fix [transform the heart of] my son and it is my job to love him.[117]

The key is to love unconditionally, the best ingredient for building bridges.

Johnson went on to say, "I also don't know all the answers. All I know is that nothing is impossible with God."[118]

I don't have all the answers either, but my life is proof of the redemptive power of Jesus. I am transformed, redeemed by God's grace. I am a new woman and I desire to serve Jesus as He calls me. Nobody can argue with the changes Jesus has made in my life. I know today that the changes in my life happened for a reason. They have been part of God's plan and part of the message He wants me to share. I ran away to the States, and then was forced to go home. I kept running. Now I understand that it wasn't God who caused me to run away.

Boyd Hopkins writes in his book, *Yes, Lord,*

> In choosing to actively let go of who we were, and in embracing who we have become in Christ, we acknowledge that we don't belong here anymore, even though we still live and work

---

[117] Barbara Johnson, "David—Gay Son & Family Restoration." March 13, 2008 (http://www.youtube.com/watch?v=x-162XmuyBsk).

[118] Ibid.

here. We are strangers who have been scattered according to the Father's will. We are where He placed us. We have a calling. We have a message.[119]

It is through love and compassion, by taking the Jesus approach, that we change the world around us. Representing Jesus well is part of building bridges and encouraging others to walk into the arms of Jesus. Could this be what matters most?

Lately, I've been pondering the concept of building bridges. I know that Jesus became the bridge between us and the Father, as He says in John 14:6: *"I am the [only] Way [to God] and the [real] Truth and the [real] Life; no one comes to the Father but through Me"* (AMP). When we claim to be true Christ followers, we too are called to build bridges. We are to be ambassadors for Christ, as though God were making His appeal through us. He gave us the ministry of reconciliation so that by our example we might bring others to Him (2 Corinthians 5:18–20).

My home group built a bridge between myself and God. Not only that, they also helped to build a bridge between myself and the church. After I shared my testimony for the first time, their response became the crucial building block I needed on my path to being able to walk into the arms of Jesus. If it was not for their loving response, I wouldn't be where I am today.

Our world is full of people who have been hurt by those who are supposed to love them. The LGBTQ community is one of those groups. They have been hurt and marginalized by the church. There is a lot of animosity and hostility between the two, and it's going to take both sides to accurately place the blocks for that bridge to be built.

As Christians, we need to corporately ask for forgiveness for our history of judging and ridiculing those in the LGBTQ community. Then we need to love, listen, accept, and treat them with dignity and respect. I believe that many churches and Christians today are working towards this goal. However, persons within the LGBTQ community need to accept our love and forgiveness. And when we don't approve of their lifestyle, because it is counter to virtue, the LGBTQ community needs to see we are *not* being hateful. My heart breaks when they think it is!

> *It is through love and compassion, by taking the Jesus approach, that we change the world around us.*

The end result of showing compassion will be astounding. We need to respond in love towards people in need, whether it be to help them out of a pit or support them on their journey to finding Jesus. We may just be able to build the bridge for them to walk into the arms of Jesus.

Will you agree? In January 2015, my testimony was filmed to air during a broadcast of *The 700 Club Canada*. The segment closed with these powerful words:

---

119 Hopkins, *Yes, Lord*, 19.

We can do better at extending our arms instead of pointing our fingers. We can do better at talking less and listening more. And no matter how complicated the issue, we are *all* called to love as *we* are loved, a love worth sacrificing for.[120]

When we take the Jesus approach, those experiencing same-sex attractions are given the invitation to discover how much God loves them. He desires to set them free, heal them, and redeem them so they can have and experience not only salvation, but life to the full until it overflows. John 10:10 tells us, *"The thief comes only in order to steal and kill and destroy. I came that they may have and enjoy life, and have it in abundance [to the full, till it overflows]"* (AMPC).

When a person has a true encounter with the living God, with Jesus Himself, what seems impossible will become possible. Redemption happens, restoration happens, transformation happens. It happened to Paul on the road to Damascus in Acts 9. It happened to the woman at the well in John 4, and it happened to me. It can happen for us and our loved ones as well.

With God, all things are possible—don't ever question that. His character and ability are never in doubt. God can handle our struggles and weaknesses because of who He is and what He is capable of. Our key goal is loving people unconditionally so that bridges can be built.

I've heard numerous stories of how unconditional love has changed people's lives. Dennis Jernigan is one of them. In one of his YouTube videos, he shares how he received unconditional love from a friend who came alongside him on his journey with same-sex attractions. His friend wasn't willing to give up their friendship, and he committed to support Dennis in his pursuit of God. He promised to be there for Dennis, whether he was in the valley or on the mountaintop. This friend motivated him not to give up on God, but to pursue Him wholeheartedly.

Having an accountability partner and someone to encourage him not only made Dennis realize that he was loved and that someone cared. He knew he wasn't alone anymore. God didn't disappoint him. His life was changed forever. Like Paul on the road to Damascus, Dennis had a true encounter with the living God who is capable of transforming lives that are headed in the wrong direction.

As a man who practiced a homosexual lifestyle, Dennis Jernigan now speaks and shares about his transformation. What Satan meant for harm, God has used for good. A few years ago, he wrote a song called "I Am Changed" to share his transformation. I love this song and I cry every time I listen to it, because I too am changed. What I have found in intimacy with Christ, I will not exchange for anything.

> Some call me a fool for daring to say I'm changed.
> If that makes me a fool, I wouldn't trade what I've found for anything.
> I am changed!

---

120 The script was written by Jeff Stout, a member of *The 700 Club Canada*'s production team. The broadcast, including my testimony, can be viewed here: http://www1.cbn.com/video/700clubcanada/2015/01/29/700-club-canada-january-29-2015. My portion begins at the eighteen-minute mark.

What Matters Most

Some call me a dreamer for daring to walk away.
From my old way of thinking, my old identity now passed away.
I am changed!

Changed from who I thought I was,
Changed by pure redeeming love,
Changed from death to life and freed from every chain.
Changed from old identity,
Freed from lies and freed to be,
Who my Father says I am, He calls me changed.
I am changed!

Some call me a hater for daring to disagree.
Come to my own conclusion of who my Father says I am called to be.
I am changed!

Some call me disillusioned, some call it a mental break.
Let there be no confusion, I am fully aware, fully awake.
I am changed!

Some call me a fool for daring to say I'm changed.
If that makes me a fool, I wouldn't trade what I've found for anything.
I am changed![121]

Change *is* possible. Our unconditional agape love *can* change the course of a life. This is what matters most!

---

[121] © 2008 Shepherd's Heart Music, Inc (Admin. by PraiseCharts.com). Used by Permission. All Rights Reserved. A video of the song can be seen on *YouTube*: https://www.youtube.com/watch?v=nVldxiw0r0Y

CHAPTER TWENTY-FIVE

Cautions in Addressing Homosexuality

God's messages of love are much more convicting than messages of condemnation. We will be much more motivated by a vision of how much God loves us and the hope He has for us than the consequences and punishments of sin. Scripture is helpful for correction (2 Timothy 3:16), but our tone and message must be infused with love. It's the role of the Holy Spirit to convict, not ours.

The topic of same-sex marriage certainly is one of the root causes for division in our churches today. Many churches have some internal meetings or have it on the table for discussion. Some merely desire to discuss this challenging topic and to bring enlightenment. However, others have set aside a period to discuss incorporating same-sex marriage. I know it is a very sensitive topic, with people being so divided between the camps of "love, accept, and endorse" vs. "love and no compromise." I applaud those who continue to stand for biblical values and truth, not approving same-sex marriage.

Churches are making decisions which cause division not only in their congregations but in society as a whole. This isn't just a North American phenomenon. The very conservative Dutch Reformed Church (DRC) in South Africa, which I grew up attending and from which I was asked to leave, changed their views in regards to the marriage of same-sex couples in the week of October 9, 2015. They decided not only to perform same-sex marriages but also to permit persons practicing a homosexual lifestyle into positions of leadership. This caused so much division that the DRC as a whole recently revisited this change; the topic of same-sex marriage and who is given leadership in the church is back on the table.

The latest news can be read on *Mamba Online*:

> At an extraordinary meeting of the General Synod this week, the DRC decided to no longer accept same-sex relationships, even if they are legal civil unions. In a statement, the church proclaimed that "marriage was instituted by God as a sacred and lifelong union between one

man and one woman and that any sexual intercourse outside such a solid formal marital relationship does not meet Christian guidelines."[122]

In reading the rest of the article, there is mention about taking legal action about this latest decision and going to court. This sounds like division with no chance of unity. This is the reality for many churches today, and to me it's not surprising.

Where there is no unity, it is evidence of Satan at work. From this, our Christian ministry to the world is greatly compromised, because we're not a unified movement to be taken seriously. When there is darkness in us, as Christians, how can we be the light of the world? We are always called to unity, for this is where God commands His blessings.

How wonderful, how beautiful, when brothers and sisters get along! It's like costly anointing oil flowing down head and beard,

Flowing down Aaron's beard, flowing down the collar of his priestly robes. It's like the dew on Mount Hermon flowing down the slopes of Zion. Yes, that's where God commands the blessing, ordains eternal life.

—Psalms 133:1–3, MSG

In our world today, as familiar as we are with the term "coming out," we're hearing a new term more and more all the time: "a change of heart." Almost daily in the news there is yet another church leader, or even politician or other high-profile individual, coming out or having a change of heart. The media gives these conversations a significant amount of airtime.

I think there's both a positive and negative aspect to having a change of heart. It can go in one of two directions.

Here's the right one: Jesus requires a change of heart when we follow Him wholeheartedly. In Matthew 11, where Jesus Himself spoke to the crowds about John, He got upset with the people in the cities who had heard the gospel and didn't repent and have a change of heart. Yes, Jesus got upset!

Then He began to censure and reproach the cities in which most of His mighty works had been performed, because they did not repent [and their hearts were not changed]. Woe to you, Chorazin! Woe to you, Bethsaida! For if the mighty works done in you had been done in Tyre and Sidon, they would long ago have repented in sackcloth and ashes [and their hearts would have been changed].

—Matthew 11:20–21, AMPC

Repentance means a change of heart—to walk away from those things which are displeasing to the Lord. God requires this from all of us. It's great to hear and see that some pastors, leaders, and

---

122 *Mamba Online*, "NG Kerk Backs Away from Same-Sex Unions in 'Disgusting' Decision." November 11, 2016 (http://www.mambaonline.com/2016/11/11/ng-kerk-backs-away-sex-unions-disgusting-decision/).

politicians recognize the need to repent for all the wrong which has been done towards the LGBTQ community over decades. For too long, this community has been judged and ridiculed, and therefore they became a marginalized group. I've listened to a few sermons (not nearly enough) of pastors in my city who say from the pulpit how sorry they are for the past and the ways in which the church has hurt the LGBTQ community.

Unfortunately, I hear more politicians and non-Christians asking for forgiveness in the media and not enough churches coming out with a change of heart. Repentance and asking for forgiveness for judgment and ridicule *is* the right thing to do, and it's characteristic of a person with a changed heart. But remember, the LGBTQ community needs to have a change of heart as well. We can't control that.

God requires each of us to be willing to experience healing. Often Jesus asked, "What do you want me to do for you?" He wants us to declare our need and choose to be responsive to the healing He is offering.

As Christians, we have to acknowledge the tragedy of our recent history. These are the facts: so many people believe that Christians are hostile towards the LGBTQ community and it's time to change this. Having a true change of the heart as Christians means turning our hearts of stone into soft, pliable, and yielded hearts.

> *And I will give them one heart [a new heart] and I will put a new spirit within them; and I will take the stony [unnaturally hardened] heart out of their flesh, and will give them a heart of flesh [sensitive and responsive to the touch of their God], that they may walk in My statutes and keep My ordinances, and do them. And they shall be My people, and I will be their God.*
> —Ezekiel 11:19–20, AMPC

This is the change of heart I believe will make God very happy. The church, and Christians in general, need to have a change of heart towards those experiencing same-sex attractions. Could the words *sensitive* and *responsive* mean that we're willing to be honest about what we've done and how we've hurt them? And could *responsive* mean that we repent and are willing to change our attitude but not our biblical standards? This is why we all need to pray like David in Psalm 51:10–13:

> *Create in me a clean heart, O God, and renew a right, persevering, and steadfast spirit within me. Cast me not away from Your presence and take not Your Holy Spirit from me. Restore to me the joy of Your salvation and uphold me with a willing spirit. Then will I teach transgressors Your ways, and sinners shall be converted and return to You.* (AMPC, emphasis added)

Our first priority must not be to point out the flaws of others, but rather to acknowledge our own. We must have an attitude of humility. This is the first step in restoring relationships. And if people see the joy we experience within this humility, maybe they'll want to know Christ deeper as well!

Cautions in Addressing Homosexuality

Humility is also the first step when we want God to hear us, according to 2 Chronicles 7:14. We must humble ourselves and repent. Asking for forgiveness paves the road for restoration. However, not all people will respond in a positive way. But we must ask for forgiveness. This will free us. Then we let go and let God.

> *Asking for forgiveness paves the road for restoration.*

Regarding changes of heart, we must also use caution in determining what our motives are. Is it to please people or to please the Lord? Is it fear-based? The sole purpose of a changed heart is to ask the Lord to teach us His ways, so that all sinners shall be converted and return to Him.

Psalm 51:13 reminds us, *"Then will I teach transgressors Your ways, and sinners shall be converted and return to You"* (AMPC). Too many people, like Saul, have a change of heart because of concern for man's approval. They fear people rather than God! 1 Samuel 15:24 tells the story, *"And Saul said to Samuel, I have sinned; for I have transgressed the commandment of the Lord and your words, because I feared the people and obeyed their voice"* (AMPC).

Living for God's approval is better than living for man's applause. Let us use caution: *"He who justifies the wicked, and he who condemns the righteous are both an abomination [exceedingly disgusting and hateful] to the Lord"* (Proverbs 17:15, AMPC). Also, *"Woe to those who call evil good and good evil, who put darkness for light and light for darkness, who put bitter for sweet and sweet for bitter!"* (Isaiah 5:20, AMPC)

God looks at the heart. 1 Samuel 16:7 tells us, *"For the Lord sees not as man sees; for man looks on the outward appearance, but the Lord looks on the heart"* (AMPC). God calls us to take a stand for Him. Therefore, a person with a change of heart can never approve of unbiblical practices. A changed heart will always aim to be obedient to what God is asking us from His Word.

It is important to remember: *"Stumbling blocks [temptations and traps set to lure one to sin] are sure to come, but woe (judgment is coming) to him through whom they come!"* (Luke 17:1, AMP) Yes, to love is certain. To apologize and ask for forgiveness is certain, too. But approving of any ungodly behavior is not. If you've had a change of heart, what were your motives? We should accept the individual without approving of a particular lifestyle.

Today, our children and youth are bombarded with gender issues. Schools and universities are promoting people to try everything. Gender fluidity and sexuality are yet more lies from Satan. People are desiring to justify and rationalize their behavior so much that rather than changing their behavior, they're creating new identities and ways to express themselves.

Consider the original umbrella term of LGBT and how the acronym has expanded over the years. Now it's LGBTQIA (Lesbian Gay Bisexual Transgender Questioning Intersex Asexual), and by the time this book is published there will probably be a few more.

Relativism is becoming the norm and biblical standards are seen as irrelevant and harsh. Parents should be aware of these societal and educational changes and make sure to talk to their children about the truth of God's Word. We must stand guard for and with our children by not allowing them to be intimidated by the different voices and pressures that speak to us, including the world, our flesh, and Satan. We must remember, *"Control yourselves and be careful! The devil is your enemy, and he goes around like a roaring lion looking for someone to attack and eat"* (1 Peter 5:8, ERV).

Parents should talk to their children about finding their identity first and foremost in Christ, while also helping them to know more than anything that they belong to His family. Parents can help their children know that they are not alone by bringing to light the reality that the virtue of chastity is something *everybody* struggles with in some way as they grow in their relationship with Christ. Also, parents should do all they can to help their children accept that not all attractions are sexual or romantic in nature, and that holy same-sex friendship is possible, healthy, and biblical. We get a great example of this kind of friendship in the story about David and Jonathan in 1 Samuel 18–20.

Parents have a vital role in educating their children according to the Word of God:

> *And these words which I am commanding you this day shall be [first] in your [own] minds and hearts; [then] you shall whet and sharpen them so as to make them penetrate, and teach and impress them diligently upon the [minds and] hearts of your children, and shall talk of them when you sit in your house and when you walk by the way, and when you lie down and when you rise up.*
> —Deuteronomy 6:6–7, AMPC

It's very important that parents actively read and practice the Word of God in order to offer it diligently to their children. In my support group, I find it challenging when some parents go to the extreme side of the spectrum, meaning that they want to change the Word of God to fit their child's behavior; they want the Bible to approve of a homosexual lifestyle. Some parents believe that loving their child and accepting the child means approving of a homosexual lifestyle. Sadly, these parents don't last long in my support group as I continue to uphold biblical truths.

Parents must know that they have a similar calling on their lives as the watchman on the wall in Ezekiel 33. They are not only to train their child according to the ways of the Bible, but they need to correct and warn them in love if they go astray.

The distinction between discipline and punishment is explained in a devotional titled "Discipline or Punishment" written by Bruce Narramore in the *Parents Resource Bible*:

> There is a world of difference between discipline and vengeful, angry punishment… You will always get better results with loving discipline. This loving discipline, intended to help our children grow, is the kind of discipline God gives to his people.[123]

---

123 Bruce Narramore, "Discipline or Punishment," *Parents Resource Bible* (Carol Stream, IL: Tyndale House, 1995), 1227.

Parents—and the church—have too often skipped straight to punishment and done a poor job of discipline. Parents must stay true to God's Word in how they raise their children. God is going to keep us all accountable one day for speaking the truth (or not):

But as for you, continue to hold to the things that you have learned and of which you are convinced, knowing from whom you learned [them], and how from your childhood you have had a knowledge of and been acquainted with the sacred Writings, which are able to instruct you and give you the understanding for salvation which comes through faith in Christ Jesus [through the leaning of the entire human personality on God in Christ Jesus in absolute trust and confidence in His power, wisdom, and goodness]. Every Scripture is God-breathed (given by His inspiration) and profitable for instruction, for reproof and conviction of sin, for correction of error and discipline in obedience, [and] for training in righteousness (in holy living, in conformity to God's will in thought, purpose, and action), so that the man of God may be complete and proficient, well fitted and thoroughly equipped for every good work.

—2 Timothy 3:14–17, AMPC

Titus warns elders to be faithful in teaching the truth, and the same warning applies to parents. They are the ones who should teach their children:

An elder must be faithful to the same true message we teach. Then he will be able to encourage others with teaching that is true and right. And he will be able to show those who are against this teaching that they are wrong. This is important, because there are many people who refuse to obey—people who talk about worthless things and mislead others… These people must be stopped, because they are destroying whole families by teaching what they should not teach… So tell those people that they are wrong. You must be strict with them. Then they will become strong in the faith… They will stop following the commands of those who have turned away from the truth.

—Titus 1:9–11, 13–14, ERV

My own parents didn't know how to address my behavior, and neither did they try to stop or encourage me to do things differently. My mom's response was one of anger, and she hoped the psychiatrist visits would "fix" me. My dad never spoke to me about it. Parents need to have open conversations with their children about everything, including a homosexual lifestyle. Avoiding this won't help. Experiencing same-sex attractions is a serious issue. It is no small thing. We can't pretend that the attractions don't exist, as healing won't come if we do.

Parents who remain timid and tentative about addressing the topic of homosexuality aren't allowing their child to speak openly about where they're at. Remember, the truth will set them free and then they will be free indeed (John 8:32). If you avoid the conversation altogether, you miss the opportunity to address the root issues. The root issues are many and complex.

It's important to deal with the root issues, whatever they may be, instead of changing a person's gender. In reality, gender change never happens. If a person is born female and then undergoes sex reassignment surgery, her physical body may change, but physiologically and psychologically she is still female. This will never change. People have the surgery and think they will become the opposite sex, but this isn't true.

There are so many tragic stories about people who thought they would be happy if they attempted to change their sex. In an article in *Charisma News*, Dr. Michael Brown comments on an article on the death of a transgender-identified person in Belgium who chose to end her life by lethal injection. These stories aren't usually shared by the media, but they are the reality.

The article tells the tragic story of a woman, Nancy Verhelst, who became Nathan Verhelst after a sex change. After seeing herself in the mirror, her reaction was that the surgery had "left her a monster."[124]

> …Verhelst said after the surgery, "I was ready to celebrate my new birth. But when I looked in the mirror, I was disgusted with myself…"
>
> …[Nathan] was allowed to die by lethal injection on the grounds of "unbearable psychological suffering."[125]

In his comments, Dr. Brown digs into the root cause of her issues; she was rejected by her mother from birth.

> And Nancy/Nathan struggled with this pain of rejection right until the time of her death, as [a Belgian news article] reports: "Hours before his [sic] death Mr. Verhelst had spoken of how, as a child, he "was the girl that nobody wanted," describing how his mother had complained that she'd wished he'd been born a boy."[126]

Does it take a psychologist to recognize that this was the real root of Verhelst's problems? Wow, this story is tragic! This is proof of the important role parents can play in a child's life, and that it can be constructive or destructive.

---

124 Michael Brown, "What the Sex-Change Industry Doesn't Tell You," *Charisma News*. October 4, 2013 (https://www.charismanews.com/opinion/in-the-line-of-fire/41250%E2%80%93what-the-sex-change-industry-doesn-t-tell-you).

125 Ibid.

126 Ibid.

In this day and age, especially when sins are more readily public and even celebrated, society is a mess. People are living together, having sex before marriage, viewing pornography, approving same-sex marriage, and so much more. So much has changed in my lifetime and in my own personal understanding of morality.

There's a life-and-death struggle going on for the minds of our children. I have a deep concern for our young generation, and I don't even have children. I do have nephews and nieces, though, and I've taken my role as a spiritual mother very seriously.

When I watch and hear about the Comprehensive Sexual Education (CSE) agenda in our schools, I realize that these things happen under our watch. And we have to do something about it. Some say it's a sign of the times and I fully agree, but we can't just sit and watch. I want to encourage parents again: you should be the teachers! It all starts at home. It's amazing what can happen in one lifetime. And just so you know, I'm not that old yet.

Recently, as I was speaking to a group of young people, I was fully aware of just how significantly things have changed since I was their age. I realized that parents have a tremendous task at hand in raising their children in a sexually "enlightened" society. The desensitization towards many unbiblical behaviors, whether sexual or moral, is of great concern to me. And so should it be for parents.

Our children are growing up in a time where *wrong* has become *right*, where holiness is rejected as an invention of Christianity. In reality, it's as simple as choosing to either align or misalign ourselves with God's order of creation, as revealed in nature itself. If people only knew!

Through consistent exposure to the world's unbiblical behaviors, we have become desensitized, and over time these false truths have become the norm for how we live. And these false truths are influencing our children and grandchildren. The media speaks directly into the minds of our children.

So how can we protect them from the lies (false truths)? How do we teach them to listen and respond to the truth from God's Word, as opposed to listening to the voice of the world? How can we help them not to be overcome by what the world urges us to do, which is to follow our hearts and do whatever makes us happy?

I believe there is only one solution, and it starts at home. This can turn the tide. Parents must lead by example. They must live a life of integrity, practice good morals, and make the truth from God's Word part of their lives. If not, trying to instill this into the minds of children will be ineffective.

Not only should parents lead by example, it's also time for them to go back to having a sacred time with their children every day. What that may look like to each family is up to the parents to decide. There needs to be a time without cell phones, TV, or distractions—a time when everyone just sits around a table and has open and honest conversation, reading the Bible, talking about it, and praying—together.

The Bible says in Deuteronomy 6:6–7,

And these words which I am commanding you this day shall be [first] in your [own] minds and hearts; [then] you shall whet and sharpen them so as to make them penetrate, and teach and impress them diligently upon the [minds and] hearts of your children, and shall talk of them when you sit in your house and when you walk by the way, and when you lie down and when you rise up. (AMPC)

Can we expect our children to stay faithful to God's instruction if they're seeing something else demonstrated at home? According to Ron Sider, author of *The Scandal of the Evangelical Conscience,* "evangelical Christians are as likely to embrace lifestyles every bit as hedonistic, materialistic, self-centered and sexually immoral as the world in general… evangelicals today are living scandalously unbiblical lives."[127]

The reality is that forty percent of so-called evangelical Christians will not only approve but also practice unbiblical behaviors, such as same-sex marriage, pornography, living together before marriage, having babies outside of marriage, abortion, teenage sex, and now doctor-assisted suicide. Peter Scazzero writes,

The consequence of this on our witness to Jesus Christ are incalculable, both for ourselves and the world around us. We miss out on the genuine joy of life with Jesus Christ that he promises (see John 15:11). And the watching world shakes its head, incredulous that we can be so blind we can't see the large gap between our words and our everyday lives.[128]

Could this also mean that our children shake their heads as they watch us? While no parent or grandparent is perfect, we *must* aim to be true ambassadors of Christ, to represent Him well. And it starts at home. As we train our children, they will watch us and follow our good example, becoming true Christ-followers themselves. As James A. Baldwin has said, "Children have never been very good at listening to their elders, but they have never failed to imitate them."[129]

How many families today take the time to eat dinner together and also read the Bible and pray while at the table? Is it not at the dinner table that we talk about our day? Yes. It's at the dinner table that our children can ask hard questions—questions about so-called false truths they hear at school, right? What and how will you answer them? If you really know the Word of God, you may just answer in the following way:

My son, attend to my words; consent and submit to my sayings. Let them not depart from your sight; keep them in the center of your heart. For they are life to those who find them, healing and health to all their flesh. Keep and guard your heart with all vigilance and above all that you guard, for out of it flow the springs of life.

—Proverbs 4:20–23, AMPC

---

127 Ron Sider, *The Scandal of the Evangelical Conscience: Why Are Christians Living Just Like the Rest of the World?* (Grand Rapids, MI: Baker Books, 2005), 13.

128 Scazzero, *Emotionally Healthy Spirituality,* 31.

129 James Baldwin, *BrainyQuote,* "James A. Baldwin." Date of access: September 18, 2017 (https://www.brainyquote.com/quotes/quotes/j/jamesabal121311.html). Baldwin was an American novelist, playwright, and social critic.

I pray that before I reach the age of one hundred, I may speak these words again to future generations: "It's amazing what can happen in one lifetime." I pray that a lifetime from now, I'll see a generation standing up and following in the footsteps of godly role models, declaring their desire to heed the voice of Jesus, obeying Him, and pursuing holiness and virtue rather than following the ways of the world.

If you aren't a parent or grandparent, you aren't exempt from leading a life of integrity. You never know who is watching you. We all need to lead by example, some more intentionally than others. Every move we make influences our environment, and our environment shapes our children most profoundly.

Comprehensive Sexuality Education (CSE) has an agenda for our children and youth. In a ten-minute video, many Christian educators around the globe voice their concerns regarding this agenda. I urge you to watch this trailer to get a glimpse of what it's all about.[130]

The trailer begins with Carrol Richards, a youth advocate from Jamaica, warning parents and fellow educators that CSE "is definitely an attack. It will affect your child rearing. It will affect your education system."[131] Judith Reisman, Director of Liberty Child Protection Center at the Liberty University School of Law in Virginia, clarifies,

> In the name of sexuality education, children are seeing obscene materials that have been ruled by Congress and by the Supreme Court impossible to show to children.[132]

Next we hear from Katharina Rottweiler, Director of International Relations and Strategy for Red Familia in Mexico:

> The focus has completely shifted from the basic needs [of students]. They get comprehensive sexual education without the consent of parents, taking and deconstructing the family.[133]

Kristine Swarts, from Power2Parent in Nevada, notes,

> One of the handouts that concerns me the most is called the Genderbread Person. They teach that gender is a spectrum that you can choose to be whatever you want. You can be all female one day and the next day feel like you are neither female or male.[134]

---

130 "The War on Children: Exposing the Comprehensive Sexual Education Agenda," *Stop CSE*. Date of access: September 13, 2017 (https://www.comprehensivesexualityeducation.org/).
131 Ibid.
132 Ibid.
133 Ibid.
134 Ibid.

Lori Porter, Director for Parents Rights in Education in Oregon, states, "Frankly it's confusing. It's mental molestation. We are confusing these kids as to what they are."[135] Mirriam Grossman, a medical doctor and the author of *You're Teaching My Child What?*, declares, "From a medical perspective, when sexual freedom is the priority, then sexual health is going to suffer."[136]

Patrick F. Fagan, Director of the Marriage and Religion Research Institute, challenges those who watch the trailer,

> It is time for parents to say, "No! My family is mine. My wife is mine, I am hers. Our children are ours." …Men have to rise up, defend their family. On matters sexual, the fathers have got to stand up. Say, "You have no place talking sexuality to my children." We resist it even with our lives, because that is what life is all about.[137]

Near the end, Judith Reisman returns to summarize the current situation: "It's happening on our watch. If we don't do something about it, it is all of us that carry that guilt."[138] Errol Naidoo, President of the Family Policy Institute in South Africa, is just as adamant: "We [have] got to stop it. We have to use everything at our disposal. We have to stand together to stop this attack against our children."[139]

All this being said, if we can't stop the CSE agenda in our public schools, does it mean parents should consider removing their children from public schools? Wow. A scary thought, I'd say.

How should parents continue to protect their children from this war? Is it the responsibility of parents to teach them how to guard their hearts? Because the CSE agenda teaches them to follow their hearts. Fathers, mothers, grandparents, spiritual mothers, and spiritual fathers… we all have a responsibility: *"Keep vigilant watch over your heart; that's where life starts"* (Proverbs 4:23, MSG). Let us teach our children, or our spiritual children, to do the same.

Specifically, the current agenda in public schools in Canada is to teach gender choice at the Grade Three level, and in my opinion that is way too soon. Kids that age can barely tell the difference between reality and fantasy; forcing them to talk or think about it so young is confusing.

---

135 Ibid.
136 Ibid.
137 Ibid.
138 Ibid.
139 Ibid.

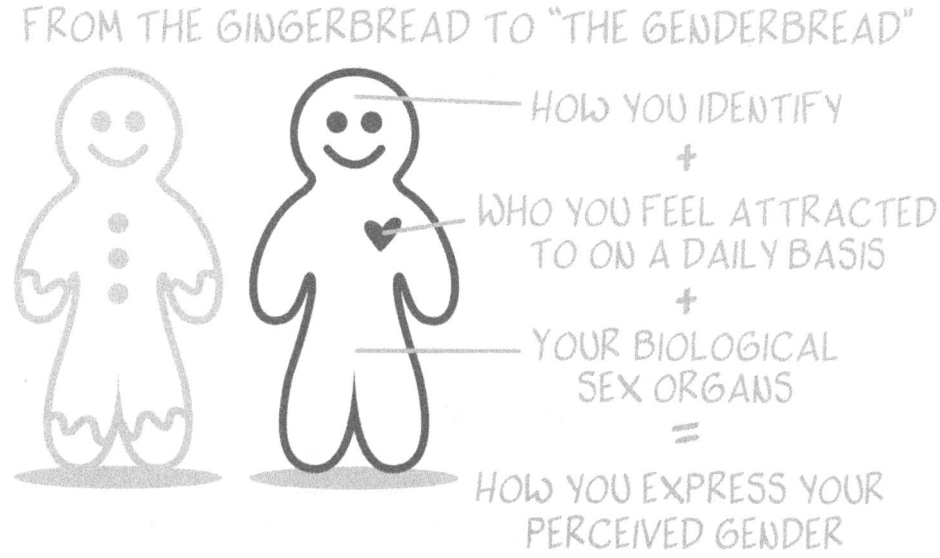

One of the ways gender choice is presented to these young children is by using an illustration called the Genderbread Person, as mentioned above. In my opinion, when people start to use something like the innocent gingerbread man—a holiday classic which is popular for the belief that its spices will heat you up—to explain gender choice, it blows my mind. It is so wrong. It's harmful to young children's innocent minds. It will lure them to believe that they can choose daily whatever gender they feel to be and be okay with it. This is confusing and abusive information to the minds of young children.

We have a saying in Afrikaans: "Vroeg ryp, vroeg vrot." It means: "If you force a fruit to ripen too soon, it will rot." This is no different. Our school systems think they are helping our kids mature by giving them a choice on whatever gender they want to be. Children need to be children. They can't handle such a responsibility. Parents are to teach them the Word of God and what their identity is—and it's first and foremost in Christ, not their sexuality.

The practice of a homosexual lifestyle is considered more the societal norm than not. In First Nations cultures,[140] there is teaching about being "two-spirited," supposedly the natural state of being attracted to the same sex. This is becoming a much more widely accepted teaching in both Canada and the United States among First Nations people. On June 9, 2016, the Native LGBTQ community had their first pride parade and many people came alongside them to support the movement. The following article explains what happened:

---

140 The Aboriginal population in Saskatchewan is expected to comprise approximately one-quarter of the province by 2031. (See Debora Steel, "Aboriginal People Will Make Up Nearly One-Quarter of Saskatchewan's Population…" *Aboriginal Multimedia Society*. Date of access: September 18, 2017 [http://www.ammsa.com/publications/windspeaker/aboriginal-people-will-make-nearly-one-quarter-saskatchewan%E2%80%99s-population]).

> The Beardy's & Okemasis First Nation made Saskatchewan history Thursday by hosting its inaugural Two-Spirit Pride Festival. It's believed to be the first two-spirit festival in the province. Kevin Seesequasis, the first openly gay councillor in the community, brought the idea to the band council. On May 31, a parade and festival were unanimously approved… "I'm just so proud of my first nation that they're doing this. I'm so happy that I'm here," [participant Angela] Gardipy said. After the parade, members of council raised the pride flag on the band office's flag pole. [Chief Rick] Gamble shared council's proclamation of the event with the crowd. Seesequasis read a letter from Prime Minister Justin Trudeau, celebrating the "inclusive initiative." The community plans to bring the festival back in 2017.[141]

While it may be true that "two-spirited" people have been around since time immemorial, only today has it been elevated to be some kind of life-defining identity that a person ought to pride themselves in. These types of celebrations go well beyond merely acknowledging one's own perceived gender non-conformance or affinity for activities associated with the opposite sex.

The United States and Canada are so connected that we often follow suit with each other. When Americans do something, it usually doesn't take long for Canadians to do the same. We Canadians not only like to shop across the border, but we like to adapt many of America's ways. What has been happening there is now happening here. Just about every day, another artist performs a song or a TV program promotes same-sex romantic pursuits or has some kind of LGBTQ newsflash.

Here's just one example of a very popular song, called "Same Love" featuring Macklemore and Ryan Lewis, with Mary Lambert. It addresses society's shift to accept same-sex marriage as a norm. Shortly after the song's release, it was performed on national television at the fifty-sixth Grammy Awards. During the performance, on February 1, 2013, thirty-three couples, both heterosexual and homosexual, came onstage to be married in a single ceremony.[142] Society accepts the idea that this defines who a person is, that they can't change and that the only reasonable course of action is to fully embrace their lifestyle choices. It makes a mockery of God and His Word and the meaning of love. What kind of love are they talking about here? Definitely not agape love. It's erotic love, the kind that pleases our sinful nature and our flesh.

Be cautious. The desire to please our sinful nature is not the will of God. We are to be set apart for Him, and we must abstain from all things that aren't pleasing to him. His will is that we not engage in our sinful nature and chase after pleasing our flesh. He's clear about what His will is for our lives:

> *For this is the will of God, that you should be consecrated (separated and set apart for pure and holy living): that you should abstain and shrink from all sexual vice, that each one of you should*

---

141 Ryan Kessler, "Saskatchewan Community Hosts First Two-Spirit Pride Festival," *Global News*. June 9, 2016 (http://globalnews.ca/news/2752879/saskatchewan-community-hosts-first-two-spirit-pride-festival/).

142 "Macklemore & Ryan Lewis—Same Love feat. Mary Lambert (Official Video)," *YouTube*. October 2, 2002 (https://www.youtube.com/watch?v=hlVBg7_08n0).

know how to possess (control, manage) his own body in consecration (purity, separated from things profane) and honor, not [to be used] in the passion of lust like the heathen, who are ignorant of the true God and have no knowledge of His will…

—1 Thessalonians 4:3–5, AMPC

To walk with God and fulfill what the above verse requires, we need to start each and every day with God and pray these words: "Lord, I need you." We need His help. We need to acknowledge that we are powerless over those things that trip us up.

To become obedient and do His will, we need the power of the Holy Spirit. In the song "Lord I Need You," Chris Tomlin sings about the fact that without Him we will fall apart.[143] He sings that holiness is Christ *in* us, and in order to have Christ in us we must make room for Him. We must allow Him into the closets and basements of our hearts. We must let Him do the work in us, from the inside-out. We must give Him our messes, and He will make messages out of them.

We become victorious through the blood of the Lamb and the word of our testimony (Revelation 12:11). Nothing is too big or too hard for Him to redeem, restore, or heal. And when the end result looks different than we thought it would, we can rejoice in it anyway. God's plans for our lives are always so much better than our own plans.

When we're single, let's celebrate singleness. This provides us with the time we need to spend with Him daily. This is a privilege and we shouldn't see it as a punishment.

When Martha complained that Mary was not helping her, Jesus said, *"Mary has chosen the good part"* (Luke 10:42, AMP). What did He mean by that? That it was better to sit at His feet, listen to Him and obey Him. To be single can be the best thing that ever happened to you. Embrace it.

As a single person, it is my desire to live in the will of God and do the will of God. It is my desire to please Him and follow His direction no matter where He leads me. I am content. I know who I am, I remember who I once was, and I am amazed at the redemption work He has done in my life. It is my desire to see others get to this same place in their lives, whether they're single or not.

There is hope, there is healing, and there is redemption in and though the power of Jesus. It truly is so satisfying to know Him on a deeply intimate level, and to listen to His voice and obey Him. He is faithful, and He keeps His promises. He is my hope and song. With Him and through Him, my life has purpose. This is the reason I was born.

May this book inspire you to get to that place, too, because without Him life has no purpose.

When gay comes home, I hope this book will help you to build bridges.

---

143 Chris Tomlin, "Lord I Need You," *YouTube*. October 12, 2011 (https://www.youtube.com/watch?v=_rR_Rdb1CTE).

APPENDIX A

The Much-Needed New Approach

Many pastors, leaders, teachers, and parents today are searching for help when it comes to the topic of human sexuality, and especially gender identity. Many have more questions than answers.

For those who have God's heart, they realize they need to do something. In answering complicated questions, they need to be sensitive yet still stand for biblical truth. This can be challenging in our world where biblical values are easily dismissed and compromised. Many people want to reach out to the LGBTQ community, a truly marginalized group, and God's heart is to see them come to Him and begin a relationship with Him.

But how? How do we incorporate truth into reality? The reality is that we have much repair work to do—we must acknowledge the tragedy of our recent history. The tragedy and facts are that so many people believe that Christians are hostile towards persons within the LGBTQ community.

The intention of this book has been to acknowledge the need for corporate repentance in the church. This is the bridge-builder, a necessary foundation for beginning to properly represent Christ in a loving and compassionate manner. It's not us versus them. We need to begin with our own repentance and seek to understand before we seek to be understood.

We truly need a new approach: the much-needed new approach. Allow me to share how I believe restoration can start to take place.

Before I address the specific points of what I believe we must do, we must accept that we are going to face some tough issues. I call them dilemmas.

> *We need to begin with our own repentance and seek to understand before we seek to be understood.*

When I address pastors and leaders, here are some things I share with them. They will face several dilemmas when they start to talk about holy sexuality in their church and community. I start by showing them a dramatization with the following script, as this type of interaction is common in many churches. I would challenge you as the reader to pick up on those aspects of the conversation that aren't ideal.

Meeting Pastor Jones:
An exploration of ministry and same-sex attractions
By Jonathan DesRoches

Pastor Jones is seated in his office, holding his Bible, when Jacob enters the room looking unsure.

Jacob:	Pastor Jones, are you busy?
Pastor Jones:	Never too busy for you, Jacob. Come on in, my boy.
Jacob:	Great, I really wanted to talk to you—
Pastor Jones:	*(cuts Jacob off)* —about Sunday no doubt. Jacob, you are a real gift to our church. The way you and Jenny led us in worship last week was so touching. Your voices, and especially your broken spirit and humility, ushered us in again.
Jacob:	Well, thanks, I don't know what to say—
Pastor Jones:	*(cuts Jacob off again)* —It's hard to believe how you've grown. I remember seeing you around here as no more than a toddler. Your folks have done a great job with you, my boy. *(Places his arm around Jacob)* A young man with zeal and character like yours is a real treasure. So tell me, what's on your mind?
Jacob:	I'm gay.
Pastor Jones:	Ohhhhh.... *(groans, followed by awkward silence)*
Jacob:	Pastor Jones?
Pastor Jones:	*(takes his arm off Jacob's shoulder)* Yesssssss....
Jacob:	Are you okay?
Pastor Jones:	Oh, I'm fine. How are you feeling?
Jacob:	Confused.
Pastor Jones:	Yesssss... *(pause)* How long have you been... been feeling confused?
Jacob:	Well, I've been wrestling with this for at least a year. I mean, since I'm gay I don't know if I'm welcome anymore.
Pastor Jones:	Of course you're welcome here. Jesus welcomes all sinners at the cross. I do have to say I'm really surprised to hear this. Are you sure you're... that way?
Jacob:	You mean gay?
Pastor Jones:	Yeah, like that.
Jacob:	Yes, I'm definitely sure.
Pastor Jones:	How can you be sure? How do you know? Are you seeing someone?
Jacob:	No, not really. I'm celibate.

The Much-Needed New Approach

Pastor Jones:	I tell you what. You should really try hanging with Jenny. You never know, these things can straighten themselves out.
Jacob:	I do hang with Jenny. We're great friends, but I'm just not attracted to her.
Pastor Jones:	Jenny's very attractive, though.
Jacob:	But I'm not attracted to women.
Pastor Jones:	Not even a little? (*Jacob shrugs*) You know, Jacob, romance has a way of developing, growing… budding, if you will. Now, I would bet that if you were to
Jacob:	(*interrupts, exasperated and frustrated*) I really don't know that will help, Pastor. I tried that in my teen years. I had girlfriends and, well… nothing.
Pastor Jones:	Did your mom put you in dresses when you were little?
Jacob:	What?! No!
Pastor Jones:	My little pony?
Jacob:	(*more frustrated*) No! Look… (*calming down*) Pastor Jones, I don't think it was anything like that at all. I don't ever remember being attracted to girls. I think I've always been this way. I just came here to figure out what to do.
Pastor Jones:	(*awkward silence*) Look, Jacob, this is going to take some time to work out. I think you should take a break from being on the worship team for the next while.
Jacob:	Are you sure?
Pastor Jones:	I think it's for the best.
Jacob:	Well, I suppose I could continue ushering.
Pastor Jones:	I'm not sure about that.
Jacob:	(*more sad and hurt*) Oh, I understand.
Pastor Jones:	(*oblivious*) Oh good, I was afraid you wouldn't understand. Jacob, could I pray for you?
Jacob:	I guess so.
Pastor Jones:	(*they close their eyes for prayer; Pastor Jones considers putting his hand on Jacob, then chooses not to*) Dear Lord, we love Jacob and thank You for him and know You love him even in the midst of his sinfulness. God, I pray that You fix this situation. Lord, fix Jacob. Rescue him from the judgment You placed upon Sodom and Gomorrah. Jesus, You still work miracles, and I pray You will straighten this all out. I pray for his future wife and family too. In Jesus's name. Amen. (*opens eyes*) Wow, I feel better now. I'll be praying for you. Jake, let's hope this is just a phase.
Jacob:	Yeah. (*Looks at audience as he exits*) What do I do now?
Pastor Jones:	What do I do now?

* * *

Let's address how the topic of homosexuality could have been better addressed in this instance, and in many similar circumstances, both in the church and otherwise.

Pastor Jones made twelve vital mistakes which we need to try to avoid. They created a lot of hurt and caused both to leave the conversation with the same question: "What do I do now?"

1. Pastor Jones was caught off-guard when Jacob told him he was gay. We all need to show compassion, care, and caution despite our lack of comfort. We need to be ready for this type of conversation as it will show up at your workplace, at home, or in your circle of friends. We need to carefully consider how we will respond.

2. A proper response begins with careful and attentive listening. Pastor Jones continuously cuts Jacob off and doesn't really listen when he shares about what's truly on his mind and heart. We must take time to listen rather than assume or interject. How can we expect to show empathy if we don't take the time to understand? Jacob came to his pastor to gain support and not be criticized or brushed aside.

3. Pastor Jones removed his warm embrace when Jacob shared about being gay. This demonstrated a lack of acceptance and created distance in the relationship.

4. Pastor Jones has bought into the concept that people who say they are gay are confused, and it can be fixed.

5. His response to Jacob's wrestling with sexual confusion is to immediately label Jacob as a sinner despite the fact that Jacob said he was living celibate. This is one of the problems in the church; we label people when they come out.

6. Pastor Jones can't even say the word "gay," which indicates he is very uncomfortable about the topic.

7. Pastor Jones's solution is to encourage Jacob to enter into a heterosexual dating relationship in the hope that it will straighten him out. Requiring this from Jacob is yet another blow to his vulnerability, as he's indicated that he had already tried that.

8. Pastor Jones attempts to assign blame to Jacob's parents. He is trying to pinpoint Jacob's confusion.

9. Jacob's vulnerability is met with dismissal. Pastor Jones asks Jacob to step down from the worship team and ushering. People who acknowledge that they experience same-sex attractions and who are living chastely should be eligible for any leadership role in the church. Dismissing Jacob from his roles in the church devastated Jacob; this kind of hurt needs to be avoided at all cost.

10. Pastor Jones assumes that Jacob understands his dismissal. He then offers to pray for Jacob as a false sense of closure without laying a hand on him. Pastor Jones is too uncomfortable to touch Jacob.

11. The prayer is about fixing Jacob and not loving Jacob. This is a prayer of condemnation and judgment. The prayer should have been about loving and supporting Jacob in a deeper relationship with Christ and coming alongside him as a community of believers in his desire to serve in the church with integrity.

12. After the prayer, Pastor Jones is most concerned about his own emotional state and minimizes Jacob's struggle as "going through a phase." He ends the conversation with the belief that being gay can go away.

If pastors are unwilling to learn and educate their congregations, we will continue to struggle as a Christian community. We all need to be educated.

How do we prepare ourselves to address the topic of holy sexuality so that we're ready when someone like Jacob comes into our lives? What will we do if we're confronted with a lack of unholy sexuality—by this, I mean practicing any unbiblical behavior—even in our own lives? You will face similar dilemmas. How can we approach them as opportunities to show love and compassion?

These are the types of dilemmas you will face.

Dilemma One: The Gay Identity

Can a person be born this way? Is it possible? Scientists have not been able to prove that there is a gay gene. And yet thousands and thousands of people, like me, say that they've felt different for as long as they can remember.

I've watched many videos from great organizations who are doing great work in helping persons within the LGBTQ community find God, and I cringe every time I hear them criticize a person for saying they were born that way. Please familiarize yourself with the content of Chapter Four, where I talk about the various factors influencing a person's identity.

When someone shares this with you, don't disregard their statement. They have struggled with this long enough. It is detrimental for them to hear "That's not possible" or "There is no gay gene" or "You're wrong." What they need to hear is that Jesus was there when they were created—remember, He formed us (Psalm 139). Whether same-sex attractions were a result of something that happened in the womb or caused by other roots, God is always present. He wants to restore us to His plan of holiness. He will forgive and take away the bitter roots and bring about beauty from ashes.

Change is possible. Our identity and entire self-concept can change, when a person becomes willing. That means it's up to us. We are the ones who accept or reject the invitation to grow in holiness and virtue.

When someone tells us that their identity is gay, we need to see their statement as a reminder to change our focus from a sexual identity to a spiritual identity. We need to come alongside him, reassuring him of our support in his desire to please the Lord and keep Christ as central to his identity. There is hope in recognizing that our identity is primarily as a son or daughter of Christ. It's a journey.

I would suggest that you revisit the chart in Chapter Fifteen where I lay out the process by which my identity changes.

Dilemma Two: The Flesh

When addressing sexuality, people often want to please the flesh above God's will. I have dealt with this in Chapter Fourteen.

While we are alive, a battle will be waged between our spirit and our flesh. According to Galatians 5:17, these two forces are constantly fighting each other. In dealing with any sexual sin, this is a big fight! That's why there was a protest when I shared my testimony and spoke about holy sexuality. The LGBTQ community hated me for preaching celibacy. Homosexual relationships are very physically orientated and celibacy isn't an option for those who want to live a homosexual lifestyle. Celibacy isn't what the flesh typically wants, unless a person is wholeheartedly orientated towards the Lord.

> *[That is] because the mind of the flesh [with its carnal thoughts and purposes] is hostile to God, for it does not submit itself to God's Law; indeed it cannot. So then those who are living the life of the flesh [catering to the appetites and impulses of their carnal nature] cannot please or satisfy God, or be acceptable to Him.*
>
> —Romans 8:7–8, AMPC

When I lived a homosexual life, I also wanted to gratify my flesh. I tried to justify it because it made my flesh feel good. But we are not called to gratify the desires of the flesh, we are called *"to abstain from the sensual urges [those dishonorable desires] that wage war against the soul"* (1 Peter 2:11, AMPC).

We need to refocus ourselves. Pleasing the flesh is fleeting, but the pursuit of holiness is necessary both now and forever. Acknowledging the pressures and desires of the flesh needs to be at the forefront of everyday living so that we can avoid it and also talk about it. We need to have an eternal focus instead of a fleshly one.

In addressing this dilemma, let us encourage holy sexuality and not the pursuit of the flesh. Wesley Hill, in his book *Washed and Waiting*, said that "faithfulness is never a gamble. It *will* be worth it."[144] We need to encourage people that putting their flesh in the back seat will be worth it in the end: "Holiness is not a feeling—it is the end product of obedience. Purity is not a gift—it is the result of repentance and serious pursuit of God."[145]

We need to acknowledge the pressure of the flesh, but also the spiritual battle we are continuously engaged in with Satan.

Dilemma Three: The God of This World (Satan)

We are in a life-and-death struggle—not between Christians and non-Christians, but within the church itself. We are in a war, and unless we understand the intensity of the power of evil, Satan will take us down with him. He is *"the god of this world"* (2 Corinthians 4:4, AMPC). We cannot serve Jesus wholeheartedly while also participating in unbiblical practices that are approved by the immoral world we live in. Light and darkness do not go together. No compromise is possible between Jesus and the god of this world.

Unfortunately, we have allowed worldly views and practices to creep into our congregations. This is how things look now:

---

144 Wesley Hill, *Washed and Waiting* (Grand Rapids, MI: Zondervan, 2010), 79.
145 Frances J. Roberts, *Come Away, My Beloved.* (Uhrichsville, OH: Barbour Books, 2002), 27.

The Much-Needed New Approach

Percentage of people who agree or strongly agree with the following statements:	People in the general population	Christians who attend church and oppose same-sex marriage	Christians who attend church and support same-sex marriage	LGBTQ Christians	LGBTQ Non-Christians
"It's okay to view pornography."	31.4%	4.6%	33.4%	57.0%	78.1%
"It's okay to live together before marriage."	43.0%	10.9%	37.2%	49.7%	74.1%
"It's okay to have casual sex."	35.0%	5.1%	33.0%	49.0%	80.5%
"Parents with kids should stay married, except in the case of abuse."	26.9%	52.2%	33.5%	22.9%	18.5%
"It's okay to engage in occasional infidelity."	7.5%	1.3%	7.5%	14.2%	26.9%
"It's okay for three or more adults to live in a polyamorous relationship."	16.3%	1.2%	15.5%	31.9%	57.8%
"It's okay to get an abortion."	37.8%	6.5%	39.1%	57.5%	71.7%
Sample Size	15,738	2,659	990	191	233

From the chart, here are some notable statistics:

- 33.4 percent of churchgoing Christians who support same-sex marriage say that viewing pornography is okay. That's even more than the general population, whose average is 31.4 percent!
- 37.2 percent of the same group says that it's okay to for couples to live together before marriage. General population: 43 percent.
- 33 percent say that casual sex is okay. General population: 35 percent.
- 33.5 percent say that married couples with kids should stay together (except in the case of abuse). General population: 26.9 percent.
- 7.5 percent think that marital infidelity is sometimes okay. General population: 7.5 percent.

- 15.5 percent say it's okay for three or more people to live in a polyamorous sexual relationship. General population: 16.3 percent.
- 39.1 percent are supporters of abortion rights. General population: 37.8 percent.[146]

As you can see, there is very little difference between the value systems of non-Christians and churchgoing Christians who support same-sex marriage.

Though we live in the world, we are not to be of it. If our lives don't differ from the rest of the world, how will we impact others? This is why the world shakes its head at us. Satan is certainly working hard to deceive God's children. He knows that when he can get Christians to approve of unholy living, they will begin to feel separated from God and eventually be cut off from their vital union with Him. This is his ultimate aim.

How do we transform this dilemma into an opportunity? We need to talk about the reality of the spiritual battle and how the imposter god of this world (Satan) uses whatever means he can find to keep us away from God. Many pastors and people of influence don't seem to want to talk about the influence of Satan and the world, but you'll face it when you address the topic of holy sexuality.

We must be prepared to challenge these views and beliefs as unbiblical. We need to have ongoing conversations about biblical standards and why they must prevail over worldly views. We cannot allow Satan's agenda to saturate our lives. Remember, greater is He that is in us than he that is in the world (1 John 4:4). God has already won and the victory is His. We need to encourage each other to live a life of victory and not defeat.

Dilemma Four: People Who Don't Know Sin Is Sin

Whether we practice heterosexual or homosexual sexual sin, it is wrong. I'm not sure why homosexuality has hit the highest rank of sin, but it has created a non-loving atmosphere and mass departure out of our churches. Persons within the LGBTQ community don't feel welcome among Christians and it's time to change this.

The truth is that any sin is unacceptable in the sight of God. Habitual sin will cause a disconnect with Him, no matter what the sin is. I urge pastors and leaders to help educate those who listen to them on the reality of sin in all our lives. Christians need to know the Word of God and be equipped in the process of maturing in Christ, thus knowing that sin is sin.

Do we have an opportunity here? Yes. Once sin is acknowledged for what it is, we have the potential to transform. We can't continue to make excuses; we must be willing to be transformed. As in the case of the prodigal son, God is willing to forgive and embrace us.

---

146 Mark Regnerus, "Tracking Christian Sexual Morality in a Same-Sex Marriage Future," *The Witherspoon Institute*. August 11, 2014 (http://www.thepublicdiscourse.com/2014/08/13667/).

The Much-Needed New Approach

Dilemma Five: Cultural Influence

We live in a perilous day and age. The reality is that people have truly become allergic to God. We definitely have a preference for pleasing people rather than pleasing Him.

There is societal pressure to conform to the world, but Scripture is just as applicable now as it was when it was first written. The biblical standards have not changed. The Word of God remains living and active in our lives. Even though Paul warned about becoming allergic to God, the message remains applicable today:

> *Don't be naive. There are difficult times ahead. As the end approaches, people are going to be self-absorbed, money-hungry, self-promoting, stuck-up, profane, contemptuous of parents, crude, coarse, dog-eat-dog, unbending, slanderers, impulsively wild, savage, cynical, treacherous, ruthless, bloated windbags, addicted to lust, and allergic to God. They'll make a show of religion, but behind the scenes they're animals. Stay clear of these people… You're going to find that there will be times when people will have no stomach for solid teaching, but will fill up on spiritual junk food—catchy opinions that tickle their fancy. They'll turn their backs on truth and chase mirages. But you—keep your eye on what you're doing; accept the hard times along with the good; keep the Message alive; do a thorough job as God's servant.*
>
> —2 Timothy 3:1–5, 4:3–5, MSG (emphasis added).

When we bring in Scripture and try to warn people, they can't stomach spiritual food. It's easier to conform to worldly views and pressures than to obey God's Word.

We have the opportunity to acknowledge that God's standards have never changed. We're called to follow His ways and support one another in Christian community. When we're weak, He is strong! We are to come alongside one another to cheer each other on in our pursuit of God.

The Bible is clear that we are to follow the narrow path, which is very constrictive. However, if we can join other Christians in our walk, we can find encouragement and accountability along the way. We may just find that the constriction can be freeing.

Dilemma Six: Compartmentalizing God

According to statistics and sociologists, one of the greatest scandals of our day is that "evangelicals today are living scandalous unbiblical lives."[147] Polls indicate that "evangelical Christians are as likely to

---

147 Scazzero, *Emotionally Healthy Spirituality*, 30.

embrace lifestyles every bit as hedonistic, materialistic, self-centered and sexually immoral as the world in general."[148]

The reason is that we are compartmentalizing God. We put Him in a box—our church box—and the rest of our lives in a different compartment. This has devastating effects on others, whether we want to believe it or not:

> ...in many crucial areas evangelicals are not living any differently from their unbelieving neighbours. The consequences of this on our witness to Jesus Christ are incalculable, both for ourselves and the world around us. We miss out on the genuine joy of life with Jesus Christ that he promises (John 15:11). And the watching world shakes its head, incredulous that we can be so blind we can't see the large gap between our words and our everyday lives.[149]

When we lack integrity, it confuses people. They see little difference between us and the world. This isn't what God calls us to do. He has called us to be true ambassadors of Him. We must represent Him well, and this means incorporating Him into all areas of our lives, not just our church box. Our walk with Him needs to be a moment-by-moment reality, not compartmentalized. We need to be asking, "How is God honored in every area of my life, including my sexuality?"

> *When we lack integrity, it confuses people.*

Dilemma Seven: Not Consistently Reading the Word

With our busy lives, we have no time for God. Therefore it's no surprise we don't lead victorious lives. Subsequently, many don't know biblical truth.

One of the biggest tasks a pastor, or any leader, has is helping those in their care to love the Word and to be in the Word daily. The Word of God is our only weapon of offense, and we must learn to use it. If we don't, the Word says, *"My people are destroyed for lack of knowledge"* (Hosea 4:6, AMPC). Many people go astray because they don't know the Word of God:

> *Jesus said to them, Is not this where you wander out of the way and go wrong, because you know neither the Scriptures nor the power of God?*
>
> —Mark 12:24, AMP

---

148 Ibid., 31.
149 Ibid.

People would rather engage in inane conversations and rationalize their behavior than discover and practice what we are called to in Scripture.

This is one of the greatest dilemmas we face today in addressing holy sexuality. People brush aside Scripture. The Bible is the measuring stick for everything we do in life. When we don't know the Word of God, our foundation for knowledge and understanding is distorted. If Scripture truly is the basis for our lives, we should be living according to absolute truth.

The Bible is uncompromising in areas of morality. However, we cannot only use Scripture to bang our gay loved one over the head; we also need to use Scripture to guide us in how to interact and come alongside them. It cuts both ways.

The opportunity? We need to find ways to encourage one another to daily be in God's Word. Abiding in Him is essential. Through abiding in Him, we will live victorious lives.

Dilemma Eight: The Lack of the Jesus Approach[150]

As same-sex practices, as well as many other unholy sexual practices, have become acceptable and approved in our society, most people have chosen to love those who engage in them. To love is not wrong, but they err by not following through with what Jesus would expect: to go and sin no more (John 8).

Many pastors teach on the love of God and also portray Jesus as a gentleman. Though I don't disagree, the reality is that Jesus was strict about expecting a change of heart, which means repentance and walking away from sinful patterns and behaviors.

This is how Jesus would do it, according to His example in Mark 8:

---

150 For a full description of the Jesus approach, refer to Chapter Thirteen.

The Jesus Approach

(Wearing Jesus Glasses)

1: Jesus Shows Compassion	See Mark 8:2
2: Jesus Is Concerned for Our Well-Being	See Mark 8:3
3: Jesus Is Willing to Engage in Tough Conversations	See Mark 8:11
4: Jesus Is Careful Before He Speaks	See Mark 8:12
5: Jesus Responds Respectfully and Assertively	See Mark 8:12
6: Jesus Goes to a Place of Solitude	See Mark 8:13
7: Jesus Doesn't Get Involved in Politics	See Mark 8:13
8: Jesus Warns in a Gentle, Encouraging Way	See Mark 8:15
9: Jesus Meets Us Where We're At	See Mark 8:22-23
10: Jesus Deals with the Real Enemy	See Mark 8:33
11: Jesus Invites People to Follow Him	See Mark 8:35
12: Jesus Warns About Eternal Consequences	See Mark 8:35-36
13: Jesus Is Not Ashamed to Share the Truth	See Mark 8:38
14: Jesus Spent Time with Sinners (Without Compromising His Holiness)	See Mark 8
15: Jesus Accepts and Loves All People (Without Approving of Sin)	See Mark 8

In loving those practicing an unholy lifestyle, we need to be willing to speak the truth at all times. We have a role to play as a watchman on the wall. We must warn people when we see that they're going in the wrong direction. This can be done in love and not condemnation.

We need to be willing to be like Jesus, to put aside our judgments and insecurities and speak the truth in love. Perhaps if more of us were to act like Jesus, showing love and upholding biblical values, we would be more compelling in drawing others to Him. This is the hope in the midst of the dilemma, that we would draw others to an intimate relationship with Him.

Dilemma Nine: Not Understanding or Practicing Holy Sexuality

This is a touchy subject that challenges a lot of people, and I believe that's why we don't hear sermons about this very often. The topic of holy sexuality both challenges people and addresses many unholy unbiblical practices and lifestyles which have crept into our churches today. Many pastors themselves struggle with some form of sexual sin; unless they address it themselves, how can they lead their congregation in the truth?

For my own journey into holy sexuality, view the chart in Chapter Sixteen. Here is a summary of the verses I use:

> *For it is God's will that you be sanctified: You must abstain from sexual immorality. Each of you must know how to control his own body in a holy and honorable manner, not with passion and lust like the gentiles who do not know God. Furthermore, you must never take advantage of or exploit a brother in this regard, because the Lord avenges all these things, just as we already told you and warned you. For God did not call us to be impure, but to be holy. Therefore, whoever rejects this instruction is not rejecting human authority but God, who gives you his Holy Spirit.*
> —1 Thessalonians 4:3–8, ISV

We need to shed light on the topic of holy sexuality. We have an opportunity to address what it looks like for each of us, single or married. When we talk more openly and authentically about holy sexuality, we have the opportunity to hold one another accountable and encourage holiness in an area that deeply affects our lives. We need to stop underestimating the effects of sexual sin.

> *We need to stop underestimating the effects of sexual sin.*

This concludes many of the dilemmas you will face. I'm sure there are more.

When Gay Comes Home

A Message to Christian Leaders

While facing these complicated dilemmas, how are you going to deal with all of this in your congregation, particularly with regards to addressing same-sex attractions? Here are some suggestions I believe you may find helpful:

1. As Christian leaders, we need to repent and ask for forgiveness for our history of showing hostility toward the LGBTQ community.

In regards to the questions I asked at the beginning of this book about the different glasses we can wear and how we see people, my question to you is this: have you been wearing your Jesus glasses? If not, you need to repent and have a change of heart, as I discussed in Chapter Twenty-Five. This will take courage and require you to lay down the pride in your own heart.

We can expect miracles in our cities when we, as leaders, take responsibility for our past and ask the LGBTQ community for forgiveness. Pastors need to repent and ask for forgiveness from the pulpit, because the attitude from the pulpit filters into the congregation. It starts from the top. Repentance among the leadership is key in order to see redemption and healing take place between the church and the LGBTQ community. Christians have hurt them deeply, and this is the reason we need to repent.

2. Educate yourself first so that you can share biblical insight, compassion, and healthy understanding with your congregations.

If you, as a leader or pastor, aren't acquainted with the topic of same-sex attractions, how will you help members of your church not only understand it, but also teach them the right approach? Our churches are fractured, and this topic impacts many of our members. As you familiarize yourself with this topic, you will need to have boldness and courage in sharing it from the pulpit. You will also be able to come alongside family members and embrace them in their pain and grief as they go through this journey. You also won't be caught off-guard by a "Jacob" in your congregation. You will know how to graciously embrace him with love and compassion.

3. Promote clear and biblical teaching. The time has come. It is your duty to promote clear and biblical teaching on the topic of homosexuality—now rather than later. Many churches today aren't educated on the topic of homosexuality, and when pressure comes they easily swing towards approval of a homosexual lifestyle. It's no surprise to hear about yet more churches who decide to marry same-sex couples. This is not biblical.

Unless we uphold clear and biblical teaching on this topic, we will cave in to the pressures of the world. Loving and accepting the LGBTQ community doesn't mean we need to compromise the truth of God's Word. We can't let ourselves be emotionally manipulated to compromise the truths upheld by the Christian faith.

As a Christian community, we cannot remain oblivious to the reality that the LGBTQ community is intentional. A pertinent recent example took place on July 11, 2016. At the Mennonite National Convention held at Teachers' Credit Union in Saskatoon, the Mennonite Church in Canada decided to open a space to consider "hearing one another" instead of outright approving same-sex marriage. The task force ended up suggesting that it's potentially the nudging of the Holy Spirit to redefine marriage.

At the same time, two-thirds of the Anglican Church of Canada, at their Synod in Toronto, decided to redefine marriage. My response? I deeply appreciate it when churches bring up the topic. It is my deep desire to see all churches do this, to open up the conversation and to discuss, acknowledge, and repent of the tragedy of our recent history. For too long the church has judged, ridiculed, and hurt persons who experience same-sex attractions. You may not like this statement, but it is a fact. Also, it's important to begin building bridges between the church and the LGBTQ community. I'm all for discussing, acknowledging, repenting, and building bridges.

However, I cannot and will not agree to redefine marriage to be something that encompasses relationships that are counter to God's created design, as reflected in our bodies. When

> *When we redefine marriage, we change the Word of God.*

we redefine marriage, we change the Word of God. We must use caution in how we attempt to build bridges. We must never compromise the truth of God's Word.

Hebrews 12:14 reminds us, *"Strive to live in peace with everybody and pursue that consecration and holiness without which no one will [ever] see the Lord"* (AMPC). Paul wrote,

> *For this is the will of God, that you should be consecrated (separated and set apart for pure and holy living)… For God has not called us to impurity but to consecration [to dedicate ourselves to the most thorough purity].*
>
> —1 Thessalonians. 4:3, 7, AMPC

We are to pursue holiness, which Psalm 93:5 defines this way: *"apparent in separation from sin, with simple trust and hearty obedience"* (AMPC). When we build bridges, we must keep this in mind.

4. Love and listen. We need to find ways to love and listen to those who tell us they experience same-sex attractions. We need to love them in a way most of us have not done. We need to show sensitivity to those who are seeking help and support so that we don't send them away empty-handed, like Jacob in the drama. Initially, we need to offer our loving and listening ear, not more talk. Trust is built through establishing rapport. We need to be respectful in developing relationship.

5. Take the lead in condemning and combating verbal or physical abuse of homosexual people. People are often insensitive when they make jokes about homosexual people. You never know when you're in a group of people who may experience same-sex attractions, or who may have a family member or friend who experiences same-sex attractions.

Our insensitive comments may hurt others. This is one of the reasons people hesitate to come out; they are afraid to be ridiculed. As Christians, we should have no part in such ridicule. Yet I still often hear negative comments and it's like a knife stabbing through my own heart! We must use caution before we speak.

6. We need much better teaching on how parents should respond if children say that they're gay. Christian families should never reject a child, throw them out of their home, or refuse to see them if a child announces he is gay. Yes, we should disapprove of unbiblical behavior, but we shouldn't refuse to love and cherish a child who engages in it. We ought to shift the conversation to the pursuit of holiness, so that our conversation applies to all people instead of singling out only a few.

7. We need to develop programs. Our congregations need to be known as safe places where persons within the LGBTQ community, or those who are questioning, can come to seek and find God. Our churches must embrace, love, and listen instead of shame, ridicule, judge or exclude.

How do we create a safe place? If our congregation is educated, enlightened, and well-equipped about the topic of homosexuality we won't be afraid and uncomfortable in our interactions with those experiencing same-sex attractions. Programs may look different in every congregation. Ultimately, we need to ask the Holy Spirit to guide us.

In Saskatoon, two men who have been together for twenty-five years (married in 2008) began Camp Fyrefly in 2009. In 2014, the news recognized their efforts by naming them Saskatoon's citizens of the year. According to a local newspaper, Camp Fyrefly is "intended for sexual minority, gender variant and allied youth."[151] The goal is to establish a safe place where youth are told they are okay and loved in an environment where a homosexual lifestyle is approved: "instead of being told you're different or you're no good or you're a deviant, you're an important person and there are other people like you."[152]

When I initially read the article, I wanted to jump on my criticizing wagon. I wanted to criticize the two men for daring to mislead so many young people. Then I had a second thought: *Where is the church? Why don't we have similar camps to create a safe place for those young people who struggle with their sexual identity, to help them understand their true identity in Christ and come alongside them without judging yet teaching them the truth of the Word of God?*

The LGBTQ community is being intentional. Why are we not being intentional?

I then realized that if the whole church was transformed and we were speaking about holiness, they would know immediately that they are on a shared journey with people like them. The focus would merely be shifted from the attractions themselves to the overall pursuit of virtue and holiness.

8. It's time to teach and nurture biblical sexual practices. We must talk about holy sexuality while at the same time not ignoring, marginalizing, or driving away from Christ those who experience same-sex attractions, or those who struggle with living chastely. Our children and families are bombarded with new sex education programs, and through the media they receive all kinds of unbiblical messages.

It is the role of the pastor to impart biblical wisdom. What is the message you're sharing with them? If you don't educate your congregation as the pastor, who will? I'll tell you: gay activists and supporters of gay rights, who are diligently fighting and pushing their agenda on all of us. They are certainly targeting

---

151 Jonathan Charlton, "The Joy of Belonging," *Bridges*. February 25, 2015, 6.
152 Ibid.

The Much-Needed New Approach

our youth. We all know about the recent attacks on biblical marriage. It is therefore vital to nurture, train, and support a generation who wants to keep their marriage vows and model a healthy family life.

9. Our churches and homes should be widely known as safe places. In a safe place, people can be open about their orientation. They won't be scared or ashamed to share about their journey. They will also feel welcomed and embraced. This can occur wherever we truly place Christ first!

10. We must be consistent in how we disciple and discipline. True followers of Jesus who engage in unbiblical sexual practices, whether heterosexual or homosexual, should be discipled and disciplined by the church and not allowed to be leaders or members in good standing if they persist in their sin. This should also be applicable to those who engage in unbiblical practices of any kind, including greed and racism.

Remember, sin is sin. We must be consistent with this and not elevate homosexual behavior above any other sin. However, Christians who openly acknowledge that they experience same-sex attractions, but commit themselves to living a chaste life with Jesus as their focus, should be eligible for any role in the church (such a person should have a proven track record of living chastely over time as per 2 Timothy 3:10). This is because God desires our hearts first, and the choice to strive to live chastely is evidence of a person's commitment to follow Jesus wholeheartedly.

> *Christians who openly acknowledge that they experience same-sex attractions, but commit themselves to living a chaste life with Jesus as their focus, should be eligible for any role in the church.*

11. It's time to take the church into the world. Due to years of ridicule and being marginalized, the LGBTQ community doesn't currently feel welcome in our churches. We need to take the church to them in ways that don't compromise our own journey to holiness.

How will this look? As radical as this might sound, for some (who are already spiritually well fortified) this may mean visiting gay bars or attending pride parades—not with flyers saying "God hates you" but rather with the message of asking for forgiveness for not taking the Jesus approach in the past.

We are all called to pray, and many of us are called to have conversations with persons who self-identify as LGBTQ and build relationships with them. Spend time with them. Jesus did! He spent time with people from all walks of life. Prayerfully, we should too. He meets us where we're at, and we need to meet others where they're at.

Not everyone is called to visit gay bars. Not everyone is called to attend pride parades and stand on the street corners to pray. Ask the Holy Spirit to guide and direct you in your interactions. When we go out into the world, we need to have the heart of God, a heart of love, kindness, and compassion.

12. Last but not least, publicize people's testimonies. I believe you need to allow testimonies during sermons—especially testimonies and stories like mine, of those who have overcome the struggle with

pornography and other sexual sins. I'm convinced that biblical testimonies will inspire others and give them hope that transformation is possible. They need to know that they're not alone in their journey. Jesus told stories all the time, so why don't we? Revelation 12:11 says that we are to overcome Satan through the blood of the Lamb and the word of our testimonies.

I have no illusion that this new approach will be easy. In fact, I expect resistance. And don't be surprised if you find yourself in a storm. Living this way will be highly countercultural, contrasting both with our society at large and the church's past. This process will require patience, endurance, faith, and persons of valor!

If we've already compromised in regards to the vision for biblical marriage, this may take generations, not a few years. But do we have generations? If churches, and Christians in general, can choose this countercultural, biblical way for several generations, the tide can be turned. My prayer today is that God will help us to make what was wrong, right. It is time.

We are at a crossroads: one road consists of tragedy, tradition, and failure, and the other road is the much-needed new approach, consisting of truth and love. Jeremiah 6:16 says, "*This is what the Lord says: 'Stop at the crossroads and look around. Ask for the old, godly way, and walk in it. Travel its path, and you will find rest for your souls*" (NLT).

I believe it's time for churches to dig deep, look at what has been done, evaluate what has been done wrong, and make a decision to not go that route again. Choose the new approach, as this will bring life. It will build bridges, not walls. And if we choose life, which isn't always the easy path, we may be astounded at what God can do.

Encouragements to Take to Heart

Be brave and don't lose heart. Galatians 6:9 provides a necessary encouragement and caution:

And let us not lose heart and grow weary and faint in acting nobly and doing right, for in due time and at the appointed season we shall reap, if we do not loosen and relax our courage and faint. (AMPC)

When you're walking to the pulpit and your knees are shaking, how do you proceed and say what you need to say? You can't do it in your own strength. You must rely on the Holy Spirit's power. Worldly views are pushed on us from all different directions. Unless you address them courageously from the pulpit, who will address these hot topics?

Use caution in whom you ask for advice. When I watched a Baptist pastor announce to his congregation that he had changed his views and approved same-sex marriage, it was clear that he had made two vital mistakes. I don't want you to make the same mistakes.

The first mistake is that he didn't use the Word of God to guide him; he didn't seek God's advice. And second, he only talked to persons within the LGBTQ community, not to any persons like me who have found victory through Jesus Christ in regards to living and practicing a homosexual lifestyle.

Also, I will caution you about the resources you use to educate yourself and others. In January 2015, it was brought to my attention that a new gay bible had come out. It is called the Queen James Bible as opposed to the King James Bible. According to the Christian Apologetics and Research Ministry, "In [the Queen James Bible], the 1769 King James Bible has been reproduced with only a very few select verses altered—the ones that relate to homosexuality."[153]

Note: if a resource isn't talking about our hearts being open to virtue and the importance of having our identity in Christ, be on guard. There might be a lot of good in it, but it may be inhibiting the fullness of truth.

Let the Holy Spirit be your guide and don't cave in to the pressure of the world. Too many people have a change of heart because they fear people and not God. As Saul said to Samuel, *"I feared the people and obeyed their voice"* (1 Samuel 15:24, AMPC). Leaders who cave in to pressure lead others astray, and God is going to hold them accountable. Many shepherds today are leading their sheep astray, which will have devastating eternal consequences (Ezekiel 34).

There are too many stories of so-called reputable leaders changing their minds. Philip Yancey's *What's So Amazing About Grace?* talks about a leader who later does just that. He mentions the story of Tony Campolo, who was once slandered for his stance:

> I also talked with Tony Campolo, a high-profile Christian speaker who opposes homosexual practice… He holds up an ideal of sexual celibacy…Tony has been slandered by other Christians, resulting in many canceled speaking engagements. At one convention, protesters distributed purported correspondence between Tony and gay leaders at Queer Nation, a letter that was proved spurious, part of a smear campaign.[154]

More recently, the same Tony Campolo made this statement on his website, changing his views, from once opposing same-sex marriage to now approving same sex marriage. A very disappointing statement to me and more reason to pray for Christian leaders who cave in to the pressure of our immoral world:

> It has taken countless hours of prayer, study, conversation and emotional turmoil to bring me to the place where I am finally ready to call for the full acceptance of Christian gay couples into the church.[155]

We must only allow the Holy Spirit to guide and lead us, not humans. The Holy Spirit will always lead us toward holiness, which is where God's creation is upheld and respected. It is where nature, not

---

153 Matt Slick, "The Queen James Bible, the Gay Bible," *Christian Apologetics & Research Ministry.* December 20, 2012 (https://carm.org/queen-james-bible).

154 Philip Yancey's *What's So Amazing About Grace?* (Grand Rapids, MI: Zondervan, 1997), 168.

155 Tony Campolo, "For the Record," *TonyCampolo.org*. June 8, 2015 (http://tonycampolo.org/for-the-record-tony-campolo-releases-a-new-statement/#.WbrmK8iGPIV).

what "feels" natural, is acknowledged. It is where the art of the divine Artist is held in high esteem and not rejected in favor of following our own ways, inclinations, or conscience.

Be open and honest with your congregation. Even if you have to admit your incapability to discuss homosexuality, your fear, or your lack of love and compassion towards the LGBTQ community, be honest. If you've had a change of heart towards the LGBTQ community and you share your transformation in an open and honest manner, including repenting of your past behavior, this will open a door for others to do the same. This is the beginning of building bridges between your congregation and the LGBTQ community.

If you've struggled with unholy sexuality, get it in the open and get help. Sexual sin is like a cancer. It will kill you—not only your body, but your soul. 1 Corinthians 6:18 reminds us of the seriousness of sexual sin: "*Shun immorality and all sexual looseness [flee from impurity in thought, word, or deed]. Any other sin which a man commits is one outside the body, but he who commits sexual immorality sins against his own body*" (AMPC).

Sexual sin is pervasive and affects every part of you. Proverbs 7 says explicitly that if you seek or give in to unholy sexuality, you are seeking to destroy your soul, body, and spirit. If a doctor discovers cancer in your body and he calls you and says you need cancer treatment, will you put it off or will you deal with it right away?

> Sexual sin is like a cancer. It will kill you—not only your body, but your soul.

Don't fear the financial committee who cuts your paycheck. You must preach God's Word. You will stand before Him one day and be accountable for speaking the truth. Some pastors are concerned that if they address hot topics, they will lose monetary congregational support, so they refrain from addressing these topics.

Be courageous. Know that those who choose to stand for the truth will pay, whether in reputation or in status. You may not be popular anymore. The reality is that what is right often isn't popular.

Become unstoppable by trusting God and doing what is right. It is vital to stand for the truth and nothing but the truth. May your new approach be like a stool held up by the following three legs:

1. Put on your Jesus glasses and approach others through love and compassion.
2. Let the Word be the lamp to your feet and a light to your path.
3. Let the Holy Spirit be your Comforter, Counselor, Helper, Intercessor, Advocate, Strengthener, and Standby.

Through a loving and compassionate Jesus approach, we can show God's tangible presence to those around us. When we apply the new approach, we may just be astounded at what God will do in the world around us.

God, through Jesus, reconciled us back to Himself and then gave us the ministry of reconciling others into harmony with Him (2 Corinthians 5:18). This is what I hope the new approach will accomplish: reconciliation between the church and the LGBTQ community. When there's reconciliation, relationship can develop. And out of having relationship, in which we are salt and light, many may desire to also drink of the living waters Jesus offers.

APPENDIX B

Questions and Answers

I have decided to add this section to help with any questions the reader may have. During my presentations, I get numerous and sometimes very difficult questions. Due to the complexity of the questions, I'm not always able to answer them during a presentation. I will attempt to do so here.

I have divided these questions into sections, depending on the audience.

Saskatoon, Saskatchewan—September 23, 2013

The following questions were posed by an audience on September 23, 2013 in Saskatoon. This was a mixed audience, containing many persons from the LGBTQ community who had come to protest the event. It also included several counselors, pastors, psychiatrists, psychologists, and the parents, family, and friends of homosexuals.

Most of the questions were asked by the LGBTQ community. I can easily identify with them asking the difficult questions, because I have been there myself. There was a time in my life when I justified, or wanted to justify, my homosexual behavior. I try to answer these questions in the context of understanding while not compromising the truth from God's Word.

Q: Why are heterosexual people called straight? To me we are all crooked!
A: This is one of the painful realities of the society in which we live. People use names and terminologies without thinking that they may hurt others. In my culture as a South African, people still use a lot of words that, when they are mentioned, feel like a knife piercing my heart. Personally, I agree that we are all crooked, whether we are homosexual or heterosexual. Romans 3:23 states, *"Since all have sinned and are falling short of the honor and glory which God bestows and receives"* (AMP).

The best information I could find came from a response on *Yahoo! Answers*, from user Ariana:

The actual definition of straight is the quality or state of extending in one direction without turns, bends or curves.

In the mid-20th century, "gay" was well-established as an antonym for "straight" (which had connotations of respectability), and to refer to the lifestyles of unmarried and or unattached people.

Here's a brief history of the original term:

The word started to acquire sexual connotations in the late 17th century, being used with meaning "addicted to pleasures and dissipations". This was by extension from the primary meaning of "carefree": implying "uninhibited by moral constraints". By the late nineteenth century the term "gay life" was a well-established euphemism for prostitution and other forms of extramarital sexual behavior that were perceived as immoral.

The use of gay to mean "homosexual" was in origin merely an extension of the word's sexualised connotation of "carefree and uninhibited", which implied a willingness to disregard conventional or respectable sexual mores.[156]

Q: It was God who helped me love myself, it was God who helped me not kill myself for being gay, and it was God who brought me to women I love. Why then would God want me to practice love in any way other than the way he showed me?

A: I will agree that the Bible teaches that we should love the Lord with all our hearts, souls, and minds. The second command is to love our neighbors as we love ourselves (Matthew 22:37–39). We need to love ourselves in healthy ways, and it's certainly not God's will for us to kill ourselves.

However, with experiencing same-sex attractions, humans tend to focus too much on "self," and then justify following the flesh instead of following the teachings of God. Living a homosexual lifestyle isn't God's will or plan for our lives, so we can never assume it to be true when a woman says, "God brought me to women I love." This is a lie. *"Satan himself masquerades as an angel of light"* (2 Corinthians 11:14, AMPC), deceiving many and making them believe that bringing this person to them is God's will and God's doing. It's not. It counters virtue, and thus counters holiness. It counters the order of creation, nature, and the art of the divine Artist.

Q: Does God not love or accept gay people who happily live a gay lifestyle?

A: God always accepts and loves all people regardless of their race, lifestyle choices, or demographics. God certainly loves and accepts all gay people who happily live a homosexual lifestyle. However, He does not approve of their choice of living and practicing a homosexual lifestyle, because it is counter to what He authored in our own bodies.

---

156 Ariana, "Why Are Heterosexuals Called 'Straight'"? *Yahoo! Answers.* Date of access: September 14, 2017 (https://ca.answers.yahoo.com/question/index?qid=20080508200036AAnVbKH).

Any sin we commit in our lives will create separation between us and Him, and so He hates what sin does to us. He does not hate us. And the beautiful thing is that God will always meet every person where they're at in a loving, non-condemning way.

When we reject God and His order, we condemn ourselves. But He requires and desires for us to live in obedience, meaning that He requires us to walk away from anything we do that's not pleasing to Him. During His encounter with the woman who was caught in adultery (John 8:1–11), He accepted her, regardless of her guilty state, and sent her away with this expectation: *"Go on your way and from now on sin no more"* (John 8:11, AMPC).

I will also caution against believing that living a homosexual lifestyle is a *happy* lifestyle. In his article for *Charisma News*, David Kyle Foster writes,

> It does no good to pretend that it is good and natural and holy. That's called denial. Statistics overflow with evidence that homosexual sex causes damage to body, soul and spirit. It actually damages the body of the partner. It tears at the body in ways that result in homosexual sex being the number one risk factor for contracting AIDS in this country. In fact, an entire cottage industry of scientific study and medical care has arisen from the proliferation of gay sex in our modern culture.
>
> Homosexual behavior also tears at the soul, causing much higher rates for substance abuse, suicide, depression, domestic violence, early death—even in the most gay-friendly regions of the globe. Why? Because active homosexuals are trying to find something through gay relationships that can never be found there. The happiness that they seek can only be found in submitting their sexuality to the Lordship of Christ and allowing Him to bring healing to the broken areas that have caused their homosexual desires. Yes, it's a slow and sometimes arduous path to take, just as it is for the addict, but the only one that leads to joy, peace and eternal life with God.[157]

Q: God has changed me (a lesbian), from somebody who hates myself for loving women into somebody who loves myself and loves the way that I have relationships. Is the way God changed me wrong?

A: See my answer to question two. This is another example of how God is being associated and connected with making the change, yet the change does not glorify Him.

> *When you bear (produce) much fruit, My Father is honored and glorified, and you show and prove yourselves to be true followers of Mine.*
>
> —John 15:8, AMPC

---

[157] David Kyle Foster, "Former Homosexual Reveals 'Unmitigated Disaster of Gay Marriage,'" *Charisma News*. July 18, 2014 (https://www.charismanews.com/opinion/44691%E2%80%93former-homosexual-reveals-unmitigated-disaster-of-gay-marriage).

Light and darkness don't go together. The "change" is not God's doing, yet people want to believe it is. I will agree that God does not want us to hate ourselves, and He can help us not to do that. God will never change us to desire to practice a homosexual lifestyle, because this is counter to growing in virtue and holiness. The idea that God wants us in same-sex relationships is another lie from Satan. It is contradictory to what God has revealed in our bodies. When God transforms us, the fruit we bear will be the fruit of the Holy Spirit, which will always include an increased desire to grow in the fullness of virtue.

Q: What is your response to the teens committing suicide because they want so badly to have someone special in their lives but instead feel that they will be too alone for the rest of their lives? Some people have no one and long for someone to love.

A: Experiencing loneliness can have deep root causes which need to be dealt with. Experiencing same-sex attractions indeed can bring about many unwanted feelings, including the reality of being single for the rest of their lives. All of this can lead to deep depression, and the end result can be to have thoughts of committing suicide.

That is why support in the struggle is vital. The church must become equipped to deal with this so that a person can be helped. Youth must be educated not only about the topic of homosexuality, but singleness should be celebrated and not talked about as if it's the worst thing in the world.

Satan and the world want us to believe that we are doomed when we are single. We must be sensitive and meet them where they are, coming alongside them. Build friendships and trust. Never ridicule or judge a person who experiences same-sex attractions. This will not support them in their struggle.

Singleness is not a bad thing. It is a good reason to follow Christ and to choose things which will please the Lord. And the wonderful promise from God's Word affirms that single persons don't miss out. In fact, if we choose those things which please the Lord, we get a name better than sons or daughters.

> *For thus says the Lord: To the eunuchs [most likely single people] who keep My Sabbaths and choose the things which please Me and hold firmly My covenant—to them I will give in My house and within My walls a memorial and a name better [and more enduring] than sons and daughters; I will give them an everlasting name that will not be cut off.*
> —Isaiah 56:4–5, AMPC

Q: Why can't gay or lesbians experience holy sexuality in a committed, faithful relationship? I am a lesbian Christian who feels called to be in a faithful relationship with Christ at the center.

A: Holy sexuality, as described in the Bible, entails far more than merely having Christ at the center of our hearts. It requires obedience and submitting to God's authority, following Him wholeheartedly. Living and practicing a homosexual lifestyle is not part of God's plan and does not qualify as a valid relationship in Gods eyes. No gay relationship, even if it is committed or where faithfulness is practiced, can contain any form of holy sexuality.

David Kyle Foster said,

> God created a man and a woman to become one flesh in a lifelong covenant of love (i.e., "marriage"), and to be fruitful and multiply when possible. God invented marriage. He designed it as a prefigurement of the marriage between Jesus and His Bride, the Church (Ephesians 5:31–32), and laid out its parameters from the dawn of time. Even cultures that do not know Him have followed that design from the beginning. There is no ambiguity about His design nor His description of it in the Scriptures. Indeed, every departure from that model is universally condemned and forbidden by Him, for what it does to our bodies, our souls and to the image of God that is stamped into the one flesh, marital union of male and female.[158]

Q: Why can't I be a daughter of Christ and a lesbian? What is so wrong with these two worlds becoming one? I do not believe I'm an abomination or a sinner any more than anyone else here today.

A: For these two worlds to become one, you must choose to live chastely. However, it is impossible to live chastely within a same-sex sexual/romantic relationship. You can't pursue a same-sex relationship while pursuing the fullness of virtue at the same time.

Q: Let it be known that I am a gay man who has and continues to be in loving same-sex relationships. I share the love of Christ with others in my life and do not feel "disconnected from God." No walls block me from Him! I testify that God is with the LGBTQ community. I used to be blocked from God when I was confused. Now I am closer to God than *ever*.

A: There is a very interesting fact that I see throughout these questions. Most of the audience mentions that they are in loving same-sex relationships—plural. To me, this means they go from one relationship to the other and that gay relationships tend to follow that trend, meaning they are not healthy.

I can't speak for any person—all I know is that when we profess to be in a deep, intimate relationship with Jesus, we will not only tell others, but the fruit of our lives will be proof that we have been with Jesus (Acts 4:13). Same-sex relationships and living a homosexual lifestyle are not God's will for our lives and so cannot be part of the fruit we bear as a result of knowing Him intimately. In Matthew 7:20, Jesus said, *"Therefore, you will fully know them by their fruits"* (AMPC).

Secondly, Satan deceives us by making us believe there is no blockage. He makes us believe that it's good to be in loving gay relationships, because God is with the LGBTQ community and He approves their lifestyle choices. God *is* with the LGBTQ community; He loves them very much. Yet He does not approve of their lifestyle choices. He desires for all of them to enter into a genuine intimate relationship with Him and allow the Holy Spirit to work. In the process of surrendering, He will open their eyes to see those blocks. This was how He did it for me.

---

158 Ibid.

While operating in the flesh, we are blind to see and recognize blocks which create in us a base mind where we believe that it's okay in God's eyes to live and practice a homosexual lifestyle. This lie becomes the veil over our eyes. It blocks our ears from hearing the truth, and it makes us unable to discern between what is from God and what is from the devil.

They do not know or understand, for their eyes God has let become besmeared so that they cannot see, and their minds as well so that they cannot understand.
—Isaiah 44:18, AMPC

I would suggest this challenge: give God one full year of your life. Stay out of bed and invite Jesus into your closet. You may be astounded at what He will do.

Q: Why is being gay a sin?

A: Being gay is not a sin, but living a homosexual lifestyle is. Many people experience same-sex attractions. While experiencing it, we are not doing anything wrong. But when we act on it, it becomes wrong and therefore a sin.

Q: What do you think Jesus would say to a practicing Christian homosexual about being a leader in a church?

A: God requires us to obey and live a life of example. Practicing a homosexual lifestyle is not God's will and not pleasing in His sight. A person who participates in this lifestyle should not be eligible for any leadership role while still practicing it because we first and foremost must lead by example.

Are we willing to truly put Christ first? Or are we clinging to this idea that we could live a homosexual lifestyle and somehow reflect an openness to grow in the fullness of holiness? No person who unrepentantly participates in any habitual sin should be eligible for any leadership role.

Any person should be welcome to become a member of a church while agreeing to follow the mission statement of faith of the particular church's denomination. In my opinion, the statement of faith should include what they believe a marriage looks like and how God intended it to be. It is between one naturally born male and one naturally born female. All members of the church should follow this statement of faith. If not, I will caution pastors to be consistent with discipling and disciplining all members who don't follow the statement of faith.

The book of 1 Timothy (especially Chapter 3) and Titus contains the qualifications for leadership roles. Living and practicing a homosexual lifestyle is a sure disqualifier for any leadership position. As true ambassadors of Christ, we can't be practicing homosexuality and leading a church. We want and need to welcome homosexuals into the church. For too long, the church has ridiculed and judged persons within the LGBTQ community. Yet we need to be consistent in disciplining all leaders.

Everyone needs to be held accountable for practicing any habitual sin—and they shouldn't be eligible for any leadership role until true repentance happens and after they have proven to be trustworthy.

Speak the truth in love. Jesus wouldn't speak to people with condemnation, therefore speak in love and conviction.

Q: If God wants unity in His church, we can all still live together in Christ despite our differences in beliefs. Every denomination has differences from others.

A: Yes, God requires unity, but we can never compromise His Word to fit our own beliefs or agenda. We must always uphold His Word, which is our ultimate measuring stick and instruction for how to live our lives. I will caution you to be on guard in regards to differences. We must always uphold the truth from God's Word, and those who believe otherwise are not serving the Lord truthfully. Romans 16:17–18 says,

> *I appeal to you, brethren, to be on your guard concerning those who create dissensions and difficulties and cause divisions, in opposition to the doctrine (the teaching) which you have been taught. [I warn you to turn aside from them, to] avoid them. For such persons do not serve our Lord Christ but their own appetites and base desires, and by ingratiating and flattering speech, they beguile the hearts of the unsuspecting and simpleminded [people].* (AMPC)

Q: Are you advocating that counselors and therapists use your ideas in client sessions, or are your ideas only for your ministry? I ask because I must only use ethical and researched ideas in sessions, and you state, "I am no scientist."

A: I can't force any person to use my ideas in client sessions. I can only hope that my story reveals the faithfulness of God and that redemption and restoration are possible through the power of Jesus. I am only faithful to share my journey and how I made sense out of it. Also, even though I state in my presentations that I'm not a scientist, my journey and the experience I have had in living as a former lesbian, and my journey now as a redeemed daughter of the King of Kings, is enough evidence of the power of God. Though I respect that your discipline relies on scientific evidence, I feel that we need no scientist to prove what God can do. The fruit of a redemptive life is proof enough.

Q: What is the gay agenda?

A: Using any means to convince society to believe that to live a homosexual lifestyle is good, that God made them this way, and that they can choose to love whoever they want and marry whoever they want. They will infiltrate schools, the church, the state, media, or wherever they can to convince the world of these things. They will push this on everyone, everywhere, and will even bully Christians when they don't approve of their lifestyle choices. Their agenda is so fierce that it's now creating persecution for every person who doesn't agree with their beliefs. Their voice is heard daily on national television, and the voice of Christianity is being heard less and less. This is the gay agenda.

Q: You said being gay is a choice. Is it?

A: I have never said being gay is a choice, so you must have heard wrong. I've said it's not a choice, but it becomes a choice in terms of what we will do with our same-sex attractions. Many people believe that they've come into the world having been born gay. This was not a choice either. Bashing them or telling them that they're wrong, or that there is no gay gene, is not the solution. This is where we must come alongside them, sharing the good news of Jesus and that there is healing in His name. Nothing is impossible.

We don't have a choice about how we come into this world. We all enter into it broken. We do have a choice as to how we live in a fallen, sinful world.

Q: Do you think that all gay people should practice celibacy in order to remain close to God?

A: Yes, because practicing a homosexual lifestyle will create separation from God.

> *But your iniquities have made a separation between you and your God, and your sins have hidden His face from you, so that He will not hear.*
> —Isaiah 59:2, AMPC

Q: Would you say that social context triggers a same-sex attraction gene, and if that social context isn't experienced do you think the gene will never surface?

A: There is no gay gene, but I do believe there are many root causes for a person to start to experience same-sex attractions. I also believe that many people, even those claiming to be heterosexual, can fall into the temptation of a same-sex relationship. There are numerous stories of persons who were in monogamous opposite-sex marriages, getting a divorce, and after being so hurt in their marriage, entering into a same-sex relationship.

No person is exempt from temptation. It is about the right person at the right place at the right time—or more accurately, it can be the wrong person at the wrong place at the wrong time. We must be on guard. Satan will lure and deceive us into anything that will drive us far away from God. Furthermore, even many gay activists are now saying that environment does play a factor in the development of one's attractions.

Q: Wilna, you are entitled to live the calling in your life. What is your response to gay people who testify that their same-sex love does not affect their relationship with God?

A: I cannot speak for any other person, but I do listen to the stories of many people who have walked away from living a homosexual lifestyle, and they too testify that they weren't able to experience true intimacy. They tried, thus confirming what I believe and experienced.

I honestly do not believe there can be true intimacy while living a homosexual lifestyle. A person may try. As I have shared during my interview with *The 700 Club Canada*, while I was living a homosexual lifestyle I tried to do all the right things. I did read my Bible, I did go to church, I even led my former partner to the Lord. Yet there was no closeness, and I could never sense His presence and true peace in my heart. This brought dryness and leanness to my soul, which drove me back into His loving, waiting arms.

Q: Why is sex a sin?

A: Sex is not a sin. It is actually a beautiful thing. It was created by God only to be had in a loving relationship between a naturally born male and a naturally born female joined in marriage. Lived out in this way, sex reflects many aspects of the creative design of the divine Artist. Like all good art, this masterpiece will teach us about the Artist Himself. The joining of husband and wife in a sexual union that honors God reflects generosity, faithfulness, intimacy, and pleasure. We bear His image, especially in sex where two become one. This is glorifying to God and certainly not a sin!

Q: If experiencing same-sex attractions isn't wrong, why is acting on them wrong?

A: Same-sex sexual and romantic attractions are among the things humans started to experience after the fall of man. When the fall happened, things started to happen to us that went against God's will, design, and purpose for us. Yet some people do experience it. By having those attractions, our flesh is opposed to our spirit (Romans 8:5–7). The same passage also mentions that the mind of the flesh is death.

Galatians 5:17 states that the desires of the flesh are opposed to the Holy Spirit. You can read about the doings of the flesh in Galatians 5:20–21, which adds that those who practice it will not inherit the Kingdom of God. Acting on or giving into our fleshly desires is against what God wants for our lives, making it wrong and a sin. God is clear in His Word that to live a homosexual lifestyle is an abomination.

In saying that, there is no limit to God's mercy for those who turn to Him with their whole heart.

Q: Dear Wilna, do you view sexuality as a right or a gift? If a gift, can it be withheld by God? Thank you for your obedience.

A: God created us as male and female, which gives each individual their sexuality—the gift, however, is not our sexuality, but the Holy Spirit who lives inside of us. In 1 Corinthians 6:19–20 states,

> *Do you not know that your body is the temple (the very sanctuary) of the Holy Spirit Who lives within you, Whom you have received [as a Gift] from God? You are not your own, you were bought with a price [purchased with a preciousness and paid for, made His own]. So then, honor God and bring glory to Him in your body.* (AMPC)

We do not belong to ourselves. We are owned by Him. Our sexuality is part of who we are, but it is never to be our true identity. Our identity is and should be in Christ, as a son or daughter of the King of Kings.

First Presentation of "When Gay Comes Home"—November 16, 2013

In November 2012, God clearly spoke into my heart to write a seminar called "When Gay Comes Home," a title which has now extended into the name of the ministry I lead in Canada, a teaching DVD available on my website, and this book! I made my first presentation in November 2013 and received great and challenging questions. It took place in a church setting and the audience was mixed.

Q: If straight couples can love each other and still have Christ as their focus, why do you feel that a same-sex couple isn't able to do the same in a loving and monogamous relationship?

A: God is love, and if you truly loving another, God is present. When Christ is the total focus and hub of your life, He will reveal to you that living and practicing a homosexual lifestyle is not His will. Many people believe that their loving and monogamous relationship is what pleases God. It is not. Having a heart that puts God first is what pleases Him.

Q: Were any of your lesbian relationships with women who had a faith relationship with Christ?

A: Yes, and this caused more struggle. We all knew it was wrong, yet we loved to be together and to feel a sense of belonging. We worked hard to justify the relationship, yet were unsuccessful. The distance from God, which happened because I chose to walk away through my disobedience, proved to me that what I was involved in was wrong. Even though I led my last partner to the Lord, this did not justify our behavior. That being said, God can use anything to bring lost sheep back into His fold.

Q: What do you think would have happened if you had become pregnant while experimenting with men?

A: I am thankful I did not. If I did, I would have had to deal with the consequences of my wrong choices to have sex with a boyfriend outside of marriage. Our choices in life matter, and even though God doesn't spare us from the consequences of our choices, He will graciously help us through life, even though we sometimes make poor choices. He forgives (if we repent), and then we need to accept it, forgive ourselves, and move forward with Him.

Q: By showing love and acceptance for the person, without expressing disapproval for the behavior, are you not showing acceptance for the behavior?

A: We must always be bold enough to share our disapproval, but this is always most effective in the context of relationship. We don't have to hammer a person with it every time we see them. By holding this in balance, they will always know our stance on the issue, while we continue to love and accept them as persons.

Prince Albert, Saskatchewan—November 23, 2013

These questions arose during a presentation I made in Prince Albert. The audience was comprised mostly of Christians and parents with gay children.

Q: Do you believe there are some women living the gay lifestyle because of their past history of being sexually assaulted or abused by men and therefore feel like men can't be trusted?
A: Yes, pain and hurt can easily turn into offense, bitterness, hatred, or unforgiveness. All of these can become roots which will bear bitter fruits, one of those could be same-sex attractions. Or women can feel safe with women, and it can become sexualized over time as it happened in my own life.

Q: You make it sound as if the only choice a heterosexual person has is to be married—isn't that choice also what God's will must be for me? Can a heterosexual person be called to a celibate life?
A: Of course! God is our ultimate matchmaker and He calls many of us, whether we are heterosexual or homosexual, to live for Him and devote our lives to Him. If a heterosexual person stays single, the same rules apply—to live celibate and refrain from all forms of sex, practicing holy sexuality.

Q. How do people living a gay lifestyle respond to your workshops and acceptance of God?
A: My workshops aren't aimed to reach persons within the LGBTQ community who aren't open to growing in holiness. They protested an event where I spoke, because they don't like the fact that I preach celibacy, and some don't like the fact that I preach holy intimacy with God.

Not many persons within the LGBTQ community attend my workshops. If they do and if they acknowledge that they struggle with their same-sex attractions, and if they want help, they will benefit by attending it. It will be very helpful, uplifting, and encouraging for them to discover that transformation and redemption is possible. My workshop is aimed to educate, equip, and enlighten the whole church.

Q: Have you encountered any legal threats or consequences for your current views?
A: Yes, I am not popular. The LGBTQ community hates me for my stance on celibacy. During the protest in Saskatoon, I was threatened with legal action. But nothing came of it.

Q: Do you feel it is possible to skip a few stages of grief?
A: There is no specific order when a person goes through a grieving process. It's possible to skip some steps, yes. Every person's journey looks different. I do, however, encourage people to give themselves time. The process of grieving is healthy and it may not be helpful to try skipping some stages.

Q: Do you think your relationship with your dad had any bearing on your orientation? If he had embraced you and if you'd had a healthy father-daughter relationship, how do you think it would have shaped you in your orientation?

A: I do believe and am convinced that things could have looked different. My tremendous fear of my father created huge walls of bitterness and hatred around me. It pushed me into the arms of women, a place where I felt safe and cared for.

I'm not putting all the blame on my father. I, too, made choices. From the very beginning, in my mother's womb, I began to reject men. I chose to continue that throughout my life, which caused me to keep all men at a distance. It was only recently that I learned my role and that I, too, needed to ask for forgiveness.

As a young person, I certainly was not open for him to get close to me. As a child, I tried the best I could to survive and protect my little girl heart. I made many wrong choices. We all do. For those wrong choices, I needed to ask for forgiveness.

I believe God could have redeemed our relationship, if my father had been open to the work of God in his own brokenness. Hurt people hurt others, and he most likely responded and acted out due to hurt in his own life.

I can never blame my father for the same-sex attractions I experienced. The bitter roots in my own life defiled not only my relationship with my father but my relationship with all men. Healing started to happen when I renounced those vows. When Jesus set me free, I was able to forgive myself and feel God's forgiveness, too. A lot of things have changed since then.

It remains that our earthy fathers and mothers can affect us deeply in how we view ourselves and what our identity is. This is why I believe that when parents decide to have children, they have such a huge responsibility to raise them in a godly way. This includes parents evaluating their own behavior constantly and making sure they live with integrity and as a godly example to their children.

Q: Should I be involved in my gay daughter's partner's life like I am with my other daughter's boyfriend's life? I don't ask my daughter anything about her partner.

A: It is desirable to love and accept this person. The reality remains that you need to be ready, though. In the process of working through the initial shock, you most likely will not be ready. You must give yourself some time. If you choose not to embrace the partner, your daughter will choose her partner above you.

Please take into consideration that you may be the only person who is "Jesus" to her, so you have a responsibility to represent Him well. This will help to build bridges so that this person may one day walk across into the arms of Jesus. If you mistreat her, she will not be interested in becoming a Christian. As we are called to be salt and light, it is our responsibility to love others well.

Many parents will love and accept their daughter's boyfriend, even if they live together, but when a daughter has a same-sex partner they treat them differently. Sin is sin. We must be consistent in living our faith. Shifting the focus to virtue and holiness will help.

Q: If we can be addicted to lust and allergic to God, can we become allergic to lust and addicted to God?
A: God's desire is to be in intimate relationship with us daily. He created us for Himself—if only we could see and experience it. Choosing daily to abide in Him will help us to become allergic to worldly things and addicted to God and His ways.

Q: Should I attend my friend's gay marriage?
A: This is a very sensitive question that requires honest answers. Before I say anything, there are things you must consider. Have you and your friend had a conversation about his choice to live a homosexual lifestyle and get married? Does he know your stance on it? If no, then this is the time to do so.

If you aren't open and honest about your stance, your attendance not only says that you approve, but gives your blessing to something God forbids. My personal answer always remains a clear no. I will never attend a gay wedding.

If you've talked to your friend about it, this will be a sensitive conversation where you gently let them know that you can't attend, explaining to them that you believe God has something better.

If you have young children, attending is a big no-no. You cannot expose them to something which God forbids in His Word.

Youth Group—November 2016

Our teenagers are bombarded with all kinds of confusing messages, especially when it comes to the sex education program which is now common in the Canadian public school system, as well as the school systems in many other countries. They are confused and come home with all kinds of questions. In addressing youth, I get a lot of difficult yet relevant questions.

Here are a few that I addressed during a presentation to a group of young people in Saskatoon.

Q: What do I do if a friend tells me he's gay?
A: If the friend is a true friend, you will assure him that you love him. You may ask why he thinks he's gay. In the process of him sharing, just listen and show that you care by listening to his story. Sometimes people just need to know that they're in a safe place with a safe person they can trust.

You don't have to bang him over the head with the Bible. He needs someone who will listen. When the conversation comes up about living a homosexual lifestyle, that's when you can share the truth from God's Word. But your friend needs to know you are there for him regardless of his journey. If he knows you love him, you can help him become disarmed from the misinformation that tells him that he is hated by the church.

Q: Can a gay person be a Christian?

A: It's important to clarify a question: is the person merely acknowledging that they experience same-sex attractions or are they living a homosexual lifestyle? If they merely express their attractions, they surely can live a life fully devoted to Jesus, being single and celibate. Living and practicing a homosexual lifestyle while being a true follower of Jesus isn't possible, though some people may say it is. Satan wants us to believe it's possible. You can't have one foot in the world of Christ and one foot in the world of the devil. Living and practicing a homosexual lifestyle is not God's will for our lives, and it is a sin.

Q: Does homosexuality equal promiscuity?

A: In many cases, it does. But there are some who have monogamous and committed relationships and won't have numerous sexual partners. I was one of them when I lived a homosexual lifestyle years ago. But monogamous homosexual relationships are still unchaste, even though they don't include promiscuity. Thus they are counter to holiness.

Q: What should I do if a friend becomes a homosexual? How can I help?

A: Be their friend. Listen to them. Love them. Live a life of integrity and excellence. Shine the light. You don't have to talk about their lifestyle choices every day, but share the truth from God's Word when the time is right. Pray for that opportunity and ask the Holy Spirit to guide you when that conversation comes up. If your friend isn't a Christian, be Jesus to them. When they see how you live your life, they may start to desire the same. They may start to ask questions.

Don't talk about the elephant in the room every day. Many of your friends know the truth, if they have a biblical background, so we don't have to remind them every day. Yet we must have the conversation at some point, so they know we stand for the truth from God's Word.

Q: How do you change from gay to straight?

A: God did not call us to be straight… He called us to be holy! Actually, we are all born crooked. Not by our choice, but by original sin. The Bible teaches us that we all fall short of the glory of God: "*None is righteous, just and truthful and upright and conscientious, no, not one*" (Romans 3:10, AMPC). Psalm 14:3 says, "*They have all turned aside; together they have become corrupt; there is no one who does good, not even one*" (ESV).

Yet God can do impossible things. He can change us; we don't change ourselves.[159] The change I'm talking about is a change of identity which reflects the state of our hearts and our willingness to humble ourselves before Him. It is far more important to focus on identity than sexuality. Embracing your identity drives you to pursue fulfillment in a particular direction. My heart changed and I

---

159 Inner healing is something we must pursue as broken people. Even though no inner healing ministry can guarantee change, many people have received transformation (I am one of them). This includes the diminishing of same-sex attractions. For others it can even ignite heterosexual desires.

shifted my identity from being gay to being a beloved daughter of the King of Kings. And when we obey the Lord by truly putting Him first, and by following Him and doing what is right, our paths *become* straight, even though we remain crooked.

The path of those who do right is straight and smooth. O God, You who are upright, You make the way of the righteous level.

—Isaiah 26:7, The Voice

Q: What was the reason for you to make that change?

A: I sensed that God's presence had gone away from me, and I felt distant from Him. I felt that He was far away. There was a wall. I felt guilt and shame. I wasn't even sure if I was going to heaven if I continued to live in disobedience, following my flesh. This separation drove me back to Him. I became desperate. I was hungry for more of the Lord, as I had tasted and seen that He was good prior to me caving in to my sexual desires. I wanted to feel that closeness with God again, so I ran back like the prodigal son in Luke 15. I repented, asked for forgiveness, and chose to walk away from a homosexual lifestyle.

Q: What was your biggest struggle in making that change?

A: My flesh. It was hard to stay celibate in the beginning. It was a big fight, but when I focused on Jesus in the times when I felt weak, I became victorious. I also got accountability partners who started to journey with me.

Q: Can homosexuals go to heaven if they are followers of God?

A: Again, we have to clarify the terminology. Do they merely experience same-sex attractions or are they living a homosexual lifestyle? We cannot judge and decide who goes to heaven or not. I do know the Word of God: He is clear about how He wants us to live our lives. He calls us to be set apart and to live holy before Him. Practicing and living a homosexual lifestyle is not a holy life before the Lord. But God alone will decide; it will be between that person and God. All I know is that when I lived it, I did not feel peace and I was worried that I wouldn't make it to heaven. I always want to make sure I am ready to meet Jesus.

Q: What do I say if someone says it's right or okay to be homosexual?

A: First, we need to be brave. We need to learn how to answer this in love and compassion, yet we need backbones of steel. We need to speak the truth and share that it is not natural to experience same-sex attractions, and acting on it is not pleasing to the Lord. God made us male and female. In sharing biblical truths, you will most likely offend people. And some will tell you because you disagree with them, that means you hate them. Be encouraged; Jesus offended many. So stay strong, and don't be afraid.

Q: How do I make friends with homosexuals?
A: Be there for them, show you care, talk to them, listen to them, and love them. Don't push them away if they are weird or do weird things. Meet them where they're at on their journey. Don't try to change them. That is the work of God. Instead try to humbly lead them towards desiring holiness.

Q: What makes you change? Why would you decide to change?
A: As I answered earlier, I changed when I felt separated from God.

Q: I had a friend who is lesbian. We were really good friends before. After I told her that I believe in Jesus, she pushed me away. I felt really sad. Please tell me what I can do and how I can help her.
A: It is sad when this happens. Your friend most likely felt convicted in your presence, as you are carrying the light of Jesus in your heart. This is what happened: light and darkness don't go together, so she felt uncomfortable. I will say that you need to continue to be there for her, pray for her, and ask that Jesus will draw her to Him. Stand in the gap for her and don't stop.

Q: When did you realize you like girls? How was your feeling when you realized that? Why did you change your mind?
A: I realized it when I went to university, but I was confused because I dated men at the same time. Dating women felt wrong, but at same time it felt wrong to have sex with a boyfriend. I was confused. I wanted to feel attracted to men, but there were no signs. When I was with a woman, I felt those butterflies in my stomach, so I wanted to be physical with them, holding hands, kissing, etc.

Because of my knowledge of the Bible, I knew it was wrong and unnatural, so I tried to fight it. It was very hard. I really didn't want to live a life that was displeasing to the Lord.

Q: What does homosexual mean to you?
A: When a person says to me that they're gay or homosexual, I will always ask them this: do you experience same-sex attractions and are you living celibate, or do you have a same-sex partner? It's always good to clarify and hear from the person firsthand before we make assumptions. We always need to ask the right questions and make sure we listen to them and try to understand their heart and where they're coming from. We need to not judge them, but it's important to clarify how we speak and that we understand what they mean, too.

Q: How do we talk to people who are homosexual and don't know about Jesus?
A: We need to be patient, build trust, and work on the friendship. Share your story with them, if asked. Over time, as they see you living a life of excellence and integrity, shining the light of Jesus, they will recognize that you are different from the world. And they may start to desire the same. When we are salt and light, the salt makes them thirsty… and when we shine the light, it will

illuminate the darkness in them—but also in us, as we all sin. Then the Holy Spirit will convict them that they need Jesus.

Our unconditional love towards them, and the way we live our lives, bearing fruit, will want them to have the same. Don't give up on people—Jesus never did.

APPENDIX C

Who Is Your Master?[160]
Study Guide

For Youth, Parents, Teachers, and Pastors on the Topic of Holy Sexuality and How to Win the Battle Between the Spirit and the Flesh

I believe that this teaching, even though it was developed for children, is for *all* of us. I have included it in this book because I know it has the potential to help many people, young and old. The truth is that we need to get back to basics, not only in regards to the topic of homosexuality, but also many other aspects of our Christian walk.

The Bible talks about our need to have faith like children. As was mentioned in earlier chapters, the church has remained an infant in regards to learning how to approach and love persons who experience same-sex attractions.

In this teaching, I use my dogs and very simple language to explain the complex and challenging topics of homosexuality and holy sexuality. I also use other simple illustrations to explain the vital necessity of abiding in the Vine, Jesus, every day. High English, scientific evidence, and theologians can sometimes make things seem very complicated. We need simple illustrations which will stick. We need the amazing truths from God's Word to lead us and guide us.

In this study guide, I also address the consequences we face for our sometimes poor choices, and for choosing not to obey the Lord. I discuss in detail what we can do to become victorious, regardless of what we struggle with.

This material can be used by parents with their children (from the age of nine, supervised) or it can be used as a Bible study guide by church groups, including youth (from the age of thirteen, unsupervised).

---

160 This workbook and study guide is also available as a video presentation. The DVD is available through my website (http://wilnavanbeek.com/resources-2.php), or it can be viewed on *YouTube* (https://www.youtube.com/watch?v=uilCUYI4e0s).

A Little About Me and This Study Guide

For as long as I can remember, I knew I was different. I always wished I had been born a boy. At the age of twenty-one, I began to live a homosexual lifestyle. Having been taught the Word of God from a young age, I felt so ashamed. I knew I was living a lifestyle that was displeasing to the Lord.

Struggling under the weight of my lies and leading a double life, my fear, shame, and guilt kept me silent. Yet deep down I hoped that someday, somehow, my story would be brought into the light.

Today, God is using my story to heal and bring hope to many people. My seminars and resources (like this one) help to educate, equip, and enlighten the body of Christ about some difficult and relevant issues of our day: sexuality and identity. I try to share authentically about my struggles, the consequences of my choices, and how through the power of the Holy Spirit I was able to walk away from a homosexual lifestyle. I continue to be victorious in this area of my life!

This study guide is based on a session that was filmed in front of a live audience at Regina Christian School in March 2016. Although recommended as a student resource (for those over the age of thirteen), it is also highly beneficial as a teaching tool for parents and leaders. If you personally need help understanding homosexuality or holy sexuality better, this is for you.

It doesn't matter what you struggle with: the battle is real. But with the help of the Holy Spirit, you can win the war! May God bless you as you set out on the path to victory.

Love, Wilna.

Wilna van Beek

WHO IS YOUR *Master?*

STUDY GUIDE

What people are saying

There are so many voices today attempting to address the issue of sexual identity that confusion and calamity reign supreme. It is, without a doubt, one of the most controversial and contentious issues facing the church in this present generation. Christian young people, especially, are assailed from every direction with contradicting views, both from within and without the church, as even the church itself is polarized to the extreme.

Some are wholly embracing the most liberal views, while others have adopted the views of the most legalistic Pharisees. The former contends that homosexuality is an "act of God" and is to be celebrated; the latter condemns persons ascribing to homosexuality and its variants in the most despicable terms imaginable.

Finally, into this darkness and theological chaos, God has said, "Let there be light!" I believe this light to be in the person and message of Wilna van Beek. It is a message of love and understanding. It is a message of holiness and consecration. It is a message that reconciled my heart and my theology. It is the voice of experience. It is the voice of reason. I believe it is the voice of God.

—Todd Harrison[161]
Principal, Harvest City Christian Academy

This material is necessary for teenagers.

—Easton, Age 15

Get ready to be confronted with hope and truth. Wilna masterfully simplifies the complex issues of homosexuality, capturing the attention of all with her three adorable dogs. It is a magnificent teaching tool filled with rich truths, insight, and practical answers for tough questions. Wilna speaks with courage and grace, having formerly experienced same-sex attractions. She understands the pain and the shame and leaves us with a longing to know the One who can truly set us free. She reminds us that "all things are possible with God." You will not be disappointed!

—Elisabeth Martens
Parent and Mentor

We were pleased to have Wilna speak to our student body and staff on what can be a very difficult subject. She was non-judgmental, compassionate, and loving as she shared openly from her own experience and the truth of God's Word. It's evident that Wilna's greatest desire is to see people set free from pain, confusion, and condemnation by the power of the Holy Spirit. She is an excellent communicator with

---

161   Todd Harrison is the principal of Harvest City Christian Academy and has been an elder and member of the leadership team of Harvest City Church in Regina, Saskatchewan for almost thirty years. His experience in working with Christian youth in various roles spans more than thirty-five years. Harvest City Church is a member of LifeLinks International.

a clear understanding of Scripture and God's love for each person no matter where they are at in their lives. I would highly recommend her presentation to schools and churches.

—Rod Rilling
Principal, Regina Christian School

Wilna van Beek presents a straightforward presentation about choices and homosexuality. Her perspective as one who lived a lesbian lifestyle and made a choice for Christ lends weight to her message. She challenges us to choose Christ and backs that call with Scripture and illustrations from her own testimony. She shares in such a way as to make this study guide a great tool for parents teaching their children, or for church and youth groups wanting to discuss the topic.

—Boyd Hopkins, M.Div.
Spoken Word Ministries Association

Introduction

Then you will know the truth, and the truth will make you free.

—John 8:32, NCV

The notes to this study guide are based on a presentation I made to a group of adolescent high school students (Grades Eight through Twelve) attending a Christian school. In this short study guide, we are going to take a look at this question: who is your master? We will also explore the term "holy sexuality" and what it means to live a chaste life.

As we consider our central question, I hope you will agree that when we accept Jesus into our hearts, when we say yes to Him, we make Him our Master. Right? We ask Him to come into our hearts and reign there. Correct? It is my prayer that you have done this already, but if you haven't yet made that decision, this is your opportunity to do just that.

So, from that starting point, if Jesus is our Lord and Savior, we have a new identity. This makes us children of God, sons and daughters of the King of Kings.

Imagine that you and I are sitting together and having a heart-to-heart conversation. Let's say you were to say to me, "Wilna, I struggle with stuff in my life." What if the struggles you confessed included same-sex attractions, gender confusion, or pornography? All of these struggles may cause you to assume that this makes you a _____. You can fill in the blank!

"Wilna, if this is what I'm experiencing," you may wonder, "how can I possibly consider myself a son or daughter of the King of Kings?"

I want you to know that no matter what you struggle with in life, it should *never* define who you are. That is not your true identity! If you have accepted Jesus, you are a beloved son or daughter of God. He wants you to pursue an intimate relationship with Him on a daily basis, regardless of what you struggle or identify with. Jesus loves you very much and He always meets us where we're at.

Who Is Your Master?

I'd like you to meet my dogs!

    I want you to pay close attention to what I share about them, as there will be plenty of tidbits to take home. First, all three of them are rescue dogs. Don't you think that Jesus rescues us, too?

    We all sin, right? The Bible says in Romans 3:23 that we have all sinned and fall short of the glory of God. We all need Him. In Matthew 9:12, He asks, *"Who needs a doctor: the healthy or the sick?"* (MSG) Jesus came to rescue all of us!

When Gay Comes Home

A Loving Brother or Sister

Back to my dogs. Meisie was just added to our household six months ago, and I'll admit that she is very stubborn. Because she doesn't yet listen to her master's voice, I purposely attached her to Thursdae, who already listens to my voice and obeys me. This will hopefully help Meisie to follow her sister's good example.

Sometimes we need a loving sister or brother to come alongside us to keep us accountable, or perhaps to help us stay on the right track. Would you agree? This brother or sister may lovingly tell us to amend our ways. This may just be how God wants to help you to stay on the right track, or to turn back from a road that may lead to your own destruction. God may just use this person to bring you back to Him.

Don't try to be strong on your own. Have accountability partners. We aren't meant to journey alone. We were created for relationship!

When we make a fire with charcoal briquettes and we remove one briquette, how long will it take before the fire dies out? Not long, right? But if the briquettes stay together, the fire burns for a long time.

We need each other! Surround yourself with brothers and sisters in faith.

Craving the Master

When I adopted my dogs, I not only became their owner, I became their *master*. Dogs need a master. Or, in the dog world, a pack leader. In my house, I'm their pack leader.[162]

As I'm their master, they obey me. They want to please me. Because they love me, they do what I tell them. They want to be with me. Why? Because my presence—my love and affection—is all they're looking for. They love my touch and crave it. If only they can be with me all day, that's good enough for

---

162 At this point, however, Meisie has been trying to be the pack leader. She is a terrier, after all! So we're working on the order of hierarchy.

them. They also trust me, because I feed them and look after their needs. They also learn to recognize and listen to my voice.

The Voice of the Master

Did you know that dogs can hear and recognize their master's voice amongst hundreds of other noises?

While speaking to groups, I'll often make my dogs sit on stage. I then walk away and ask the audience to start talking to each other. Then I remove my mic and call my dogs by name. They hear my voice and respond immediately! Afterwards I take them back onstage and do it all over again. But this time I'll ask a member of the audience to call my dogs. The dogs don't respond—because they only know and trust their master's voice!

The spiritual world is no different. When we accept Jesus into our hearts, He becomes our Master—if we let Him. Ideally, we learn to hear His voice daily and respond to it. He says, *"My sheep hear My voice"* (John 10:27, NKJV), so we start listening to Him. And if we want to obey and please Him, because we love Him, we learn that there is a reward now and for eternity. As Jesus says, *"I have come so that they may have life and have it in abundance"* (John 10:10, HCSB). This means abundant life here and now, and also for eternity. When He becomes our Master, we *want* to listen to His voice, and not the voice of Satan, the voice of our flesh, or the voice of the world around us.

Jesus wants us to make Him our Master, whose voice we know, recognize, listen to, and obey. And just so you know, following Jesus wholeheartedly and being obedient to Him will always cost you something.

What has it cost you so far?

Just as my dogs have a choice whether to obey my voice, so do we. We must choose to obey God or not. Because my dogs love me, they want to please me. If we truly love God, we want to obey and please Him, and follow His commands: *"If you [really] love Me, you will keep (obey) My commands"* (John 14:15, AMPC).

When Jesus becomes our Master, we seek His presence daily. We want to sit with Him and enjoy His presence, just as my dogs want to be with me all day. This makes them very happy. When we "sit" with Him, He is faithful to direct our steps.

> *You will show me the path of life; in Your presence is fullness of joy; in Your right hand there are pleasures forevermore.*
>
> —Psalm 16:11, AMP

When He is our Master, we learn to hear, know, and respond to His voice. The Bible teaches us that He is the Good Shepherd and we are His sheep:

My sheep listen to my voice. I know them, and they follow me.

—John 10:27, ICB

The sheep that are My own hear My voice and listen to Me; I know them, and they follow Me.

—John 10:27, AMP

My sheep recognize my voice. I know them, and they follow me.

—John 10:27, MSG

So why is it that we don't hear His voice? And why is it that we don't follow or obey Him as our Master? Why do we cave in to things we know are wrong?

Personally, I think there are a few reasons.

1. We don't make time to listen.

Unfortunately, with our busy lives, we don't make time to listen. And yes, God still speaks today. How? He uses many ways. In Numbers, He used a donkey to speak to a man named Balaam.

Balaam had disobeyed God, but God loved Balaam and wanted to protect him from travelling in the wrong direction. So He sent an angel to block the road. Only the donkey could see the angel. When the donkey stopped in her tracks, Balaam was very angry and hit her. That was when God opened the mouth of the donkey.

You can read all about it in Numbers 22. It's a very compelling story!

God can use His Word. He can use other people to speak to us. He can speak to us through nature, through music, through dreams, or through dog illustrations like I'm doing now.

Journaling has also played a huge role in my life when it comes to hearing God's voice. At times when I need to make a major decision, I've often gotten clear answers through journaling. God doesn't specifically tell me exactly what to do, so I have to trust and obey Him.

Sometimes He wants us to get out of the boat and walk out into the unknown. As long as we keep our eyes on him, we won't sink.

Take time to quietly consider your responses to these questions:

- What time did you get up this morning?
- How much time did you spend reading God's Word and praying?
- Did you make time to listen to Him, or did you need to rush?
- When do you spend time with God?
- When do you make time to sit and listen to Him?

I want to challenge you as a reader to make time for your relationship with God. You may be surprised just how He'll speak to you.

To clarify, there are many voices we can listen to: our own voice, the voice of Satan, the voice of the world, and the voice of God. God's voice isn't necessarily audible, but it can be that still, small voice.

Know that when God speaks to us, it will never be negative; it will always be uplifting, edifying, and it may warn us when we're on a wrong path. Satan's voice will always lead us astray, or it will be negative. Our own voice, and the voice of the world, can also lead us astray. Both of these voices more often than not speak out of our fleshly desires.

This leads us to the second reason why we don't follow and obey Jesus as our Master.

2. Our flesh gets in the way.

Romans 8:3 says, *"For God has done what the Law could not do, [its power] being weakened by the flesh [the entire nature of man without the Holy Spirit]"* (AMPC). This same chapter of the Bible also describes the mind of the flesh like this: *"Now the mind of the flesh [which is sense and reason without the Holy Spirit] is death…"* (Romans 8:6, AMP)

So our spirits may be born again and alive, but our flesh can get in the way. There's a battle going on. While we're alive, there will be a constant battle between our flesh and the spirit man. These two are fighting each other (Galatians 5:17). It is literally a war for our souls, a war between following and being obedient to what God tells us to do from His Word or following our fleshly desires.

There is a struggle between *what the Bible says* and *what our flesh wants.*

Spirit vs. flesh

Spirit	Flesh
Sex is to be enjoyed in marriage between one naturally born male and one naturally born female. 1 Corinthians 7:1-5	I can sleep with whom I want, when I want.
"Looking" and lusting is sin. Matthew 5:28	Porn is harmless.
Acting on same-sex attraction is sin. Leviticus 18:22	God made me this way, I can love whom I want.
Your body is a temple of the Holy Spirit. 1 Corinthians 6:17-20	My body is for my pleasure, whether healthy or unhealthy.
Guard and guide your heart. Proverbs 4:22	I should follow my heart.
Serve one another humbly in love. Galations 5:13	I don't need anyone.
It is a blessing to live according to biblical principles. James 1:25	I should do what makes me happy.
Live not only for the present life, but also for the life to come. 1 Timothy 4:6-10	YOLO. (You Only Live Once.)

Who Is Your Master?

The reality is that this war will go on until the day we die.

When you wake up in the morning, Satan readies his attacks on your life. His aim is to drive you as far away from God as he possibly can. He is not only the accuser of the brethren, but he will tempt you in areas of your life where you are weak. And don't we all fall? Don't we all give in? Our spirit may be willing, but our flesh is weak (Matthew 26:41).

The Tale of Two Dogs

Consider this scenario. Two dogs are pitted against each other in a fight to the death. They're kept in separate cages, but each day they attack one another when they're let out. Eventually one will die. Which dog will win? Is it the one who is stronger? Faster? Bigger? Smarter? Perhaps the one that you like the most?

It is the one that you *feed*.

When Thursdae and Meisie play tug-of-war, Thursdae will most likely win because she is bigger and stronger. But if I were to starve Thursdae for thirty days, she wouldn't have any energy, and therefore she would no longer be the stronger one.[163]

Who are you feeding? Your spirit or your flesh? Is there a bad habit of yours that comes to mind? Perhaps you're clicking that computer button and watching things you know you shouldn't. Maybe you like to smoke or get high on drugs or alcohol. These are all ways to feed your fleshly desires.

The reality is that as long as we live, we will have to deal with our flesh *and* our spirit. And the one we feed the most is the one who will win! We must choose which one to feed.

---

163 By the way, I would *never* starve my dogs!

If we don't spend quality time with God on a daily basis, are we feeding our spirit or our flesh? And which will end up winning the fight? This is why Paul said, *"I do not do the good things that I want to do. I do the bad things that I do not want to do"* (Romans 7:19, ICB). His flesh was in the way.

Our sinful selves want what is against the Spirit. The Spirit wants what is against our sinful selves. The two are against each other. So you must not do just what you please.

—Galatians 5:17, ICB

Have you ever internally resolved "I am never going to do that ever again!" only to find yourself doing it again the next day? Why is this? Could it be that your spirit is willing but your flesh is weak?

I struggled like this too. When I entered into my first homosexual relationship, I knew it was wrong. It felt wrong. I knew it was not normal to feel attracted towards the same sex, and I knew it was not God's will for my life… but I did it anyway. My spirit was willing, but my flesh was weak.

I so desperately needed and wanted someone to love me and to be with me, but caving in cost me a lot. Entering into and living a homosexual lifestyle not only created a separation from God, but it created a dryness in my soul. I felt lost. I felt no joy. I felt shame and guilt! And worst of all, I didn't sense God's presence any longer.

My Testimony

Let me start from the beginning and tell you a bit about my journey. As long as I can remember, I was different. I believed the myth going around in South Africa that if I could run under a rainbow, it would change my sex. I tried to run under every rainbow I saw! I just wanted to be a boy.

I grew up in a Christian home, but we had much dysfunction going on, including a dad who was easily angered and abusive to my mother. I've since been told that I didn't want to have anything to do with my grandpa, and he passed away when I was just a year and a half old. I also pushed my father away. My dad took this personally, and as a result we never had the quality father-daughter relationship I longed for. This didn't help in my relationship with my heavenly Father.

I always felt uneasy around men, and I kept them at a distance. In fact, I was terrified of them! Recently, during an intensive prayer time at a ministry called Elijah House,[164] Jesus showed me why I was so terrified. While my mom had been pregnant with me, I'd picked up on what was going on in our

---

164 Elijah House "was founded with the mandate to restore the hearts of the fathers to their children, and the hearts of the children to their fathers (Malachi 4:5–6). This is being accomplished by equipping the saints with biblical tools founded upon universal laws in the Word of God, to enable discernment of root issues and allow true healing" (https://www.elijahhouse.org/page/website.aboutus).

home—the physical and emotional abuse, yelling and screaming.[165] This fear led me to vow that I would push all men away and keep them at a distance for the rest of my life.

When I was born, I wouldn't let any man near me. The fear of men then drove me into the arms of women. I felt safe with women. I didn't choose to be gay, but the fear of men created some bad fruit in my life: same-sex-attractions.

God did not make me this way. I experienced same-sex attractions because of sin and the fallen world we live in.

This sort of thing happens to all of us. Look at this picture of the roots and the fruit:

When bad things happen to us, it creates bad roots which in turn bear bad fruit. God wants to heal us from all this, but doing so means that we need to go back and cut the bad roots.

But this is a topic for another day. Back to my story.

The church my family attended didn't preach salvation through belief in Jesus, but rather that He would punish us if we did anything wrong. They preached that we had to be good before Jesus would accept us. So even though Jesus was God to me, He was not a gentle God. He was this big man with a stick, ready to club me if I did anything wrong. Nobody ever told me that Jesus loved me just the way I am.

I tried very hard to be good, but I kept struggling with the fact that I was "different." So when I was twenty-one years old, I entered into my first homosexual relationship.

I really had no clue what I was doing, as I was dating both men and women at the same time. Dating women didn't feel right, but at the same time having sex with a boyfriend seemed wrong too. I tried

---

165 After my healing time at Elijah House, I read a book called *The Secret Life of the Unborn Child*, by Dr. Thomas Verny and John Kelly (New York, NY: Dell, 1982), which confirmed the ways in which unborn babies are influenced by external factors outside the womb.

so hard to change and to feel attracted to men, but it just never worked. And when women came along, there it was—that strong attraction.

This is a reality for people who claim to experience same-sex attractions. It is there. You just can't help it! It isn't fair to tell them to just "pray the gay away." In some cases, by the power of Jesus, you can lay hands on people, pray, and they'll go away healed or cured. God can do impossible things! But there are no guarantees. Same-sex attractions may never go away. For me, it certainly didn't go away instantly. It has been a long journey.

I accepted Jesus fully into my heart at the age of twenty-six, and my life changed in a moment. Despite getting to know Jesus and living for Him, though, I still chose to live a homosexual life.

My spirit was willing, but my flesh was weak. The moment I entered into a homosexual relationship, a wall went up between me and God, and I felt separated from Him.

> *But your iniquities have made a separation between you and your God, and your sins have hidden His face from you, so that He will not hear.*
>
> —Isaiah 59:2, AMPC

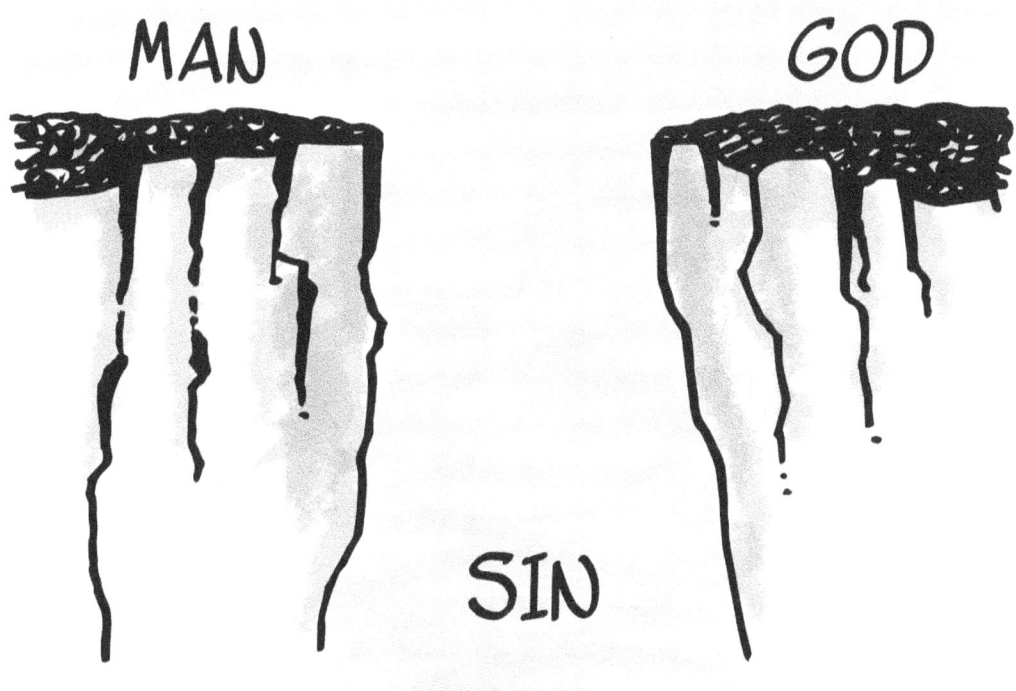

To be separated from God isn't a good feeling, and it brought me to a place of total surrender in 2003. I cried out to God to please change me, as I couldn't live without His presence in my life any longer.

At that time, I also chose to embrace chastity.[166] This means that a person doesn't engage in sexual relations outside of marriage. Chastity in marriage means that you don't use your spouse for your lustful pleasures, and that you remain faithful to your spouse—in thought, word, and action!

Embracing chastity for me means that I choose to practice and embrace *holy sexuality*.[167]

I repented of my homosexual behavior and walked away from the lifestyle. Repentance means to turn around and walk the other way. I chose to walk away out of my love for God—and because I wanted to please Him in all that I do.

Making Him the center of my life and inviting Him into my heart is the key to how things started to change. I started to experience victory!

---

166 Another word we use is "celibacy."
167 I'll discuss this term a bit more later.

The Bike Wheel and the House

Let's examine this using the example of a bike wheel:

In the middle of the wheel is the hub, which holds all the spokes together. If you remove the hub, what will happen to the wheel? Well, it'll fall apart!

When we accept Jesus, He desires to become the hub of our life wheel. He longs for us to surrender every area of our hearts to Him.

All the compartments between the spokes represent areas of our lives. When I made Jesus the hub, my whole life started to change—not only in regards to my sexuality, but in every area. This was key. I had to surrender and acknowledge that in my own power I could not change the things I wanted to. But by surrendering and allowing God to do the work, slowly but surely things started to change.

Now, I also like to explain this using the analogy of a house. You may have heard pastors, or others, share similar analogies, but note how I've made sense out of my own house story.

As a Christian, when I accepted Jesus into my heart, I invited Him into my "house." That's what I did when I initially invited Christ into my life back in 1991. I welcomed Him in, and like a good hostess I showed Him around. I gave Him the tour, explaining where the bathroom was, the living room, the kitchen, and the guest room.

I told Him not to go into my closet, as it is was full of "stuff." I also told Him that I had locked the door to the basement. My basement had stuff in it I didn't want Him to see: sin, shame, and guilt!

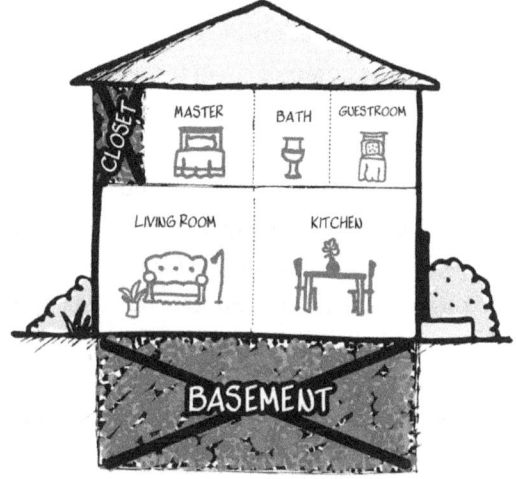

I avoided letting Him into those intimate spaces. This is a tactic of Satan, who knows that when we allow Jesus in, he must flee.

By not allowing Jesus into these locked areas, I didn't experience victory in my life. Therefore, I experienced destruction, and I didn't understand why until I had the revelation of the house in 2003.

If I would have asked Jesus to tell me why I experienced destruction, I believe this is how He would have answered: "Yes, you invited Me in, and I'm excited to be here… but you didn't give Me access to every room in the house."

By not allowing Him into my basement and closet, I was restricting Him as a guest. I didn't allow Him to make any changes to my house.

Jesus wants to live in us permanently—as an owner. We must give Him access to every room and not shut Him out. Inviting Jesus into the closet and basement of my heart was the key to starting the change that led to victory. When we allow light to come, darkness must go! Psalm 18:28 (AMP) declares, *"For You cause my lamp to be lighted and to shine; the Lord my God illumines my darkness"* (AMP).

Isaiah 42:16 reminds us that God sees what we do not, and He will be a constant companion:

I will lead the blind by a way they do not know; I will guide them in paths that they do not know. I will make darkness into light before them and rugged places into plains. These things I will do [for them], and I will not leave them abandoned or undone. (AMP)

John 1:5 informs us that the darkness doesn't win in the end:

The Light shines on in the darkness, and the darkness did not understand it or overpower it or appropriate it or absorb it [and is unreceptive to it]. (AMP)

When we allow the light of Jesus into our closets and basements, darkness has to go. We can't do this on our own!

Let me say it again: making Jesus the hub of my life and inviting Him into the basement and closet of my heart was what ultimately broke the power of sin over my life. This is why I can say today that no man, psychiatrist, self-help book, or even my own effort to change myself could do for me what the Holy Spirit has done.

You may ask, "Wilna, who are you now?" Because I've chosen Christ above everything else, I no longer self-identify as gay. My embraced identity today is this: *I am a beloved daughter of the Most High God. I seek after and pursue holiness in all I do. I practice holy sexuality through chaste living.*

I was only able to get here through a daily and intimate relationship with Jesus, as I put Him first and at the center of my heart. Jesus truly became my Master and I want to obey Him rather than my fleshly desires.

When Jesus became my all-in-all, He started to change and transform my whole life. Change is possible. Our identity can change when we realize our need and when we're willing for God to work in us. But we cannot change ourselves. Only God can change us!

Can we change other people? No! Paul had an argument with Apollos about whose work was the most important. He came to the conclusion that it is God who makes us grow:

I planted the seed of the teaching in you, and Apollos watered it. But God is the One who made the seed grow.

—1 Corinthians 3:6, ICB

He can and will do the same for you! He will meet you where you are. The only requirement is that you have to return to Him and be *willing*. He will take you as you are.

Today I am joyfully celebrating my fourteenth year of chaste living—to God be all the glory! I make Him part of every day, and through this powerful principle and habit I have become a conqueror. Through total surrender and submission to God, I can say that today my same-sex attractions are nonexistent.

But this was a journey, and it did not happen overnight. I know He isn't done with me yet. Sanctification is a lifelong process. Are any of us perfect? Is He done with *you* yet?

The fact that my same-sex attractions are nonexistent doesn't mean this will happen to every person who struggles with these attractions—and we must remember this. Every person's journey is different, but things *can* change.

He Makes No Mistakes

I have struggled for many years trying to figure out how I started to experience same-sex attractions. Things happen to us as humans—things which are not God's will, but He allows them. They hurt Him as much as they hurt us.

During a prophetic prayer and ministry time, Jesus took me back to a scene from my childhood. This was very hurtful for me.

Here's what happened.

We were sitting at the dinner table. My father got mad at my mother and began to throw plates and break glasses. There was screaming and cussing. My sisters and I just sat watching, frozen in fear.

Now, back to the prophetic ministry time—my counsellor asked me if I could see Jesus in that picture. It took me a while, but then I saw Him sitting in the empty chair next to me. And do you know what He was doing while observing this fearful situation? He was crying! I saw tears running down His face! He not only saw what happened, but *cried* for me and for the pain I was going through.

Seeing this helped me to understand Jesus better. He loves us so much, and when painful things happen to us, He feels the same pain and cries with and for us.

Even though painful things happen to all of us, the reality is that Jesus is always present and He cares deeply about us.

Knowing that Jesus is always present gives me such peace. When I go through hard times now, I know that He's with me and that He never leaves or forsakes me. And though Jesus doesn't always rescue us from hurtful situations, the fact remains that He is there and cares deeply.

I have learned that God allows things into my life to build my character. If I choose to learn from those experiences, He also uses my pain as gain for others. As Joyce Meyer once said, my *mess* is now my *message*. That's cool, right? Whatever you're going through, He knows about it! And He is with you, even though you may not feel Him or see Him.

God never makes mistakes. You are not a mistake, and neither am I. Even though I explained earlier how I got so afraid while I was still in my mom's womb, the fact is that God was there.

Here's another example of not-so-good things that can happen to us due to the fallen world we live in. Some babies are born blind, and others are born deaf or without limbs. Why? Because something happened in their mother's womb. This doesn't mean that God loves us less. He still has a plan and a purpose for our lives, regardless of how we came into the world.

> *While He [Jesus] was passing by, He noticed a man [who had been] blind from birth. His disciples asked Him, "Rabbi (Teacher), who sinned, this man or his parents, that he would be born blind?"*

> *Jesus answered, "Neither this man nor his parents sinned, but it was so that the works of God might be displayed and illustrated in him.*
>
> —John 9:1–3, AMP

Then Jesus healed him! And so this became a testimony of what God can do.

God can do impossible things. He transformed my life, and He can do the same for you. If you struggle with anything, remember that your identity remains: you are a son or daughter of God, and He loves you.

Unfortunately, today in the LGBTQIA (Lesbian, Gay, Bisexual, Transgender, Queer or Questioning, Intersex, and Asexual) world, people claim that God made them this way. Therefore, according to them, they can live the way God created them to be, whether that be L, G, B, T, Q, I, or A.

- Lesbian: A woman who is attracted romantically, erotically, and/or emotionally to other women.
- Gay: A term used to describe individuals who are primarily emotionally, physically, and/or sexually attracted to persons of the same sex and/or gender. It can also be used to refer to the queer community as a whole, or as an individual label for anyone who does not identify as heterosexual.
- Bisexual: A person who is emotionally, physically, and/or sexually attracted to both males and females.
- Transgender: A person who lives as a member of a gender other than their sex at birth.
- Questioning/Queer: An individual who is unsure about, or is exploring, their own sexual orientation or gender identity.
- Intersex: Someone whose combination of chromosomes, gonads, hormones, internal sex organs, and genitals differ from the two expected patterns of male or female.
- Asexual: Having a lack (or low level) of sexual attraction to others and/or a lack of interest or desire for sex or sexual partners.

God is clear in His word that it is not natural to experience same-sex attractions. These attractions could be a result of something that happened in the mother's womb or other painful experiences after birth. Many factors play a role in causing a person to experience these unnatural same-sex attractions.

> *…their women exchanged the natural function for that which is unnatural [a function contrary to nature], and in the same way also the men turned away from the natural function of the woman and were consumed with their desire toward one another, men with men committing shameful acts…*
>
> —Romans 1:26–27, AMP

Who Is Your Master?

Women stopped having natural physical relations with men for what is unnatural. In the same way, men stopped having natural physical relations with women and began wanting each other. Men did shameful things with other men.

—Romans 1:26–27, ICB

You must understand this: even though experiencing same-sex attractions isn't natural, some of us *do* experience it. In that experience, we're not *doing* anything wrong. However, dwelling in that experience, and acting on those attractions, is when it becomes displeasing to God—and a sin. Remember, it's not God's original intent for us to be attracted to the same sex. These attractions can happen because of sin in our fallen world.

So if you claim to be a person within the LGBTQIA community, the challenge remains to stay celibate. Living and practicing a homosexual life, or practicing any heterosexual sin, are sinful acts, and God forbids us to do them. Sin is sin.

God requires obedience from us. He requires chastity or celibacy. Chastity must continue to be practiced in marriage as well. Unfortunately, in the world we live in today, many ungodly, unbiblical, and unholy sexual practices are now widely accepted. To name a few: pornography, hookups, living together before marriage, same-sex marriage, abortion, and masturbation (which is a selfish act and can become very addicting)… the list goes on. None of the above is God's will for our lives. He requires holiness from us in all we do, including our sexuality.

Holy Sexuality

What is holy sexuality? And what does the Bible say about marriage and singleness?

God never intended for two women to be in a sexual relationship or for two men to have sex with each other. He strictly forbids it in His Word. He also forbids many other sinful behaviors. He doesn't want two people to have sex outside of marriage, either. So whether you practice a homosexual sin or heterosexual sin, it's still a sin.

Sex, however, is something beautiful. It was created by God, and it is only permissible between a naturally born male and a naturally born female in marriage. Let's look at what the Bible says about it.

1. God created male and female.

When Adam was alone in the garden, God didn't create another Adam. He created Eve, a female. When the Pharisees argued with Jesus about divorce, this is what Jesus answered:

Surely you have read in the Scriptures: When God made the world, "he made them male and female." And God said, "So a man will leave his father and mother and be united with his wife. And the two people will become one body." So the two are not two, but one. God joined the two people together. No person should separate them.

—Matthew 19:4–6, ICB

2. Some people are born to be single, and may stay single their whole lives.

Note that the Bible says,

There are different reasons why some men cannot marry. Some men were born without the ability to become fathers. Others were made that way later in life by other people.[168] *And other men have given up marriage because of the kingdom of heaven. But the person who can marry should accept this teaching about marriage.*

—Matthew 19:12, ICB

3. Singleness is not a bad thing.

As I speak, many comment, "Man is not made to be alone, so I have to get married, whether that's to someone of the opposite or same sex." No, you don't. This is what Paul writes about singleness:

Sometimes I wish everyone were single like me—a simpler life in many ways! But celibacy is not for everyone any more than marriage is. God gives the gift of the single life to some, the gift of the married life to others.

I do, though, tell the unmarried and widows that singleness might well be the best thing for them, as it has been for me. But if they can't manage their desires and emotions, they should by all means go ahead and get married. The difficulties of marriage are preferable by far to a sexually tortured life as a single.

—1 Corinthians 7:7–9, MSG

This is what the Lord says,[169] *"To the eunuchs who keep My Sabbaths and choose what pleases Me, and hold firmly to My covenant, to them I will give in My house and within My walls a memorial, and a name better than that of sons and daughters; I will give them an everlasting name which will not be cut off.*

—Isaiah 56:4–5, AMP

---

168 The word to describe this kind of a person is *eunuch*. It means that their testicles had been cut off. This is a physical representation of the cutting off of fleshly desires in order to make God's desires a priority.

169 This is what the Lord says to those who may remain single their whole lives, and who choose Him above everything else.

Wow! That is a powerful statement! A single person who follows Jesus wholeheartedly gets a name *better* than that of a son or daughter. It is worth it to stay single and celibate.

4. Marriage can and will be challenging.

The Bible says,

> *But if you decide to marry, that is not a sin. And it is not a sin for a girl who has never married to get married. But those who marry will have trouble in this life, and I want you to be free from this trouble.*
> —1 Corinthians 7:28, ERV

Part of the intent of marriage is for two people to help one another to mature—and this can be a difficult process. Marriage is designed not to make us happy, but to make us holy.[170]

5. It is not good to be unequally yoked.

You must consider this before you enter into a relationship. If your friend isn't a believer and you are, God is clear that He does not want this relationship to end in marriage.

> *Don't become partners with those who reject God. How can you make a partnership out of right and wrong? That's not partnership; that's war.*
> —2 Corinthians 6:14,8 MSG

Please don't get confused about these scriptures. God does want us to make friends with the world, otherwise how will they hear about Jesus? We are *in* the world but not *of* it (John 17:14).

6. Bad company corrupts good morals.

Paul wrote, *"Do not be fooled: 'Bad friends will ruin good habits'"* (1 Corinthians 15:33, ICB).

Did you know that forty to fifty percent of students who graduate from church or youth group will fail to stick with their faith in college?[171] Why is this? Have you made your faith your own? Have you

---

170 For more on this subject, I recommend Gary Thomas's book, *Sacred Marriage: What If God Designed Marriage to Make Us Holy More Than to Make Us Happy?* (Grand Rapids, MI: Zondervan, 2015)

171 For more information, see: "What Makes Faith Stick During College?" *Fuller Youth Institute.* September 6, 2011 (https://fulleryouthinstitute.org/articles/what-makes-faith-stick-during-college).

been abiding in the Vine?[172] Have you chosen to impact your friends, and not the other way around? Bad friends can ruin good habits. If you don't stand for something, you will fall for anything.

Nonbelievers get to know about Jesus through us, but we need to use caution to not allow them to ruin our good habits.

God's Will

What is God's will for us regarding our relationships and sexuality? Let me paint a picture of contrast. A high number of churchgoing youth are involved in unholy sexual practices. Here are some statistics for today:

- In a 2010 national survey in the U.S., more than a quarter of sixteen- to seventeen-year-olds said they were exposed to nudity online when they did not want to see it. In addition, twenty percent of sixteen-year-olds and thirty percent of seventeen-year-olds have received a "sext" (a sexually explicit text message).
- More than seven out of ten teens hide their online behavior from their parents in some way.
- Thirty-five percent of boys say they have viewed pornographic videos "too many times to count."
- More than half of boys and nearly a third of girls see their first pornographic images before they turn thirteen. In a survey of hundreds of college students, ninety-three percent of boys and sixty-two percent of girls said they were exposed to pornography before they turned eighteen. In the same survey, eighty-three percent of boys and fifty-seven percent of girls said they had seen images of group sex online.[173]

Today, close to forty percent of evangelical Christians not only approve, but will also practice unbiblical, unholy sexual practices.[174] These practices include same-sex marriage, pornography, living together before marriage, marital infidelity, and abortion. These things are *not* God's will for our lives. God requires holiness in all that we do. He wants our lives to bear good fruit!

God wants you to be holy and to stay away from sexual immorality. He wants each one of you to learn how to take a wife in a way that is holy and honorable. Don't give in to lust like people who do not know God. So do not wrong your brother or cheat him in this way. The Lord will punish people who do those things. We have already told you and warned you about that. God called us to

---

172 I will explain the concept as God as the Vine a bit later.

173 Luke Gilkerson, "Get the Latest Pornography Statistics," *Covenant Eyes*. February 19, 2013 (http://www.covenanteyes.com/2013/02/19/pornography-statistics/).

174 For more on this subject, I recommend *Emotionally Healthy Spirituality*, by Peter Scazzerro (Grand Rapids, MI: Zondervan, 2014). See page 30.

be holy and does not want us to live in sin. So the person who refuses to obey this teaching is refusing to obey God, not man.

—1 Thessalonians 4:3–8, ICB

What Does Holy Sexuality Look Like?

So what does holy sexuality look like for us, whether we are single or married?

1. I do what is acceptable in God's sight.

Because I love God, I want to please Him in everything I do. I want to do what is acceptable to Him. In pleasing the Lord, and in our pursuit of living and practicing holy sexuality, we must always remember that we cannot do it in our own strength. Jesus is clear in His word:

I am confident that the Creator, who has begun such a great work among you, will not stop in mid-design but will keep perfecting you until the day Jesus the Anointed, our Liberating King, returns to redeem the world.

—Philippians 1:6, The Voice

We are not able to do this unless we have faith in Jesus and a desire to obey Him—and Him alone.

[And try] to learn [by experience] what is pleasing to the Lord [and letting your lifestyles be examples of what is most acceptable to Him—your behavior expressing gratitude to God for your salvation]. Do not participate in the worthless and unproductive deeds of darkness, but instead expose them.

—Ephesians 5:10–11 AMP

2. I conform to God's will in thought, purpose, and action.

According to Paul in the Book of Romans,

And so, dear brothers and sisters, I plead with you to give your bodies to God because of all he has done for you. Let them be a living and holy sacrifice—the kind he will find acceptable. This is truly the way to worship him. Don't copy the behavior and customs of this world, but let God transform you into a new person by changing the way you think. Then you will learn to know God's will for you, which is good and pleasing and perfect.

—Romans 12:1–2, NLT

3. I treat my body as a temple of the Holy Spirit.

My body is a temple of the Holy Spirit, and I want to honor and bring glory to Him in and through my body. For me as a single person, I must choose to abstain from any form of sex and even guard and protect my mind and heart against any thoughts in regards to this.

> *Don't you realize that your body is the temple of the Holy Spirit, who lives in you and was given to you by God? You do not belong to yourself, for God bought you with a high price. So you must honor God with your body.*
> —1 Corinthians 6:19–20, NLT

4. I guard my heart.

The Bible says, *"The heart is deceitful above all things, and it is exceedingly perverse and corrupt and severely, mortally sick!"* (Jeremiah 17:9, AMPC)

The world tells us to follow our hearts, but God tells us in Proverbs 4:23 to *"keep and guard your heart"* (AMPC).

5. I choose to walk in obedience with God.

Paul wrote to the Colossians,

> *So put everything evil out of your life: sexual sin, doing anything immoral, letting sinful thoughts control you, and wanting things that are wrong. And don't keep wanting more and more for yourself, which is the same as worshiping a false god. God will show his anger against those who don't obey him, because they do these evil things.*
> —Colossians 3:5–6, ERV

Walking with God requires obedience. God doesn't require obedience in order for Him to love us. He loves us as we are, unconditionally. But imagine trying to maintain a close relationship with your parents if you refused to obey them. A good parent will place boundaries on their children's life in order to protect them from harm and strengthen their character.

God's design for the family is a good, though imperfect model for helping us understand the ways in which we can relate to Him. We will not be able to fully understand or emulate on earth the intimacy with our Father we can expect in Heaven—but it is worth pursuing now.

Who Is Your Master?

For now [in this time of imperfection] we see in a mirror dimly [a blurred reflection, a riddle, an enigma], but then [when the time of perfection comes we will see reality] face to face. Now I know in part [just in fragments], but then I will know fully, just as I have been fully known [by God].
—1 Corinthians 13:12, AMP

Author Wesley Hill wrote, "Faithfulness is a serious pursuit of God, not a gamble."[175] We *will* reap our reward, and it will be worth it!

Let your flesh take a back seat. Obey the Lord in all you do, even though it may not be easy. Obedience will help to build your character, and in the end you'll look more like Jesus. Jesus wants us to imitate Him all the time (Ephesians 5:1). In the process of following Jesus and obeying Him, we become holy.

Boyd Hopkins, an author and the founder of Spoken Word Ministries, has delivered seminars on biblical sexuality and dealing with pornography. He is well respected internationally and his ministry has helped many people get set free from sexual addictions. At a seminar on October 8, 2016, he said,

> I always say that holiness is first *who* you know (Jesus) and *then* what you do by living out your commitment to Him by the power of the Holy Spirit. Holiness is *not* a performance based thing that I become after I do what God says.

In pursuing God wholeheartedly and obeying Him, we must use caution to not let it become self-effort. As I've said, my own efforts didn't go so well, but through the power of the Holy Spirit I was transformed and my whole life changed. Through His power, I am also able to pursue Him. I can be obedient and allow Him to work in me and let my character become more like Jesus.

The Consequences of Unholy Sexual Practices

You may say to yourself, "But it's what I want! It feels good!" Does it? Perhaps for a time. But let's look at the consequences of unholy sexual practices. Do not be deceived. Bad roots will bear bad fruit.

1. It will cost you your life—your eternal life.

Beware the wild woman:

> *By her clever words she made him give in. By her pleasing words she led him into doing wrong. All at once he followed her. He was like an ox being led to the butcher. He was like a deer caught in a trap. But quickly an arrow shot through his liver. He was like a bird caught in a trap. He didn't know what he did would kill him. Now, my sons, listen to me. Pay attention to what I say. Don't let yourself be tricked by the woman who is guilty of adultery. Don't join her in her evil actions. She has*

---

175 Wesley Hill, *Washed and Waiting* (Grand Rapids, MI: Zondervan, 2010), 79.

ruined many good men. Many have died because of her. Going to her house is like taking the road to death. That road leads down to where the dead are.

—Proverbs 7:21–27, ICB

Keep in mind here that the woman's actions are being condemned, not the woman herself. Her wrong actions are capable of negatively influencing the man, but the man is still accountable for his own actions. Don't play the blame game!

Keep the rules and keep your life; careless living kills.

—Proverbs 19:16, MSG

For what does it profit a man to gain the whole world, and forfeit his life [in the eternal kingdom of God]?

—Mark 8:36, AMPC

2. It will kill your body.

There are serious physical consequences that come with unholy sexual practices. This is no secret. Disease and damage are far more likely to occur with these types of behaviors.

3. You will lose God's presence, and He won't hear you.

Isaiah warned us, "*It is your evil that has separated you from your God. Your sins cause him to turn away from you. And then he does not hear you*" (Isaiah 59:2, ICB).

God will never abandon His children, but He does allow us our own free will. If we desire to walk away from Him, He won't stop us. It grieves Him, but He allows it.

4. You will dwell in shame, guilt, and a loss of self-worth.

Your identity will be marred:

Adultery is a brainless act, soul-destroying, self-destructive; expect a bloody nose, a black eye, and a reputation ruined for good.

—Proverbs 6:32, MSG

A man who takes part in adultery doesn't have any sense. He will destroy himself. He will be beaten up and disgraced. And his shame will never go away.

—Proverbs 6:32–33, ICB

Not a great identity to have, right?

Our identity should be in Christ, but our willful participation in unholy sexual practices automatically brings shame, guilt, and a loss of self-worth. The devil will also continue with His lies, and instead of going back to who you really are as a son or daughter of God, you will dwell in shame and guilt, giving you an identity of low self-worth. This is not a great identity to have.

5. You will hurt others.[176]

The devil's intention in tempting us to sin is not only to harm us, but also to harm those around us. For a time, it may be easier to carry out unholy sexual practices believing the lie that "nobody has to know."

For there is nothing hidden that will not become evident, nor anything secret that will not be known and come out into the open.

—Luke 8:17, AMP

No matter how many steps we take to conceal our actions, sin and its consequences will always find a way into the open. And when we deceive others, there will inevitably be a loss of trust. The end result is broken relationships. If we sow dishonesty, shall we expect to harvest intimacy?

Even in cases where sexual sin is done publicly and we are affirmed in our unbiblical lifestyle choices, the people in our inner circle are not exempt from the repercussions of our actions. When we are confused about our identity and step outside the will of God for our lives, we are not living in abundance. We are settling for much less than what God intended for our lives when He created us.

As we live in this way, our example will point others to the same confusion and misguided beliefs about their identity as well. The cycle of negative side-effects that inevitably surface in our emotional, mental, physical, and spiritual well-being will continue in the lives of the people we have influenced. As we hurt ourselves, we hurt those we love.

But here's the good news. We can be victorious! We can live lives that are pleasing to the Lord. How?

How to Live a Victorious Life

Many times we expect God to do everything in our lives, and we just sit back and wait for Him to do it all. Unfortunately, it doesn't work like this. There are things we must do, and God will do the things we can't do.

Paul is one of my favorite writers in the New Testament, but there was one thing I didn't like when I read it for the first time. I was disappointed in Paul's words:

---

176 Note that this point is not referenced on the DVD or YouTube video.

> *Train yourself toward godliness (piety), [keeping yourself spiritually fit]. For physical training is of some value (useful for a little), but godliness (spiritual training) is useful and of value in everything and in every way, for it holds promise for the present life and also for the life which is to come.*
> —1 Timothy 4:7–8, AMPC

> *Exercise daily in God—no spiritual flabbiness, please! Workouts in the gymnasium are useful, but a disciplined life in God is far more so, making you fit both today and forever. You can count on this. Take it to heart.*
> —1 Timothy 4:7–8, MSG

Here, Paul mentions that physical training is of some value and useful for a little. As a sports fanatic, I was addicted to exercise. When I read this passage, I didn't like hearing that physical fitness is less important than spiritual fitness.

So, if spiritual fitness holds promises for the present life and also for the life to come, why is it that so many of us don't do it? Is it then any surprise that many Christians don't live victorious lives?

In order to become victorious, we need to discipline ourselves. It's almost like having a personal trainer at the gym—not to get physically fit, but spiritually fit. You cannot rely on the spirituality of others to get you through life. You have to create your own spiritual growth plan.

Discipline yourself and stick to it daily. If you want to remain faithful to God, there are practices you need to implement in your life. If you don't, you may become one of those heart-breaking statistics I mentioned earlier.

Becoming Spiritually Fit

So how do we become spiritually fit?

1. Abide in the Vine, daily.

This is one of my signature quotes. You and I will have zero power to overcome or live a life of victory unless we abide in Jesus every day. Jesus says,

> *I am the Vine; you are the branches. The one who remains in Me and I in him bears much fruit, for [otherwise] apart from Me [that is, cut off from vital union with Me] you can do nothing.*
> —John 15:5, AMP

When Martha complained to Jesus about her sister Mary, who was sitting at His feet and not helping with the chores, this was Jesus's response:

But the Lord replied to her, "Martha, Martha, you are worried and bothered and anxious about so many things; but only one thing is necessary, for Mary has chosen the good part [that which is to her advantage], which will not be taken away from her."

—Luke 10:41–42, AMP

We all need to practice this. It is vital.

Seek Me [inquire for and of Me and require Me as you require food] and you shall live!

—Amos 5:4, AMPC

To truly live, the best habit is to abide in Jesus. Daily!

2. Have an active prayer life.

Prayer is a two-way conversation. We need to make time and not be lazy! God wants to speak to all of us, but we usually don't make time to listen. When Jesus talked about prayer, He said,

And when you pray, you shall not be like the hypocrites. For they love to pray standing in the synagogues and on the corners of the streets, that they may be seen by men. Assuredly, I say to you, they have their reward. But you, when you pray, go into your room, and when you have shut your door, pray to your Father who is in the secret place; and your Father who sees in secret will reward you openly.

—Matthew 6:5–6, NKJV

In the King James Version, the word "room" is translated as "closet." The Greek word in this context is *tameon*, which means "the place where treasures are stored."[177] The place where you spend time with God is the place where the real treasures are found. A life of prayer is a powerful habit to have!

3. Read and memorize scripture, daily.

The Bible says,

This Book of the Law shall not depart from your mouth, but you shall read [and meditate on] it day and night, so that you may be careful to do [everything] in accordance with all that is written in it; for then you will make your way prosperous, and then you will be successful.

—Joshua 1:8, AMP

---

177 E4—*Champions Encounter* (Little Falls, South Africa: Little Falls Christian Centre, 1998), 9. From the second edition.

Your word is like a lamp that guides my steps, a light that shows the path I should take.
—Psalm 119:105, ERV

One way I like to memorize Scripture is by writing verses on recipe cards. I keep them with me wherever I go. I rehearse them as I go for walks or during my time with the Lord. During difficult times, or when I can't sleep, I'll recite those scriptures and it will often bring peace or clarity. We must remember that the Word of God is our weapon of defense, and we must use it! Jesus used it all the time against Satan.

4. Keep a journal.

If you don't already keep a journal, I encourage you to start. God wants to speak to us. When I've faced major decisions in my life, answers have often come to me as I was journaling.

5. Know your true enemy and clothe yourself with the armor of God.

Your enemy is not a person, though Satan may use people to hurt you. Satan is out there trying to kill and destroy, and he will go after you, especially if you call yourself a Christian. And remember that God gives us strength, even in our weakness. Clothe yourself with God's armor every day.

> *Wear the full armor of God. Wear God's armor so that you can fight against the devil's evil tricks. Our fight is not against people on earth. We are fighting against the rulers and authorities and the powers of this world's darkness. We are fighting against the spiritual powers of evil in the heavenly world. That is why you need to get God's full armor.*
> —Ephesians 6:11–13, ICB

Pray the prayer of armor before you leave your house. Understand that when we pray this way, we are actually putting on Jesus, meaning that we truly become *"hidden in Christ"* (Colossians 3:3, AMPC). Every piece of armor really *is* Jesus.[178] When we're clothed with Him, we don't have to fear anything that may come our way.

Here's an example of a prayer of armor which contains lots of Scripture, making it even more powerful. It's very important to pray Scripture out loud.

> Lord Jesus, as I start my day I choose to clothe myself with You, with Your full armor. I thank You that every piece of clothing I am about to put on is really You. And by doing so, I truly am protected and don't have to fear anything that may come my way today—not even the darts the enemy may throw at me, nor the plans he has to steal, kill, or destroy (John 10:10).
> I praise You that through Your armor, I truly am dressed for success.

---

[178] You can find descriptions of each piece of armor in Ephesians 6:13–18.

I choose to put on the Helmet of Salvation. I thank You, Jesus, that You are the Source of my salvation: *"and, once made perfect, he became the source of eternal salvation for all who obey him"* (Hebrews 5:9, NIV).

I put on the Breastplate of Righteousness, and I thank You, Jesus, that You are my righteousness: *"This righteousness is given through faith in Jesus Christ to all who believe. There is no difference between Jew and Gentile"* (Romans 3:22, NIV).

I tighten the Belt of Truth around my waist, which helps me to stand my ground. Your truth has set me free. I am thankful, Jesus, that You are the truth. As You have said, *"I am the Way and the Truth and the Life; no one comes to the Father except by (through) Me"* (John 14:6, AMPC).

I choose to take up the Sword of the Spirit, which is the Word of God. Thank You, Jesus, that You are the Word: *"In the beginning [before all time] was the Word (Christ), and the Word was with God, and the Word was God Himself"* (John 1:1, AMPC).

I lift up the Shield of Faith today, and I thank You, Jesus, that You are my Leader and the Source of my faith: *"Looking away [from all that will distract] to Jesus, Who is the Leader and the Source of our faith [giving the first incentive for our belief] and is also its Finisher [bringing it to maturity and perfection]"* (Hebrews 12:2, AMPC).

I also choose to put on the Gospel of Peace as shoes on my feet. I am thankful, Jesus, that You are my peace. You created peace through dying on the cross, through which You reconciled me with the Father, as Colossians 1:20 says, *"And God purposed that through (by the service, the intervention of) Him [the Son] all things should be completely reconciled back to Himself, whether on earth or in heaven, as through Him, [the Father] made peace by means of the blood of His cross"* (AMPC).

Lastly, I choose to pray at all times, in all the different ways I can pray. I choose to pray now and throughout the day. I also choose to not only pray for myself but for others, as Ephesians 6:18 declares: *"Pray at all times (on every occasion, in every season) in the Spirit, with all [manner of] prayer and entreaty. To that end keep alert and watch with strong purpose and perseverance, interceding in behalf of all the saints (God's consecrated people)"* (AMP).

Thank You, Lord. I am now clothed with You and I know that I will be strong throughout the day to not only stand my ground against Satan but also be victorious through Your power and the working of the Holy Spirit in and through me. I love You, Lord. Thank You for this new day. Amen.

6. Remember who you are: a child of God.

When you accept Jesus as your Savior, you are a son or daughter of the King of Kings. And even though you may struggle with your sexual identity, this should never define who you are. Your identity should always be in Christ, first and foremost.

You can tell for sure that you are now fully adopted as his own children because God sent the Spirit of his Son into our lives crying out, "Papa! Father!" Doesn't that privilege of intimate conversation with God make it plain that you are not a slave, but a child? And if you are a child, you're also an heir, with complete access to the inheritance.

—Galatians 4:4–7, MSG

Jesus loves us, and because He loves us, He says,

I do not call you servants (slaves) any longer, for the servant does not know what his master is doing (working out). But I have called you My friends…

—John 15:15, AMPC

Conclusion

Dogs are known to be man's best friend, and in the same way, Jesus wants to be your friend too. Remember, I am my dogs' master, and they are my best friends. In the same way, Jesus, our Master, wants us to be His best friends too. You become His friend and He becomes yours! Cool, right?

Let me conclude with this story. It was September long weekend and I was getting ready to pack up my camper and go home. I was going through a tough time in my life and my mom had recently passed away. I was struggling with many things.

I decided to take my dogs to the dock for their last swim of the summer. As I watched my dogs jump in, I felt a prompting in my spirit (that still, small voice) to get into the water myself.

No, thanks, I thought. After all, the water was cold and I didn't want to get wet.

The prompting continued until I finally gave in and went into the water. It was *cold*. The dogs were swimming not far from me, so I called Daisy. As I pulled her close to my body, hoping to get some heat from her, she kept swimming and her legs scratched my belly.

I then sent her off to shore and called Thursdae, pulling her close. When she also kept swimming, I gave her body a squeeze, telling her, "Thursdae, stop kicking! Trust me, I have you!"

Immediately she relaxed, turned on her back, looked back into my face, and kissed me. That was when I heard the Holy Spirit say to me, "Wilna, stop kicking! Trust me, I have you! I love you!"

Jesus loves you very much. He takes you as you are, no matter what you struggle with. When you make Him your Master, your identity changes. You are a friend and child of God!

Now… who is your Master?

Reflection

The best way to understand a concept is to explain it in your own words. The following questions are a great way to reflect on the information presented in this study guide. I encourage you to reflect on them individually and journal the answers, or better yet, discuss them with a partner or group.

The Role of Jesus in Our Lives

1. Do you believe God speaks to us? How?
2. In what ways have you heard and listened to God's voice in your life? Do you know His voice?
3. Why is it vital to love and adhere to the Word of God?
4. Is it the role of teachers, schools, or the government to educate children on these difficult topics? Why or why not?
5. What does it mean to make Jesus your Master?
6. Explain in your own words the concept of the bike wheel and the hub.
7. I described the period of my life when I invited Jesus as a guest into my house. Why was that not enough to bring victory into my life?
8. Can you think of a time when you restricted Jesus from having access to every area of your life and heart? What did you do to change that? Have you surrendered that to Him?

Sexuality and Identity

9. Does Jesus hate homosexuals? (Hint: your answer should be "No!") Why doesn't He?
10. If a person comes into the world experiencing same-sex attractions, is it natural?
11. Describe the difference between experiencing same-sex attractions and living and practicing a homosexual lifestyle.

12. Do you believe God can remove same-sex attractions? Does a person always change from a homosexual into a heterosexual person?
13. How can someone determine their true identity if they are confused about their gender?
14. What is your true identity? When you sin, what happens to your identity, and why?

Holy Sexuality

15. What does holy sexuality mean for you? For a single person? For a married couple?
16. In an oversexualized world, how can you be a role model in equipping and motivating others to walk the narrow road?
17. What is your view on sex? Is sex a bad thing? Should we warn our children against it?
18. What does chastity mean? Which group of people does it apply to? Is it only for single people?
19. How can God expect a person who experiences same-sex attractions to stay single? If you believe it is unfair, discuss why.
20. List some of the consequences of unholy sexual practices.

Marriage

21. Why shouldn't a believer marry an unbeliever?
22. Is marriage worth the commitment when it can be so challenging?
23. If someone experiences same-sex attractions, why shouldn't they just marry someone of the same sex? Why won't it meet their needs?
24. If celibacy is what God requires from a single person, isn't that too hard?
25. If same sex-marriage is not God-ordained or God's original plan, why do so many churches today marry same-sex couples?

Overcoming the Hold of Sin

26. How do you feel about the concept that a baby can make vows in the mother's womb?
27. Explain how bad root results in bad fruit.
28. Explain this concept: "My spirit is willing but my flesh is weak." What is the remedy?
29. What does repentance mean?
30. If sanctification is a lifelong process, how can we pursue it and avoid going backwards? How can we live a victorious life?
31. Do you believe Jesus can take you back to scenes from your past and heal you from them? Is He the God of yesterday, today, and tomorrow?
32. Explain in your own words the meaning of "I choose to walk in obedience with God." Do you agree with this statement?

Wilna van Beek

Wilna van Beek is an experienced and practical teacher, bringing encouragement and hope to all who will listen. Her core message, particularly surrounding human sexuality, is incredibly vital in this day and age, and it applies to a wide range of listeners. Wilna has been sharing her transformation story with large audiences since 2009. Her redemption and restoration are the driving forces behind her message, and they inspire her to teach and train others to share their own faith stories.

Wilna is passionate about seeing all people be restored and experience life in abundance, here and now. Furthermore, she seeks to fulfill the great commission and has a heart for the lost. She loves to teach believers about abiding in the vine, becoming mature disciples, and eventually being called "fishers of men." Her aim in life is to be a true ambassador for Christ!

While Wilna loves to travel and share, and today's technology makes it possible, through conference calls and live streaming video, for her to speak to audiences whether or not it's possible to be there in person. Wilna would love the opportunity to connect in this way.

As Wilna shares her story of transformation, individuals and/or couples are often stirred to reach out to her on a personal level, seeking private help or counsel, particularly in the context of responding to a friend or family member who journeys with same-sex attractions. In order to guide these connections, it is best to have a predetermined arrangement and scheduled sessions. Wilna aims to steward the time appropriately and respect the boundaries of all involved.

If you have an event or gathering where you'd like Wilna to speak, or perhaps a classroom or small group setting where a Q&A session would be appropriate, Wilna is happy to consider meeting your needs—even from a remote location!

To contact Wilna for a speaking engagement or consultation,
check out her website at www.wilnavanbeek.com or
email info@wilnavanbeek.com.

www.ingramcontent.com/pod-product-compliance
Lightning Source LLC
Chambersburg PA
CBHW080912170426
43201CB00017B/2296